Interpreters of Occupation

Gender, Culture, and Politics in the Middle East
miriam cooke, Simona Sharoni, and Suad Joseph, *Series Editors*

Interpreters
of Occupation

Gender and the Politics of Belonging
in an Iraqi Refugee Network

Madeline Otis Campbell

Syracuse University Press

∞ The paper used in this publication meets the minimum requirements
of the American National Standard for Information Sciences—Permanence
of Paper for Printed Library Materials, ANSI Z39.48-1992.

For a listing of books published and distributed by Syracuse University Press,
visit www.SyracuseUniversityPress.syr.edu.

ISBN: 978-0-8156-3455-3 (cloth)
978-0-8156-3437-9 (paperback)
978-0-8156-5359-2 (e-book)

Library of Congress Cataloging-in-Publication Data
Names: Campbell, Madeline Otis.
Title: Interpreters of occupation : gender and the politics of belonging in an
Iraqi refugee network / Madeline Otis Campbell.
Description: First edition. | Syracuse, New York : Syracuse University Press, 2016. |
Series: Gender, culture, and politics in the Middle East |
Includes bibliographical references and index.
Identifiers: LCCN 2016000183| ISBN 9780815634553 (cloth : alkaline paper) |
ISBN 9780815634379 (paperback : alkaline paper) | ISBN 9780815653592 (e-book)
Subjects: LCSH: Iraqis—United States—Biography. | Iraqis—Migrations—History—
21st century. | Refugees—United States—Biography. | Social networks—Case studies. |
Belonging (Social psychology)—Political aspects—Case studies. | Sex role—Political
aspects—Case studies. | Translators—Iraq—Biography. | Iraq War, 2003–2011—Refugees. |
Ḥizb al-Baʻth al-ʻArabī al-Ishtirākī (Iraq)—Biography. | Young adults—Iraq—Biography.
Classification: LCC E184.I55 C36 2016 | DDC 920.00892/7567—dc23
LC record available at http://lccn.loc.gov/2016000183

Manufactured in the United States of America

Contents

Illustrations

Preface

Young Iraqis come face-to-face with questions of everyday security, their family's expectations and aspirations, and their country's future. At the time of this work's inception in 2008, Iraq was under the occupation of US troops at the "surge" of American militarism there and also confronting militias and movements vying for control of the country. At least 134,000 civilians died as a result of war and violence in Iraq between 2003 and 2013, according to Brown University's Costs of War analysis.[1] At the time of this book's writing in 2015, Iraq is under the power of competing sovereign and quasi-sovereign powers, and the United States has once again deployed thousands of troops to the country.

Questions of security, family expectations, and national futures abound in the transnational Iraqi diaspora as well, where many young Iraqis attempt to carve out a home. As they do, dilemmas of identity and identification—political, regional, religious, and ethnic, among others—continue to grip them. In speaking to dozens of Iraqi twenty- and thirty-somethings in the US-based diaspora over the years I spent researching this book, I encountered Iraqis who were passionate about their country, who told stories of Iraq's rivers and its poetry. I met Iraqis who made the grave decision to leave their homes in hopes of *protecting* their families because, as former employees of the US occupation, they had targets on their backs. These Iraqis grapple every day with the consequences of that decision.

1. See Neta C. Crawford's report, "Civilian Death and Injury in the Iraq War, 2003–2013," at brown.edu.watson/costsofwar/. The Iraq Body Count Project (Iraqbodycount. org) has estimated that the death toll may be nearly twice that at 250,000.

By 2015, some of the men and women who became key interlocutors in this book were poised to redeploy to Iraq in American uniforms. Several young men I met had served as military interpreters in the Iraq War, immigrated to the United States, returned to Iraq as US soldiers in the waning days of occupation, and now are on the verge of redeployment in a campaign to counter the rising power of Da'ish (*ad-Dawlah al-Islamiyah fi 'l-'Iraq wa-ash-Sham*), or the Islamic State. These events make all the more pressing the questions of identity that young Iraqis confront in the diaspora. My interlocutors represent a particularly contentious corner of the Iraq War's diaspora due to their association with the US military. But their dilemmas of identification speak to broader dilemmas of belonging and betrayal across the diaspora in the aftermath of war and displacement—dilemmas that unfold on multiple registers and in complex ways. This ethnography focuses on one embattled network of refugees in the Iraqi diaspora in situ and at one moment in time (2010–12). Their intimate dilemmas of identity remain as relevant today as ever for broader discussions about Iraq's future.

Acknowledgments

This book represents a collective effort of my intellectual communities and ethnographic interlocutors, though I take full responsibility for any of its shortcomings. The culmination of my doctoral dissertation research at the University of California–Davis (UC-Davis), this project was made possible from its inception by the support I found in the UC-Davis Anthropology Department and the Middle East and South Asia Program. My doctoral research was supported at different stages by a generous University of California Graduate Research Fellowship, a Boren Fellowship, and a Foreign Language and Area Studies Grant.

At UC-Davis, Doctors Suad Joseph and Omnia El Shakry were outstanding mentors throughout my doctoral study. Under Suad and Omnia, I received rigorous training as an ethnographer, writer, and theorist that has profoundly shaped my career as a feminist scholar. Both Suad and Omnia supported my decision to take a leave of absence from graduate study to work with the US Refugee Admissions Program in the Middle East. Both were instrumental in my ability to synthesize that experience, my academic study, as well as my professional, personal, and political commitments in the course of research—and in these pages. I wish to thank Suad, in particular, for encouraging me so steadfastly to write this book.

My intellectual community at UC-Davis would not have been complete without Cristiana Giordano, Lena Meari, Timothy Murphy, Adam Brown, Bettina N'gweno, Sunaina Maira, Donald Donham, James Smith, Bascom Guffin, Leah Wiste, Jacob Culbertson, and Vivian Choi.

In the Boston area, I have been overwhelmed by the generosity so many in the Iraqi refugee network have shown me—and equally by the interest they have taken in this research. I owe this project's success entirely to these young Iraqi women's and men's willingness to open their homes to me, share their voices with me, and participate in my painstaking process trying to get these pages "right." Time is only one way to measure the tremendous commitment to this work that my ethnographic interlocutors have shown, but I am deeply grateful for their willingness to make time for interview after interview—after work, between shifts, or before breaking the fast on hot summer days during the Ramadan season—and even for several-day-long "shadowing" sessions in which I would accompany them in their everyday lives at home, work, and school. I am humbled by the openness and candor many young Iraqi women and men showed in the course of this research. Even in the face of misgivings among and between many participants in the research, I am thankful for the measure of trust many of my interlocutors put in this project.

This book would be impossible without the contributions of several people in particular in the Boston area: Ridhab Al Kinani, Yaqoob Al Kinani, Mohammed Intisar, and Ahmed Al-Mostafay. Thank you also to Sarah, Yoseph, Sofia, and Tamara for your warmth and friendship.

I am indebted to my colleagues who have read portions of this work in different stages, including Qussay Al-Attabi, Kevin Smith, Tanzeen Doha, Rim Zahra, Razzan Zahra, Chris Kortright, Connie McGuire, Kregg Hetherington, Michelle Stewart, and Nicolas D'Avella. I am also deeply grateful for the invitation by Alexandra Filindra, Dana Janbek, and Paola Prado to present portions of this work at Brown University, Lasell College, and Roger Williams University, respectively. Additionally, I thank the participants in the UC-Davis Middle East/South Asia Arab Studies conference and the members of the American Anthropological Association panels in which I have shared this research over the years.

My sincere gratitude to the editor-in-chief at Syracuse University Press, Suzanne Guiod, for supporting this project. Thanks also to the generous reviewers at the press for their attentive and insightful feedback on the work. Your support has enabled me to develop this work with care and precision into its current form.

Finally, I wish to thank my family and friends who supported me so faithfully through research and writing. Thank you to my mom, dad, Katharine Otis, Kathy and Ron Campbell, Kassandra Showers, Eileen

Volquez, Langan Courtney, Tatiana Andia, Lenne Klingaman, and Tim Murphy for their support. Above all, I want to thank my children, Louisa and Phillip, who continue to inspire me, and my husband, Jeremy, who saw this coming long before I did.

Abbreviations

A-file	alien file—held on all applicants for refugee status
09 Lima	temporary linguists serving in the US Armed Services
ACUs	army combat uniform
ASVAB	Armed Services Vocational Aptitude Battery, the Armed Services entrance exam
CAT 2 linguist	Category 2 linguist—a contracted government employee, requiring security clearance and US citizenship
FOB	Forward Operating Base, a US military base in an active combat zone
IED	improvised explosive device
P1 Refugee	priority 1 refugee—refugee applicants referred to the US Refugee Admissions Program by the United Nations High Commission on Refugees
P2 Refugee	priority 2 refugee—refugee applicants who apply directly for refugee status with the US Refugee Admissions Program due to their membership in a designated population of interest; that is, former allies of the United States in Iraq
SIV	Special Immigrant Visas
Terp	a local national contracted interpreter for US Forces, also called Category 1 linguists
TRIG	Terrorism Related Inadmissibility Grounds in immigration procedures

USRAP   US Refugee Admissions Program, the multiagency
                refugee resettlement program

volag   voluntary agency, the paragovernmental agency
                responsible for aiding resettled refugees in the
                United States

Cast of Characters

The following individuals make up the key ethnographic interlocutors in this book. I have provided some distinguishing biographical information about each person as well as an indication as to where they appear in the pages to follow. *Note*: Names and other identifying information (e.g., individuals' hometowns or neighborhoods or current locations) have been changed for the protection of their privacy.

Max—A twenty-nine-year-old Baghdadi born to a Kurdish mother and an Arab father, Max speaks four languages fluently and became an interpreter for US Forces straight out of college. He was quickly stationed in Abu Ghraib, to interpret in the base's military prison and hospital. Max resettled alone in Lowell, Massachusetts, in 2011, where he remains, working several jobs. See section on "The Tongue" in chapter 2.

Mohammed—Mohammed is a former cell-phone vendor from Basrah, who worked as an interpreter for several Marines units from the war's beginning, though he quit the job many times. Frequently called "Mo" by colleagues in the Marines, Mohammed became "Mo" permanently in Providence, Rhode Island, where he settled in 2009. Now thirty-two years old, Mo has moved back to Iraq to marry, and is uncertain about where his new family will land. See sections "The Bridge" in chapter 2 and "Mohammed: Antiwar American Ally" in chapter 4.

Meena—From Adhamiya, Baghdad, Meena worked as an interpreter with a US-Iraqi Transition Team on Loyalty Base near the Green Zone, after graduating from college with a BA in English. Thirty years old, Meena resettled in Chelsea, Massachusetts, independently in 2010. She is now living in Texas, and continues to visit her mother in Iraq annually. See the section "Meena: The Perfect *Bint Iraqiya*" in chapter 3.

Joe—Joe became an interpreter for the US Army's 101st Airborne division after completing a master's degree in civil engineering at Baghdad University, near which his family continues to live. Joe was kidnapped for several days by an insurgent group in the west of Iraq and, upon being released with the payment of a ransom, applied for refugee status. He resettled to Lynn, Massachusetts, in 2011 where, after working as a doorman in a hotel, he began the process of enlisting in the US Army as a private. Thirty-one, Joe hopes to join the Army Corps of Engineers in the future. See the section "A Generation without a Model" in chapter 4.

Tariq—From Al-Amil, Baghdad, Tariq is a thirty-four-year-old husband and recent father of two twin girls. A trained agronomist, Tariq became an interpreter for a US-Iraqi Transition Team when his office in the Iraqi government was disbanded after the invasion. He and his wife resettled in Dorchester, Massachusetts, in 2007. Shortly thereafter, he joined the US Army as an 09 Lima, a military linguist, and was deployed to Iraq until the end of US military operations. His wife remains in Massachusetts, while he is now deployed to a military base in Arizona. See the sections "Tariq: Returning to Iraq as an American Soldier" and "Hyperpatriarchy Unbound" in chapter 4.

Tamara—A twenty-eight-year-old trained electrical engineer from Yarmouk, Baghdad, Tamara began working as an interpreter for the US Army after graduating from college. Tamara spent much of her time with army units at Camp Victory that were involved in training the new Iraqi military. Resettled in South Boston in 2010, Tamara has moved multiple times, finally landing in Chelsea. She served as Meena's sponsor and has begun a PhD program in engineering in the Boston area. She continues to visit her mother in Baghdad frequently. See the section "Tamara: A 'Liberation War' Refugee Rebuffs Salvation" in chapter 5.

Hussein—Hussein is a thirty-two-year-old from Dora, Baghdad. After a one-year Fulbright Fellowship in the United States in 2005, Hussein began interpreting for a US Army Command office in Baghdad. Threatened by al Qaeda, Hussein applied for refugee status and resettled in Worcester, Massachusetts, in 2009. There, he serves as a refugee caseworker for a resettlement agency serving predominantly Iraqi clients. See the section "Hussein: Rebuilding Iraq as a Refugee Caseworker" in chapter 5.

Abbas—A thirty-year-old originally from Sadr City, Abbas began working with the US Army on a voluntary basis in his neighborhood in the early days of the war, eventually accepting a full-time position in which he was stationed on bases to the north of Baghdad. Resettled in South Boston, Abbas lived with his sponsor, Husham, on and off for several years before moving back to Iraq and marrying. He is currently building a house in Al-Kadhimya. See the sections *Sexy Female Interpreters!* in chapter 3 and "Abbas: Husband and 'New Man'" in chapter 6.

Husham—Husham is a twenty-nine-year-old musician from Al-Mansour, Baghdad. After studying in a musical conservatory, Husham worked briefly as an interpreter with the Marines. During the period of his work with the US Marines, Husham received indirect threats on a visit home and decided to apply for refugee resettlement. Now in South Boston, Husham is studying music in a local college and working several jobs. See the sections *Sexy Female Interpreters!* in chapter 3 and "Abbas: Husband and 'New Man'" in chapter 6.

Hiba—A thirty-three-year-old from Basrah, Hiba is the wife of Tariq and mother of two twin girls. She resettled in Dorchester, Massachusetts, in 2007 (later moving to Revere) and has served as the immigration sponsor to three separate interpreters-turned-refugees while her husband has been on deployment with the US Army: Frank, Yoseph, and Anwar. See the sections "Hiba: From 'Single Woman' to Perennial Sponsor" in chapter 6 as well as "Tariq: Returning to Iraq as an American Soldier" and "Hyper-patriarchy Unbound" in chapter 4.

Interpreters of Occupation

Introduction

Global Routes—Baghdad to Boston

Approaches

The flight from Amman to Baghdad International Airport on an American C-130 was full of US government officials and contractors, sitting face to face, knees interlocking. A perverse sense of adventure filled the plane during its "corkscrew formation" descent over the city's neighborhoods, rivers, families, and memories. No one in the plane, aside from the military personnel piloting the aircraft, could see the city below. In our approach, the government personnel on board saw neither decimated homes nor blast walls. We saw none of the city's ubiquitous checkpoints or bare streets, once lined with lush trees. The plane was full of officials who could not see beyond the colleague seated in front of them, by design of both the plane and the government mission that had deployed it.

Stepping off the plane onto a massive US military base named "Camp Victory," we entered into a dehistoricized geography, an unmoored time-place, the signposts for which were distant headlines or our own fantasies. It was 2009, at the end of the so-called surge in Iraq. I had chosen to enter these embattled spaces in an effort to understand what the "war on terror" looked like in practice—from within an official subject-position structured by myopia, as I experienced on the plane. Just as important, I took that flight to Baghdad to begin a longer journey to study and subvert that myopia—to begin to glimpse how the US war machine had impacted, in every way imaginable, the lives of everyday Iraqis. I was working in Iraq on a short-term basis as a refugee officer in the US Refugee Admissions Program (USRAP), on leave from my doctoral program at the University

1

of California–Davis. Most of my work entailed interviewing Iraqi "allies" of the US mission in Iraq—drivers, security guards, and, above all, interpreters—who were applying for refugee status in the United States. I had completed similar assignments in Syria, Egypt, Jordan, and Lebanon, interviewing Iraqi refugees for the year and a half I worked with the US federal government. In Damascus and Cairo, I interviewed families escaping violence and chaos in their Iraqi towns and neighborhoods. But in Baghdad, I met young men and women fleeing dangers that emerged due to their alliance with a government that I now represented—dangers stemming from these men's and women's strategic deployment within a military mission that I deeply opposed.

This book is part of my attempt to make good on the responsibilities I assumed by taking that flight to Baghdad. It is an ethnography about and dedicated to the young Iraqi men and women whom I met in Iraq, across the Middle East, and eventually in New England, where, after completing my work as a refugee officer, I conducted two years of fieldwork in the emergent diaspora of US "allies." My aim is to provide a window into the occupation of Iraq from the perspective of young Iraqis who left their homes and families because of their sacrifice in the Iraq War.

These diverse young Iraqis' accounts crack open windows into the war where I had found none—as on American-filled C-130s—or where I had found windows fogged by the limits of imagination and empathy in the presence of fear-driven ideology, such as during my visits to American boardrooms and classrooms. More broadly, I share these accounts of the young Iraqis who bravely contributed their stories in order to expose and challenge the structured myopia that conditioned their lives as allies of the US Forces. To be sure, this represents only a partial view into a massive war and a multifaceted diaspora. Attending to the unique experience of wartime interpreters propels us to face the complexity and cruelty of the Iraq War's enduring impacts.

Interpreters of Occupation

As an ethnography of a distinctive refugee network inside the Iraq War diaspora, this book considers how former US-allied interpreters now living in the Northeastern United States grapple with dilemmas of identification. Every identification practice implies a checkpoint of sorts, whether militarized, legal-juridical, or socio-discursive. This study set out to investigate how young, single Iraqis negotiate the especially troublesome checkpoints in the diaspora of former US allies. As interpreters in Iraq, members of this refugee network had urgently honed identification strategies amid chronic suspicion: from the US Forces, to whom they represented potential threats to American security; from fellow Iraqis, some of whom saw their work with US Forces as a betrayal to Iraq; and, not least of all, from each other. They faced recurrent checkpoints in which their identities were scrutinized from all sides. The strategies that these diverse young men and women carved out on US bases and in their Iraqi homes have multilayered histories and surprising futures, unfolding now in the diaspora.

"Red flag!" shouted Husham, referring to his Boston-area roommate Abbas, whom he believed was approaching "anti-American" because of his expression of sympathy for his family's political views in Iraq. "Watch out for that guy," Abbas later advised me speaking of Husham, who, in Abbas's view, had forgone so much regard for Iraq—even for his family still living there—that he had nearly lost himself. Both part of the refugee network of former interpreters and on-again-off-again roommates, Husham and Abbas continue to find themselves embedded in mutually mistrustful relationships vis-à-vis the US state, the wider Iraqi diaspora, and, above all, each other. The specter of state and diasporic checkpoints—material and discursive constructs—only magnify the mistrust they express toward one another.

Unique socialities of suspicion took root among interpreters on US bases, where they had worked behind pseudonyms and military uniforms (sometimes even facemasks) to interpret the linguistic and cultural "terrains" of Iraq. As "cultural translators" (Asad 1986) of the so-called human terrain in Iraq, they interpreted potentially suspicious places and faces, including each other's. In the diaspora, these socialities morphed and their modes of expression varied. Members of the refugee network explained their apprehension around one another in terms of self-protection: to trust others could endanger oneself or one's family. But, just as in Iraq, interpreting others' actions with an eye toward suspecting their motives appeared to serve a more fundamental role: in the diaspora, suspicion became a prominent technique for survival.

In parallel activities, Husham and Abbas perform identification strategies they sharpened under occupation, which had dynamic histories in the years leading up to the US invasion. Their everyday speech vis-à-vis one another, the diaspora, and the US state persistently evokes family duty—natal and national families alike—and casts doubt on other network members' filial attachments. That their fervent assertions of filial devotion were performed oceans away from family only heightened the refugees' mutual doubt about each others' claims, making the claims all the more pressing. However, imperatives to perform and police assertions of familial duty are not entirely new to these young men and women. Their strategies are citations of techniques they developed under conditions of war and dictatorship as members of the last Ba'thist generation. "My responsibility is to protect my family—my mother most of all—and then all of my Iraqi brothers and sisters. I did it all for them," Abbas reveals, reflecting on his decision to work for US Forces as we ate lunch with Husham on the Boston Common. In that encounter, I represented a checkpoint of sorts—my questions about his work, an imperative to identify—and this, his tactic in navigating potentially hazardous terrain. Over the years that followed, Abbas became a close friend: we shared weekly dinners, helped each other move, went on hiking trips together, lent each other cars when the other's was in the shop; he even wrangled my partner into skydiving. Still, the specter of hundreds of checkpoints haunted us over every dinner as we spoke of his life in Iraq and his work for US Forces—often upon his initiation. In each case, he called on patterned language of filiality. Hand-in-hand with his assertion of familial duty came questions about that of others.

As I grew to know Husham, I found that he put to use similar discursive strategies to negotiate the haunts of past and present checkpoints—including those that Husham and Abbas would foist upon each other, where filial attachments were used as an index of cultural and national identities as "anti-American" or not Iraqi enough. In their patterned usage across both sides of those mutually imposed checkpoints, Husham and Abbas's identification strategies were situated and changing practices.

Meena—a shared acquaintance of both men in the Boston network—similarly evoked filial duty to navigate the diaspora's checkpoints but from a distinctly situated subject-position, and with different valences and stakes, as a single woman, reflecting: "What choice did I have? I did not want to work for the Americans, but my family needed money."

Scholars of the Middle East, including notably Suad Joseph, have long observed the centrality of relational filial identity to selfhood, politics, and sociocultural configurations (Joseph 1999, 2005, 2008).[1] Scholarship of US-based Arab communities demonstrates the heightened stakes of policing the family in the diaspora (Naber 2012). Critical to understanding young Iraqis' evocation of filial duty in this case are two distinct factors: (1) their situation as members of what I call a "war generation," who came of age amid back-to-back conflicts and are now refugees of war; and (2) their situation as "cultural translators" during the US war in Iraq. Over their lifetimes in a country at war (and under brutalizing sanctions) as members of the war generation, shifting constructs of filial duty emerged as avenues for this generation to lay claim to cultural and national belonging, both intensely policed. "War experience" narratives about male protection (in both military and domestic spheres) and female sacrifice in natal and national families evolved over the Iran-Iraq War, Gulf War, the sanctions era, and the US occupation, serving to regulate claims of belonging according to gendered constructs of filial attachment (Khoury 2013). The same structures of power that incited these strategies also encouraged Iraqi citizens to question each other's faithfulness to models of filial obligation.

To understand network members' widespread evocation of filial duty one must also appreciate their situation as former "cultural translators" for US Forces in Iraq. Complexly layered upon their experiences as members of the war generation, network members' identification practices are shaped by the narratives they crafted as wartime interpreters, translating complex and contested social historicities into military grids of

---

1. See also Barakat (1983) and McClintock (1993). For an elaboration of the position of the familial in national and cultural projects more broadly, see Collins (2000).

intelligibility. Their translations were often overdetermined by discourses of terrorism and liberation. Interpreters like Husham, Abbas, and Meena found themselves suspended in structures of US military power in which they were hired to speak as experts on Iraqi culture. From that subject-position, interpreters translated historically situated, pliant, and deeply political idioms around Iraqi "culture" for US Forces, giving life to new narratives. The hiring of thousands of Iraqi interpreters to navigate the "human terrain" of Iraq was the bedrock of the US military's approach to the Iraq War. This military approach sought to win hearts and minds on the field of culture, through greater cultural appreciation and understanding of cultural threats (Brown 2008).[2] Tropes about gender and family in Iraq—men's duty of patriarchal protection and women's attachment to home and vulnerability there—emerged as central themes in interpreters' cultural translations. "Believe me, more than Sunni-Shi'a or Arab-Kurd," Abbas once told me, "you will not understand Iraqi culture if you don't understand how important the family is to us, and if you don't understand how Iraqis think about men's and women's roles." In Abbas's formulation, echoed by former interpreters across the refugee network, gender and family were as important as any matter of "culture" in Iraq.

The singular act of cultural translation both called upon earlier "war experience" narratives—in particular, public constructs of gender and filial duty that had circulated since the Iran-Iraq War—and translated those constructs into US war on terror frameworks. In translation, historically situated narratives took on lives of their own as reductive and unmoored cultural truths, wherein women might be thought to require liberation from "traditional" men. Those cultural truths would haunt interpreters throughout the US immigration process and in the diaspora, structuring both the institutions of power they confronted and their strategic,

2. Interpreters inherited a longstanding role as "cultural translators," a role that has served a variety of orientalist projects, as Talal Asad has discussed (1986). This weaponization of culture ultimately culminated in the Human Terrain System (HTS) in 2007, in which social science "experts" were deployed to navigate the "human terrain" of Iraq. For summaries of the military policies surrounding the Human Terrain System and the "weaponization of culture," see also Gonzalez (2008, 2009, 2010).

sometimes subversive, responses. This book sets out to interrogate the citational acts that come alive within the militarized encounter of cultural translation, which become formative of interpreters' identification strategies under occupation and in the diaspora.

In that encounter, interpreters were subjectivated as subjects of US power, employed to render the Iraqi "other" intelligible. They were also subjectivated as cultured subjects themselves: they were hired both to represent Iraqi culture and to stand above it in a privileged position as authoritative speakers. These dual processes of subjectivation produced an impasse—an unwieldy discursive knot—for Iraqi interpreters-turned-refugees, from which mutual suspicion was an understandable outcome. Interpreters' suspicion of one another's claims to cultural tropes of filial devotion positioned them both as potential guardians of authentic culture and as the "reasonable" subject standing above culture, suspicious of all cultural claims. Talal Asad writes: "Suspicion seeks to penetrate a mask to the unpleasant reality behind it: . . . a hidden motive to commit a crime . . . a terrorist in disguise . . . when a 'reasonable' person comes to a conclusion" (Asad 2004, 285). With this in mind, let us return to the Boston Common, where my exchange with Abbas now takes on a new dimension. Abbas had said, "My responsibility is to protect my family—my mother most of all—and then all of my Iraqi brothers and sisters. I did it all for them." That this utterance comes miles away from family makes it all the more urgent, and all the more suspicious to others in the refugee network. Did he really do it for his family? Or did he represent a "group" (*majmuʿa*)? Was he an apologist for US militarism in Iraq? Or, maybe worse, was he looking for an adventure? Checkpoints materialize in which network interlocutors like Husham become judges of Abbas's claim on culturally dynamic constructs of filial duty in the very midst of US structures of power, where they had once been hired to be the "reasonable" cultural translators of that suspicious cultural terrain.

An ethnography of the refugee network reveals that mutual suspicion along filial lines predates the US war in Iraq. Indeed, those socialities of suspicion were a formative condition of wartime interpreters' experiences of occupation. The contested meanings of belonging and betrayal in the wake of occupation become particularly clear in the case of wartime interpreters. Interpreters were pressed to translate the suspicious "essences" of Iraq for a military occupation that was itself suspicious of them. In response, interpreters appeal to the familial to parry one another's doubts. So too, in due course, do familial invocations become the very indexes of suspicion.

The Network

The network of former interpreters in Boston did not make up a "community" in the sense that anthropologists generally use the term. Instead, this network is an assemblage of individuals who have followed a common global "route" in James Clifford's formation (1997), and find themselves in fractured and short-lived relationships constituted by chain migration and immigration sponsorship. Building on Clifford's formulation, my theorization of this network is akin to Gilles Deleuze and Felix Guattari's concept of the "rhizome," a network whose constituent parts exist in relation and in a continuous process of rupture, by which new "lines" of relation are drawn.[3] The origin of this diasporic network's shared "route" or "line" was, of course, the momentous decision to work for US Forces under occupation in Iraq and the equally momentous decision to leave Iraq.

Quite unlike the networks imagined in transnational studies or refugee studies, this network is an assemblage of people that seek to strategically disconnect from one another, rather than connect. Scholarship in refugee studies examines how different populations—often imagined as homogenous ethno-national groups—re-form social networks in new homes (see, e.g., Holtzman 1999). Similarly, research in the field of transnationalism often take for granted that networks are defined by connectivity or pursuits

---

3. In *A Thousand Plateaus* Deleuze and Guattari write: "A rhizome may be broken, shattered at a given spot, but it will start up again on one of its old lines, or on new lines. . . . Every rhizome contains lines of segmentarity according to which it is stratified, territorialized, organized, signified, attributed, etc., as well as lines of deterritorialization down which it constantly flees. There is a rupture in the rhizome whenever segmentary lines explode into a line of flight, but the line of flight is part of the rhizome. These lines always tie back to one another" (1987, 10).

at connectivity—whether economic, intimate, or otherwise (see, e.g., Parreñas 2005). The network at the center of this study comprises individuals who are tied together through immigration procedures that privilege "sponsorship," encouraging one refugee to serve as a temporary host to another refugee—even if that person is a distant acquaintance. The result has been chain migration of former interpreters to common areas, like the Northeast, who are distantly acquainted but are forced into close quarters as host and newcomer. In the Northeast, they also forge new acquaintances with individuals in the network, whom they often wish could remain "distant" but are only too close. The sponsorship chain—combined with refugee service agencies, employment agencies, and select social spaces—keep these individuals in continued uneasy relation to each other.

In the first instance, a common choice to ally with US Forces binds the members of this refugee network, as do nagging doubts about why others in the network made that life-altering choice. Though the refugees' assertions of filial duty emerged as an answer to mistrust around their alliance with the United States, it never proved satisfactory. Nor could such an explanation fully satisfy the curiosity and concern of other refugees, as they knew nothing of each other's families. These young men and women had generally immigrated alone and now lived *apart* from any relatives in the diaspora. Members of this refugee network met expansive Iraqi definitions of *shabab* (unmarried youth, under thirty-five years old), aside from the inescapable fact that they lived without family—highly unusual for unmarried "youth."

So too had network members shared similar structures of opportunity and necessity in Iraq, which motivated their contentious decision. Members of the refugee network came from comparable class and educational backgrounds. Though diverse in regional, religious, and ethnic backgrounds, most of the network comprises urban Iraqis from middle-class families with degrees of higher education—bachelor's degrees and also often master's and doctoral degrees. A majority in the network were Baghdadis, though there also were members who hailed from Basra, Mosul, and other urban centers. That they spoke English as a second or third language was an index of both their education and class positions, having studied in secondary and post-secondary education. Paradoxically, a large number of network members' parents were former employees of the government—whether as professors or doctors in the public medical system. The overthrow was a peculiar challenge for families whose income was tied to government work. These families were not necessarily the hardest hit by the war. But given US policies of "de-Bathification" across all government sectors, many middle-aged government servants with low-level affiliations to the Ba'th Party lost their jobs and had little chance of employment outside of the government.[4] In these and other families, younger generations of university-trained engineers and computer scientists represented a new wave of potential household earners under occupation.

While network members would have widely preferred to find work in their fields, they found that English was their most marketable skill. Just as the government had been the biggest employer in Ba'thist Iraq, the military occupation that now replaced it, and had cut their parents' jobs, emerged as a leading avenue of employment for the younger generation. Network members decided thus to work as interpreters for US Forces for a range of reasons, including a sense of obligation to bring home income; a hope for individual professional advancement, which held the promise of family advancement in the long run; or a desire to qualify for refugee resettlement and to immigrate to the United States, which also held the promise of helping family in the form of immigration petitions for "family reunification." In this way, a sense of family obligation mixed with a desire for professional opportunity to motivate this weighty decision. For most network members, it was not the case that their family wholly depended upon their income for survival, but neither was it the case that these young individuals made the decision to work for US Forces without support for their families in mind—as others in the network might accuse them.

Interpreters worked for an American defense contractor, most notably, San Diego's Titan Communications.[5] Viewed by some Iraqi opponents

4. Hazem Saghieh provides a useful discussion about the motivations of US policies of de-Baathification in "Vie et Mort de la Débaassification" (2007).

5. While a great deal of scholarship has scrutinized private defense contracts in Iraq (see Avant 2006; Isenberg 2008; and Kwok 2006), little research has examined Titan in

of the American-led war as collaborators, interpreters were targeted with death threats, kidnapping, or violent and sometimes deadly attacks by groups such as *Jama'at al-Tawhid wal-Jihad* (Al Qaeda in Iraq) or *Jaish al-Mahdi* (the Mahdi Army). As a result, thousands of interpreters fled Iraq for surrounding countries and applied for refugee resettlement in the United States when Iraqi refugee processing began in 2007.[6] Soon after, due to the ongoing violence against US allies, the US Refugee Admissions Program introduced a priority channel for Iraqi allies of US Forces, for which Iraqis could apply from Baghdad. Some network members had been directly threatened and were in immediate peril, while others feared future life-threatening danger was just around the corner.

Of Sponsors and Suspects in the Diaspora

In the United States, the cluster of former interpreters grew in New England as a product of chain migration. Constituted by a system of immigration sponsorship, this network of individuals took shape by one former interpreter serving as an immigration sponsor to another. An immigration sponsor serves as the point of contact and host to the newly arriving refugee. Because it allows for more choice in one's resettlement destination and expedites the process, to list a sponsor—even if he or she is a distant acquaintance or perfect stranger—was favored over unsponsored resettlement in a chance US city. (Because it saves state resources, the government also prefers this method.) Network members began their lives in

---

particular. Accounts of Titan and its treatment of interpreters are, however, abundant in the media (see chapter 2 for further discussion).

6. A smaller number have applied for "Special Immigrant Visas" (SIVs) available exclusively to Iraqi interpreters. Theoretically, SIVs' immigration process is streamlined and, unlike refugees, SIVs arrive in the United States with a green card in hand. However, very few Special Immigrant Visas are granted each year. While Iraqi refugee admissions were based on soft "targets" in the tens of thousands, SIVs for interpreters are strictly limited to 500 per year. Once in the United States, SIVs received similar benefits as those refugees received. In this text, I use the terms "refugee" and "refugee network" expansively to include SIVs within it.

the Boston-area apartments of sponsor-hosts, who had in turn once lived in the apartments of their sponsors. Thrust into uncomfortably intimate relationships with strangers or near strangers, these associations were usually short-lived.

On US bases in Iraq, interpreters had known each other by pseudonyms and had relied on the veil of anonymity that came with military-issued uniforms or even facemasks. Now in each other's apartments, the pseudonyms or masks were off; network members developed other methods of carefully guarding their personal information. For example, refugee roommates might calculate their return to a shared apartment around mail delivery to reduce the risk of the other seeing their personal mail, or they might create alternate Facebook accounts for their interpreter acquaintances, listing false information. These measures were not only to protect their own privacy, but also to protect their families at home, whom they believed could be at risk if word traveled through diasporic channels back to Iraq that they were in the United States.

Network members generally moved out of their sponsor's apartment as soon as they could manage it. What continually surprised me was the fact that those same individuals would not hesitate to become sponsors of a new wave of interpreters-turned-refugees. Usually, they agreed to do this as a favor to a mutual acquaintance who had put them in touch or because serving as a sponsor allowed them to access state resources—in the form of rent and food expenses for the newly arriving refugees—at a time when many found their own refugee assistance dwindling or found work difficult to come by. That new wave of refugees, too, would quickly move out and become sponsors themselves.

The network of former interpreters continues to be defined by its itinerancy—its members moving around the region for available jobs or housing options. Dispersed around New England, members of this network tend to see very little of each other. When they do, it is typically by happenstance in commonly frequented professional spaces, such as refugee service agencies or temp agencies and, to a lesser degree, social spaces like restaurants or cafés. In a few instances—as in the case of Husham and Abbas—network members decide to remain roommates despite the challenges of this arrangement. To the extent that network members sought out social relationships in the Boston area, they appeared to prefer to associate with single young professionals or students from elsewhere in the Middle East rather than members of the Iraqi diaspora. Yet, corresponding with families in Iraq made up the centerpiece of interpreters' daily lives and support system in the United States. Unlike many in the wider Iraqi diaspora, and unlike other refugee populations, members of this network also frequently travel back to Iraq to see their families, which highlights their unique position as single, middle-class young men and women.

In the Boston area, the network had ambivalent relationships with the US state. On the one hand, some network members—typically young men—sought out work with state or parastate agencies given their professional backgrounds in Iraq. Strikingly, some network members that I met would join the US military, and even deploy back to Iraq. Others became caseworkers in refugee service agencies, charged with dispensing state resources for other Iraqi refugees. One applied for a job with the National Security Agency (NSA), translating tapped phone conversations, though he did not get the job. On the other hand, network members were wary of the state's intrusion into their lives. That they had to "report to" caseworkers made many network members uncomfortable; there were also concerns that they were so closely monitored that if they traveled back to Iraq their state benefits could be suspended. Network members were frequently stopped by the police and harassed on the street. They sometimes coped with harassment by appealing to the police. (One of those members would years later apply to join the police force.) To ward off harassment or prejudice by the police—as well as to bolster their employment or housing applications—network members would frequently share aspects of their life histories. They told stories of their work for US Forces, their difficult positions as refugees, and the dire circumstances of their families back in Iraq to gain the trust of the figures in power. For example, Meena pled with her landlord for a slightly reduced rent, because she had to send money back to her mother monthly and had little left over for food or phone credit. Though a few organizations, such as the List Project, set out to assist former interpreters in the Boston area, network members by and large felt that their sacrifices in Iraq were not matched by sufficient support in the United States. Instead, they felt they were received as foreigners who had to prove their belonging in the United States with war stories and tales of victimization. While their past work with US Forces was invisible in everyday life in the United States, their perceived foreignness felt very visible. The identification strategies that interpreters developed on the battlefields of "cultural translation" in Iraq dynamically shaped how they identified in the diaspora. Performance and policing of filial duty emerged as a modality to claim belonging both in the diaspora and vis-à-vis the US state.

Subject Formation in Translation

As they navigate dilemmas of identification, network members' identification strategies represent this book's core ethnographic object. I offer the concept of *subject formation in translation* to frame the conditions of subjectivation and agency of which military interpreters are a part—the conditions that give rise to interpreters' dilemmas and strategies of identification.[7] Subject formation in translation describes a process in which subjectivities are formed through linguistic, discursive, and physical displacements across steep power divides. It is, in other words, the process of being translated—and translating oneself—across structures of power and recognition. The process bespeaks a lived experience of disjunction in and through channels of recognition—and experiences of recognition in and through conditions of disjunction.

This process, as in any performative process of subject formation, is indeterminate. The seemingly stable contours of discourse are products of repeated citational performance. The power of discourse, as Judith Butler has shown, is to "produce the phenomena that it regulate[s] and constrain[s]" (1993, 2). That subjects necessarily come into being through subjectivation in discourse does not mean that they lack self-reflexivity in the process, or that they perform social scripts just as institutions of power desire. Further, interpreters' self-reflexive interventions in those

---

7. Etienne Balibar's "Subjection and Subjectivation" (1994) provides a succinct elaboration of Foucault's concept (1991).

scripts—their subversive translations—are also potentially significant material interventions within broader social fields. The concept of self-reflexivity or agency is distinct from that of "free will." Reflexive agency suggests the possibility for creative and critical responses to systems of knowledge/power. In this sense, agency is often strategic and is sometimes subversive. Michel de Certeau conceptualizes strategy as subjects' "calculation (or manipulation) of power relationships" (1984, 218). The breadth of interpreters' agency is not limited to strategic action, though much of the action they took as conduits of US power—and now as members of the Iraqi diaspora in the United States—is strategic.

Members of the refugee network face the US state as well as the Iraqi diaspora with a rage of strategic identifications as gendered and filial subjects—daughters, brothers, would-be fathers, for example—within regulatory regimes that have emerged out of the translation encounter between discourses of US power and of Iraq "culture." These identifications reveal, as Stuart Hall suggests, the "points of temporary attachment to the subject positions which discursive practices construct for us" (2000, 19). In the diaspora, network members continue to find themselves in structures of power and recognition within which they translate themselves and are translated.

My use of the concept of *subject formation in translation* posits identification as a discursive, state-mediated, and physical practice. As such this work intervenes into three related scholarly discussions about subject formation and identification. First, engaging with the work of Judith Butler (1990, 1993) and Stuart Hall (2000), among others, who have theorized how "identities" cohere, transform, or dissolve around our subject-positions in discourses, this work examines how identification arises out of contested discursive practice. Identification represents our fleeting attachment to the subject-positions that discourses of power call into being: the nexus between discourses of power that hail us into particular subject-positions and our subjective self, which as it inhabits subject-positions, signifies and resignifies them.

My interlocutors' range of identification practices as filial subjects—patriarchal protectors-to-be or sacrificial daughters, for example—represent "temporary attachments" to the subject-positions available to them at the intersection of Iraqi public discourses surrounding wartime filial responsibility and American discourses around terrorism and liberation in Iraq. Network members strategically, if fleetingly, attach themselves to Iraqi wartime narratives that position Iraqi women as heroic victims of war and soldiering men as their defenders. Those tropes take on new meaning upon their translation into authoritative US discourses about "liberation" (*tahrir*) and "terrorism" (*irhaab*), within which Iraqi women in particular were figured as victims in need of outside protection from internal threats, and to which network members also strategically attach themselves, if subversively.

Practices of identification such as these are embattled responses to an imperative to identify a checkpoint. Indeed, practices of identification would not exist but for checkpoints that call them into being. I situate this process of "hailing" in relation to the state and other forces of governmentality.[8] Under structures of US military and immigration services, Iraqi interpreters-turned-refugees are subjectivated as cultured subjects and as the "reasonable" interpreters of suspicious cultural terrain. This work contributes to discussions about the ways in which states "administer" cultural difference. Elizabeth Povinelli (2002), Aihwa Ong (2003), and Talal Asad (2003) demonstrate how state structures that aim to accommodate "multiculturalism" become administrators of difference, deciding what cultural forms are acceptable and what are suspect. The imperative to identify is thus steeped in suspicion and, unsurprisingly, gives rise to suspicious identities vis-à-vis structures of power. Depoliticized or culturally reductive interpretations of my interlocutors' identification practices would not only misunderstand them, but may well serve the interests of US state power whose rhetoric about victimized Iraqi women and violent Iraqi men would only find new fodder.

Finally, my theorization of subject formation in translation situates practices of identification in place. Rather than essential and timeless, practices of identification reflect local material conditions: of war and

---

8. Situating practices of identification in relation to state power, I thus draw on the work of Louis Althusser (1970) and Michel Foucault (1991).

occupation. Building on the work of Edward Said (2001) and James Clifford (1994), I understand my interlocutors' identification strategies in the diaspora to be complexly layered products of displacement processes. Their strategies in the diaspora respond to situated conditions there, and call upon previous strategies used in other time-places: behind US uniforms and pseudonyms under occupation, and under surveillance as members of the war generation. Some have used the term "diaspora of empire" to refer to diasporic networks that are products of military or economic imperialism (Naber, 2012). Building on postcolonial scholars who figure diaspora as the "reminder and remainder of the nation's historical past" (Mercer 1994, 7), Naber's "diaspora of empire" aptly describes contemporary Middle Eastern diasporas formed in the wake of US-led or US-backed wars over the past half century. The unique global-political and intimate-memorial conditions in a diaspora of empire distinguish the diasporic identities that take shape there from other diasporic communities or "transnational" identities writ large (Ferguson and Gupta 1992). An appreciation for these individuals' unique positionalities as embattled imperial subjects and agents contributes to the wider literatures on diasporas of empire. As Nadine Naber (2012) and Louise Cainkar (2009) show, diasporas of empire face distinct problems of belonging and threats of "de-Americanization" in the era of domestic and global war on Arab and Muslim populations.

In light of my interlocutors' multifaceted strategies of identification, a distinctive politics of policed belonging come into view. To probe the political and affective ties of belonging in the diaspora, I build on concepts of cultural citizenship and transnational citizenship. I conceptualize citizenship as a legal-political and sociocultural set of relationships among people, states, and national bodies (Ong 2003). As a process of self-making and being-made, citizenship refers to the encounter between individuals and the state as well as intersecting sociocultural matrices of membership. These processes materialize in individuals' practices of identifying, claiming belonging, and coping with exclusion. Building on the work of Aihwa Ong, I define cultural citizenship as the structures of belonging that cohere around dominant sociocultural categories and that underlie legal citizenship in the nation-state, while transnational citizenship refers to structures of belonging that cohere around interlocking sub- and supranational communities of membership. This book intervenes in the historically masculinist study of transnational practices, which too often assume women's attachments to home make their relationships to diaspora more "provisional" than those of men. Such assumptions can produce a feedback loop that shapes immigrant service agencies and produces gender inequalities based on reductive notions of gender. Revealing that despite expectations young Iraqi women appear more rooted and less "provisional" in the diaspora than do young men, this book opens new discussions about gender and transnationalism.

Network members' identification strategies translated into gendered practices of cultural citizenship vis-à-vis the United States and transnational citizenship with respect to the global Iraqi diaspora, and with some surprising outcomes. Especially by taking jobs within state and parastate infrastructures, men appear able to assume an assimilationist stance regarding the United States, identifying as binational citizens. Paradoxically, they also appear more able to imagine a future in Iraq. At the time of this writing, Husham has found a job working at a refugee service agency as a caseworker, and recently he became a US citizen; Abbas has moved back to Iraq, though he returns to the United States to work seasonally. By contrast, women in the network assume a more "insulationist" stance vis-à-vis both US and Iraqi national communities, frequently expressing both instrumental and affective ties to the identity of a "refugee." Meena, like many of the women I met, does not see a life for herself in Iraq, nor does she consider herself "American." She finds a place for herself betwixt and between both national communities, insulated as best as possible from the dangers of each for a single woman. Yet, far from provisional, women's diasporic lives appear more rooted and permanent than do men's.

An "Écouteur" in the Diaspora

I was both an intimately familiar and a foreign kind of "écouteur" or listener in the diaspora, and the accounts gathered here are products of a distinct kind of listening or "écoute" (Pandolofo 2006). Perhaps the best way to capture the unique research encounter that unfolded in my fieldwork is to elaborate on the linguistic dynamics that emerged. To my surprise, the accounts I gathered were overwhelmingly rendered in English. My conversations with young Iraqis often began in Arabic and included Arabic phrases.[9] Almost always, however, we found a way back to English. This puzzled me. I considered the possible explanations: almost across the board, their English is better than my Arabic; they *worked* as English interpreters; and it was largely about this work that we were speaking. Each of these likely had a role to play. Eventually, though, I settled on the explanation that I began with: that I was a certain kind of "écouteur" or listener, and our encounters lent themselves to a unique kind of "listening." We meandered between languages but we landed in English. In English, they enunciated certain subjectivities, which I was uniquely able to study in English—to the exclusion of others.

In English we carefully positioned ourselves vis-à-vis our past and present trades—for me, immigration work and academic anthropology, and for my interlocutors, military interpretation and work in the armed services or refugee agencies—across which we shared many features of a dominant discourse. In this way, our relationship was laden with immediate interpersonal and historical-discursive power relationships. My connection with many interlocutors evolved well beyond a professional relationship; I connected with various participants as neighbors, fellow students, and activists. Still, our trades remained very present in our relationships. In the recent past, interpreters had encountered refugee officers serving in the capacity that I once had. Though all understood that I maintained no connections to the federal government, my past employment shaped how my interlocutors viewed me and, in some relationships more than others, it created a formal dynamic that took time to overcome. A few interpreters remarked on the fact that my working for the US immigration services seemed as unlikely as them having worked for the US military. One friend continues to call me *thabita* (officer) ironically to this day.

9. I have studied Arabic for over a decade and received multiple grants to study both *Fuhsa* (and *Hassaniya* dialects) across the Middle East; I have also conducted other field research in Arabic (see Campbell 2010). For this research project, I followed the lead of my interlocutors in deciding on the language of the interviews.

Given my past work with the US federal government, I reflected with refugee network members about the degree to which we occupied a common body of knowledge. We had been wartime professionals of sorts—a field with many overlapping acronyms, acquaintances, and geographies, which also involves the exchange of adrenaline-soaked war stories, activist petitions, or book reviews. These exchanges were almost always in English. We were in similarly liminal positions, balancing seemingly opposed commitments and identities: they, Iraqi sons, daughters, or citizens and US allies and residents; and me, anthropologist, researcher, activist, and former government official, passenger on that C-130 landing in Baghdad. We were wartime professionals, with extremely alterious histories and asymmetrical power dynamics to be sure, but with reference to a discourse that continued to call us back, again and again. The language we spoke—literally and figuratively—reminded me of the deep histories—of imperialism, Western orientalism, and US occupation, which made our encounter possible.

That C-130 descent into Baghdad was, therefore, formative of this work. My uneasy relationship to the US state in an era of global war shaped my intellectual, political, and affective relationship to the "warscape" I entered (Hoffman and Lubkeman 2005). My personal and scholarly commitments to the Middle East (and its diasporas) also shape my approach to this research. My preexisting and ongoing ethnographic research across the Middle East—in Algeria and Jordan primarily—on issues of refugee displacement, my longstanding involvement in New England diasporic networks, and my training in Middle Eastern studies and critical ethnography within the vibrant intellectual communities of the Bay Area dynamically inform my approach to this work.

This fieldwork experience proved starkly different from projects I have conducted elsewhere, such as in the Saharawi refugee camps in Tindouf, Algeria, where I lived conducting research in a delimited place, but where accessing a space of ethnographic inquiry that was mutually shaped and trusted with interlocutors proved difficult. In Tindouf, living with a family in their camp home, my role as an écouteur was shaped by the fact that: (1) I was a woman, positioned within the family's gendered division of labor, rarely in contact with men, and almost never alone; and (2) I was an outsider with a passport, in an impoverished camp, who was at best observing or at worst interrupting everyday life there. Given these social and power dynamics, I gained a partial snapshot in a holistic picture of (a woman's) daily life in the camp, but lost much of the larger sociological or historical view. By contrast, in this research project, I was not able to glimpse a holistic view of my interlocutors' lives—I did not know them in Iraq, I did not meet their families, and our relationship was, as I have indicated, indelibly shaped by our past and present trades. I sometimes regretted this. But the conditions in the refugee network—and my position in it—guided a distinct and ultimately fruitful method of fieldwork, also inspired by transnational ethnographic methods, which reject the notion of "bounded groups that are tightly territorialized, spatially bounded, or culturally homogenous" (Appadurai 1990, 196). I found that some of my interlocutors ardently wanted to talk to me—one-on-one and anonymously. I received calls from interpreters whom I had never met requesting a meeting with *me*. Through individualized relationships with members in the network, I was able to take a larger view of their present subject-positions, contextualizing them within a network of others who were similarly situated. Thus on an individual basis I was able to delve deeply into the everyday experience of the dilemmas and strategies that I found they widely shared.

Giving an Account: Field Methodologies

I used a combination of participant observation and oral history methodologies to bring into focus my interlocutors' lives inside the refugee network.[10] A total of fifty network members became active interlocutors

---

10. The data I share from my time in Iraq consists largely of observation on US bases and in the immigration bureaucracy. While working for the federal government, I had firsthand experience working on US military bases as well as meeting with Iraqi refugees and adjudicating their claims for asylum. In this work, I do not include any personal information about the Iraqi or American men and women I encountered from this period. I include no data whatsoever about specific refugees I met in my capacity as a refugee officer. All of the observations included relate to institutional contexts and procedural matters. After ending my work with the government, I also conducted online surveys with US soldiers and currently employed interpreters. One network member

in this research, though I interviewed over 125 people involved somehow in the refugee network (including, for example, refugee resettlement officials or roommates of the key research group). I spent the majority of my fieldwork in the Boston metropolitan area, but also spent time with Iraqis living in Central Massachusetts and Providence, Rhode Island. I met Iraqi interpreters living as far north as Portland, Maine and as far south as New Haven, Connecticut. In the New England region, I became acquainted with former interpreters through mutual Iraqi acquaintances—sometimes mysteriously, other times mundanely. For example, one of the first research contacts I made was through a friend of mine in another state. My friend told me simply: "There is a really tall Iraqi guy in Rhode Island, named Mohammed. Just ask any Arab there for the Iraqi, 'Mohammed Tawiil' [tall Mohammed]." Sure enough, through friends of friends I tracked down "Mohammed Tawiil." He, in turn, introduced me to a few other Iraqis in Rhode Island (his sponsor, for example) over coffee and hookah—Iraqis he would later warn me to "avoid."

In this delicate way, I participated in the everyday life—at home, work, and school—of each of my interlocutors. Given that this was a dispersed network, one of the most effective methods to immerse myself in members' everyday life was to "shadow" them for several days at a time. In addition to everyday meals, meetings, and errands, I took part in special events and holiday *iftars*; I talked to network members' families over Skype; I joined them at their US naturalization ceremonies; and I lived for periods of time in the apartments of female network members. My everyday engagement in the refugee network provided the grounding to the oral life histories and discourse analysis that would constitute the driving force of my research.

Oral history is both a method of scholarly inquiry and a modality of subjects' self-accounts in everyday life—much like Meena finds herself

---

in Boston, who maintained many contacts with US Forces and interpreters, sent out an e-mail requesting participation in an anonymous online survey about "The Role of Terps in the US Iraq War." A total of forty-nine interpreters participated; thirty-three US service members participated. While not the focal point of the study, these surveys shed light on the broader themes studied through participant observation and oral history.

giving accounts of herself to her landlords. As an investigative methodology, I understand oral history to broadly describe a dialogic field method that captures subjects' "history of the present." Scholars have utilized oral history as a mode of empowering or authorizing frequently silenced voices (Thompson 2000, 3). A key way that oral history methods "transform" knowledge production is by shifting typical structures of intellectual authority toward a configuration of shared authority (Frisch 1990). Questions of power and authority within structures of knowledge production remain central concerns of mine in this research. At the same time, the social life and significance of oral histories are not limited to the academic purposes to which they might be put. Oral histories also represent performative moments of self-making in everyday life, as Luisa Passerini has shown (1992, 1998).

The oral history method is thus dialogic in two important senses. First, oral histories hinge on the presence of an interlocutor in addition to the subject and a dialogue between the two (Abrams 2010, 54). In this situation, both subject and interlocutor are discussant and historian. To the extent that they both are involved in setting the parameters of the dialogue, they are both involved in producing the text and the analysis that may arise from it. The genre of account captured through oral history is not comprehensive precisely because it emerges from situated dialogue and not "objective" interpretations of static texts. A second way in which oral history methodologies are dialogic is their nonlinear approach to memory, in which accounts contain multiple historical frames within them. Within the context of the dialogue, there is no firm division between "past" and "present." Annette Kuhn writes that memory "is neither pure experience, nor pure event. Memory is an account, always discursive, always already textual" (2007, 264). I found this particularly true doing diaspora-based research in the midst of an ongoing conflict. Pasts layered upon one another in subjects' utterances in the present.

I collected network members' oral histories under two different circumstances: during the space of interviews and in casual conversation.[11]

---

11. For each of the fifty key interlocutors, I accumulated hours of tape. With each hour of tape, I transcribed and (when necessary) translated each word and reviewed

The topics covered in oral histories were left open-ended. However, I aimed broadly to address four areas of inquiry: interpreters' family life, memories, and background; interpreters' learned and lived narratives of Iraqi history, with reference to a few historical benchmarks, such as the Iran-Iraq war, sanction, and the US invasion; interpreters' memories and accounts of daily life working with US Forces; and, finally, interpreters' accounts of resettlement and daily life in the United States.[12]

The excerpts of oral history that I have included as case studies in this work shed light on broader phenomena across the refugee network. Patterns that emerge across the particularities of my interlocutors' accounts speak to common experiences of displacement, dilemmas of identification, and creative responses in everyday practice. I chose the central "characters" in this book because their stories—and their telling of them—were especially compelling in illuminating issues I saw among many others in similar situations. I have quoted excerpts from interpreters' oral histories word-for-word and often at length. The choice to quote interpreters

transcripts with interlocutors, who revised or responded to the text; some were more interested in involving themselves in that process than others. I did this not to correct a text in order to find a truer meaning, but to continue the dialogic process. In addition to interviews, I also recorded everyday conversations between individuals, their roommates or friends, and myself over dinner. In both instances, these were useful transcripts with which to juxtapose interview accounts. Neither instance is more "real" than the other, though the affect and tenor varied.

12. I examined these spoken texts at three interrelated levels: at the level of syntax, at the level of the speech act, and at the level of broader sociohistorical context. At the level of syntax, my analysis focused on the correspondence between particular constructs and signs; for example, I was interested in tracking slippages in subject usage from "we" to "they" when talking about Iraqis. At the level of the speech act, my analysis focused on the social parameters and audience of an utterance; centrally, I was concerned with the immediate power dynamics at play in the performance of speech, such as the terms of the question to which an utterance might respond and the language in which it is spoken. Finally, at the level of sociohistorical context, my analysis focuses on the intertextuality of speech, considering how one evokes particular vocabularies, narratives, or tropes both directly and indirectly. For more on critical discourse analysis, see Fairclough (2001, 2003).

at length both allows interpreters to speak for themselves and to enable narrative context to build for the reader. I strive to present the interpreters who chose to share their life histories in this book as interlocutors rather than "informants." They have co-shaped the project and text. Short, decontextualized quotes would do a disservice both to their stories and to the readers who have chosen to take them on.

Especially given the conditions of suspicion in the network, protecting the identities of my interlocutors was a guiding concern in my fieldwork. My interlocutors always chose where we met and under what terms. In this book, I have used pseudonyms, selected by my interlocutors themselves. To guard their privacy, I also changed certain identifying information, including the suburb or city in which individuals live. With permission and often upon request, I have also altered certain elements of historical/ biographical information that are particularly sensitive, such as the military unit with which they were deployed in Iraq.

Still, this ethnographic study, like most others, did not come without quandaries. I became friendly with people who were not necessarily friends with one another. Perhaps most challenging was the fact that my relationship with any particular former interpreter could become—and often was—subject to the suspicions and probing of another. When friends learned that I had met with certain members of the refugee network, they might initially advise me to "never to speak with him again" or they might ask me what he had said. Navigating these situations with grace was sometimes challenging. My tactic in negotiating such scenarios involved constant reminders to my friends about my unusual position in the network as a researcher; though my relationship with network members was friendly, I would belabor the point that I had to follow the codes of research. With my appeals as a researcher, my interlocutors learned quickly that I never spoke about the interviews I had had with others, as much as they baited me to gossip. However, *their* commentaries on my meetings with other network members remained prevalent for the entirety of my fieldwork. The degree to which I included those commentaries in my work depended on the wishes of those involved. For example, Husham and Abbas each gave permission to include their quarrels, briefly introduced above. Where network members' commentaries refer to individuals not represented in this work, I have changed names, locations, and other identifying information to protect those individuals' identities.

In addition to the complex relations among my interlocutors, I was also an essential actor in the social frame that unfolds here. Therefore, my analyses reflect my positionality as an interlocutor in that frame. What follows is, to be sure, *my* interpretation. However, I do not presume to be the final interpreter of the accounts that follow. Rather than a silent, all-knowing analyst outside the frame of the ethnography, I attempt to position myself on every page as an interlocutor, with quandaries of my own.

1

The Last Ba'thist Generation

In their powerful Introduction to *We Are Iraqis*, Nadje Al-Ali and Deborah Al-Najjar ask: "What happens when a community—be it a political group, an ethnic or religious community, or a whole nation—deals with devastating events? How is the identity of communities implicated in and reshaped by overwhelming circumstances? How are violence and mourning encoded into collective narratives and how are such narratives psychologically, sociologically, and culturally implicated in the interpersonal dynamics of trauma?" (2013, xxv). To understand the identification struggles of US-allied Iraqi youth requires an appreciation of the war-torn milieu in which they grew up and the collective narratives of war that were circulated and contested over their early lives in Iraq.

Iraqi interpreters' identification strategies under US occupation and in the diaspora can be contextualized against the backdrop of decades of war, when their national identities were sites of active signification, resignification, and resistance. Over the years of international conflict and sanctions, pliant gendered tropes of filial attachment became tools by which young Iraqis—like Iraqis in general—made claims of citizenship and national belonging. Born between the early 1970s and the late 1980s, the interpreters who follow the global route I track here came of age in a country engulfed in seemingly ceaseless wars. Though varied in regional, class, religious, and political backgrounds, their shared experiences of loss in the Iran-Iraq War; their shared memories of cities under siege, a faltering Iraqi military, and ensuing intifadas during the Gulf War period; and their shared endurance of a decade of austerity under an international embargo, paired with state decline, combine to make these children of war a generation with distinctive dilemmas and sensibilities.

27

This generation of war, characterized by steadfastness (*sumud*) in public narratives of the 1990s, sharply contrasts with the generation that came before, dubbed by the Ba'th Party the "revolution generation." This older generation, born between the early 1950s and late 1960s, witnessed or participated in the 1968 revolution, the ascendance of the Ba'th Party, and the rise of Saddam Hussein to power. In both the case of the "revolution generation" and the generation characterized by steadfast endurance—what I term the "war generation"—the Iraqi state deliberately sought to cultivate generational sensibilities in line with Ba'thist ideologies and the national needs of the day. If not those Ba'thist efforts themselves, then the shared political conditions under which the two generations came of age (roughly 1963–83 and 1983–2003),[1] succeeded in establishing discrete generational identities tied to national visions of Iraq as "ascendant" and in crisis, respectively (Davis 2005). The mark of success is apparent today in lasting divides between the two generations. As historian Dina Rizk Khoury has observed: "The state's attempts to elevate and manipulate the . . . birth of a new sensibility for a Ba'thist generation [the revolution generation] of Iraqis has left a memory that continues to play themselves out in the present. It has created generational fissures between Iraqis whose formative years were in the 1960s and those who grew up under the Ba'th and have no memory of life without war" (2013, 217).

Even prior to the US-led war and occupation of 2003, distinctive generational politics took shape between the revolution generation and the war generation revolving around multiple axes. First, the projects of Arab nationalism and socialism of the 1960s—broadly supported among many in the revolution generation—had declined to such a degree by the 1990s that the war generation appeared widely disenchanted from both,

1. 1963 marks the first Ba'thist revolution in Iraq, beginning a political era defined by the party's powerful political presence. Though it was ousted shortly after its 1963 revolution, the Ba'th was reinstated in the successful 1968 revolution. The year 1983 marks a midway point in the Iran-Iraq War, when military realities and the political climate began to dramatically shift from a revolutionary outlook of an Iraq on the ascent to a view of Iraq as in crisis and under threat. The year 2003 marks the beginning of the US-led war and occupation.

and especially from the Ba'thist appropriation of them. Second, diverging relationships to the "outside" (*barra*) of Iraq—that is, international media and politics—distinguished the generations' daily experiences and aspirations: while the revolution generation had transnational experiences and ideologies that informed their Iraqi nationalism, many in the war generation grew up with a deeply felt sense of isolation from the world that sowed a desire to connect with a world beyond Iraq. Finally, increasing urbanization and government policy undermined historically rural-based tribal practices during the revolution generation, while the war generation experienced a resurgence of (neo)tribalism given economic turmoil and government frailty.

The US-led invasion was a watershed moment, which sharpened generational fissures by precipitating a series of somewhat contradictory developments: the mobilization of youth within an array of political or military projects in the context of occupation and contests over the new Iraq; the growing sectarianism among some youth and, simultaneously, a growing cynicism about religion altogether among others; and a generational exodus of young men and women from Iraq—a significant portion of the larger refugee outmigration. Perhaps one of the clearest of generational fissures, however, related to practices of gender and prescribed filial roles over the turbulent decades between the 1960s and 2000s.

During the formative years of each generation, publicly sanctioned gender constructs were disciplinary mechanisms by which the state defined the sensibilities of each generation and by which the generations' members came to understand themselves. The revolutionary gender norms and family practices of the late 1960s, 1970s, and early 1980s— when the revolution generation came into adulthood—gave way to reactionary and conservative gender norms and family laws in the mid- to late 1980s, 1990s, and 2000s when the war generation came of age. Each generation was dynamically shaped by hegemonic constructs of the Iraqi man, the Iraqi woman, and the Iraqi family, which were tied to the nationalist narratives or wartime patriotism of the moment. The centrality of gender identity to national identity is not unique to Iraq and is the focus of extensive research in Middle East studies. Emerging out of colonial contexts, women became markers of the nation—and men bearers of the state—in diverse sociocultural contexts as shown by Leila Ahmed (1992) and Lila Abu-Lughod (1998), for example. What may distinguish this case is the rapidity with which the contours of that construct morphed in a matter of a generation.

Here I investigate the changing ideologies of gender—and the changing family structures in which gendered relations are embedded—as a framework for understanding the generational politics between Iraq's first and last Ba'thist generations. Positioning the experiences of the war generation in relation to the revolution generation clarifies the manner in which life under the Ba'th shaped this distinctive generation's choices, strategies, and structures of desire under occupation. Drawing on the work of historians Dina Rizk Khoury and Eric Davis who are among a few scholars to theorize generational politics in Iraq, I discuss the defining historical events of each generation—revolutions, wars, popular uprisings, and sanctions—and the distinguishing ideologies surrounding gender and family that came to define each historical period and generation. This historical analysis helps bring more sharply into view that crucible moment of 2003, into which the war generation was foisted as key players in military and political battles, confronting them with gnawing questions of performed national identity, gender performance, and filial duty. I intersperse the voices and recollections of my interlocutors—members of the refugee network in Boston—who belong to that generation and whose choice to ally themselves with the United States becomes all the more poignant in light of these embattled histories.

Generational Histories Part I: Precursors

Dina Rizk Khoury observes that Iraq's war years are a "perpetually present past" (2013, 245). The Iran-Iraq War and the First Gulf War were organizing forces in these young people's lives, and they remain so today. Members of this generation in the diaspora recount memories of war—some embodied, others narrated, both personal and collective. My interlocutors recall the shift in the meaning and purpose of their childhoods and the total reorientation of daily life during the Iran-Iraq War; they remember the sorrow that accompanied mourning relatives who were lost in the war, mixed with the comfort of rituals to honor war martyrs. Iraqis in the diaspora recollect the sound of nearby airstrikes, the shrieks of neighbors crying in fear, and the numbing terror that set in during the urban warfare of the First Gulf War. The subsequent sanctions era between 1991 and 2003 was just as formative, as these young men and women attempted to carve out paths of their own in a society shaken by war and an economy shattered by the international embargo. By the time that Operation Iraqi Freedom began in March 2003, my diverse interlocutors were in their late teens to early thirties and considering their next moves.

They had lived through a lifetime of transformative events in a matter of decades. Yet, rather than beginning their life histories with significant historical events through which they had lived, members of the refugee network began their stories with the Ba'th Party's consolidation of power, British colonialism, or even earlier events. Though they had not lived through Iraq's formation in the early twentieth century or the rise of the Ba'th Party in the middle of that century, these young men and women did not narrate their own experiences in Iraq—or the choice to work with US Forces—except with reference to the country's larger historical milieu. The personal histories they shared with me were deeply interwoven with national histories. Such a weaving of the national into the personal and vice versa had been an explicit goal of the Ba'th Party for Iraqi citizens— especially for children and youth. Eric Davis has shown that the Ba'th deliberately sought to inculcate a hegemonic historical memory, so that Iraqi citizens saw themselves as part of grander historical projects. The Ba'th sought to "restructure the younger generation's understanding of the past" (Davis 2005, 161) in an effort "to build a new Iraqi man and society" (ibid., 146). Instead, as Davis argues, the Ba'th Party "became captive to its own historical memory—namely one of cruelty, torture, war, and economic degradation" (ibid., 277). Appropriating one of the Ba'th Party's technologies of power for their own purposes, young Iraqis continually spoke of their lived experiences of "cruelty, torture, war, and economic degradation" within a larger historical narrative about cycles of externally and internally imposed injustice and tyranny.

Colonization

Members of the refugee network continually reminded me that the contours of the current Iraqi state were a creation of the British—as was the notion that the peoples living in its territory belonged to a common nation (compare historical analyses along the same lines by Zubaida 2002 and Dodge 2003). So too were certain enduring structures and strategies of rule in Iraqi legacies of the British. Though the nation-state was an absolutely seminal force in young Iraqis' lives, they did not take the state for granted. For example, Tariq belongs to a historically large, transnational tribe, and he informs me that many in his grandparents' generation felt a greater affinity to the tribe than to the nation-state. While he and his parents' generation felt "national pride" because of wartime patriotism, he suspects that Iraqis' loyalty may once again splinter into supranational tribal, religious, and ethnic channels in the future. By contrast, Mikhaeil, a Christian from Mosul, dreams of establishing a new political entity, a semiautonomous region for all of the Middle East's Christians—who are now weakened by their dispersal across artificial national borders—within Iraq's borders. Each of these national visions is steeped in a historical memory of the colonialism—of the drawing of borders and the movements of people, both physical and affective—that accompanied colonial state formation.

Indeed, Iraq's centuries of colonialism cast a long shadow over Iraqis' historical memory. Before British colonialism, the Ottoman Empire governed Iraq from the sixteenth century to the early twentieth century as three distinct provinces: Mosul in the north (populated by a largely Kurdish population), Baghdad in the center (largely Sunni Arab), and Basra in the south (largely Shi'i Arab). After the dissolution of the Ottoman Empire, the British Empire integrated the formerly autonomous and demographically distinct Ottoman provinces—an expansive territory that also contained significant populations of Assyrians, Christians, Jews, Yazidis, and Sabeans. After that time, the definition of Iraqi nationhood became a political project of the colonial state, anticolonial movements, and Iraqi intellectuals (Bashkin 2009). Though the north and south of the country were putatively as much a part of the new Iraqi state, urban Sunni

Arabs of central Iraq were privileged with positions of power under the British colonial government. Both the Kurds in the north and Shi'a in the south lobbied the colonial government for independence from the new state, in 1919 and 1920 respectively, and both failed.

The British governed the heterogeneous territory through a heavy reliance on customary law, which empowered tribal leaders in Iraq's diverse regions to govern locally according to "tribal law" (Sluglett 2007; Efrati 2013). As Efrati has observed, "The 'tribe,' not the individual, was the lens through which their [British] interpretation of society gained coherence" (2013, 25). Through the implementation of the Tribal Criminal and Civil Disputes Regulation (TCCDR), shaikhs of Iraq's diverse communities were given support, arms, and titles to land by British officials, bolstering the role of local-level patriarchs—sometimes even "small men of no account" or "petty village headmen"—over those communities.[2] Those same colonial policies had significant impacts on gender in Iraq, effectively "tribalizing" women. The TCCDR subjected Iraqi women to intensified and now state-sanctioned interpretations of "tribal law" (Efrati 2013, 37).

That the sanctions era of the 1990s and the US invasion would see a "retribalization" of society—and of women—was clear in the accounts of my interlocutors, who critically reflected on the genealogies of Iraq's neo-tribalism. It was not only for this reason, however, that young Iraqis began their life histories with this period of national history. They appeared to do so for several other significant purposes: first, to show that the nation-state of Iraq was from its birth a contested artifact of colonialism; and second, to show that Iraq is an exceptionally diverse nation-state with historically rooted fractures and inequalities among the nation's regions and populations, which have only been exacerbated by foreign rule. (This move to historicize their lives in this way was often a strategy to counter metanarratives about primordial tribal, sectarian, and ethnic enmities,

---

2. These quotes come from Major Pulley, Political Officer, Hilla, to Civil Commissioner, Baghdad, August 6, 1920, quoted in Farouk-Sluglett and Sluglett (1983, 496); and "Administration Report to Sulaimaniyah Division for the Year 1919" sourced by Robert L. Jarman (1992, 4:719).

or Iraqis' inability to govern peacefully—metanarratives into which some found themselves drawn during their work as "cultural translators" for US Forces.) The third and perhaps the most urgent of reasons for these young Iraqis' autobiographical shift was to situate themselves and their families within the context of longer historical experiences of foreign occupation, national politics, or marginalization, which they understood to have informed their choice to work with US Forces.

Independence

When Iraq gained nominal independence in 1932, the state maintained close political and economic ties to Britain, which received the majority of oil contracts in Iraq. The British-backed Kingdom of Iraq remained a Sunni Arab–dominated government and persisted in governing through "tribal law," which "continued the process of tribalizing women" (Efrati 2013, 50). Anticolonial movements created a platform for forging novel Iraqi identities and visions. Under the leadership of the Communist Party, large-scale uprisings erupted in 1948 against de facto British control. A 1958 revolution marked the country's full independence from Britain; urban Sunni Arabs retained control of the government. Much of the national politics of the 1940s, 1950s, and early 1960s revolved around class rather than sect or ethnicity, however. Iraq's Communist Party was the largest in the region, and class struggle emerged as a focal point of national debate. While present, sectarian politics in this period were secondary to anticolonial and class-based political identifications (Haj 1997).[3] Further, a strong women's movement, represented by the Iraqi Women's Union and the League for the Defense of Women's Rights, grew in size and strength, challenging "tribal law" and women's disenfranchisement.

3. Hanna Batatu provides an adept summation for the rivaling revolutionary parties and movements of this period in *The Old Social Classes and the Revolutionary Movements of Iraq* (2012). It was not at all clear at this point in history that sectarianism would play such an important role in the country's politics and internal conflicts in the future.

Later Ba'th Party efforts strove to decidedly split from this era of con-tested politics in cultivating a newly unified revolutionary generation: the shaping of a generation meant to "set them apart from an earlier genera-tion whose sensibility had been formed in the melee of . . . politics" before the 1968 revolution (Khoury 2013, 182).[4] Though the goal of the revolu-tion may have been to unite Iraqis in one vision for Iraq, it was as clear after the 1968 revolution as it was at independence that no single Iraqi vision encompassed all of its citizens, given the regional, class, ethnic, and religious diversity of the country and the state-sanctioned exclusions and repression rooted in those differences. Instead, as my interlocutors attested, what it meant to be Iraqi, today as much as at the moment of national independence, was a varied and vernacular matter that depended on "who one was, where one was, and how one was raised, and how close to the government in power," as Meena put it. She insists that the multi-plicity of Iraqi national identities in no way suggests that the country of Iraq or Iraqis' feelings of nationalism were not "true and real." A diversity of citizens or national visions, she asserts, are not themselves threats to the existence of Iraq. Instead, it was and is the politicization of certain differ-ences—a pattern left by the British, and reinvigorated by the US occupa-tion—that threatened the cohesion of the country.

A politicization of ethnic and religious differences came to define Iraq in the aftermath of independence. Having consolidated power with independence, the dominant Sunni Arab Iraqi government responded to newly reignited uprisings by the Shi'i and the Kurdish populations by decisively quashing these rebellions and punishing their populations as a whole. Kurdish attempts at independence resulted in a series of brutal wars between the central government of Iraq and the Kurdish Peshmerga that would last for much of the late twentieth century. Another revolution, in 1963, put the Arab nationalist Ba'th Party in power. After falling briefly

---

4. Iraq's 1968 revolution occurred in the context of worldwide revolutionary move-ments, adding a particular sense of legitimacy and fervor to the generation's political sensibilities.

from power, the Ba'th would retake power in a decisive 1968 revolution and would remain in power for nearly forty years. In a large and diverse country, employment and educational opportunities were concentrated among urban, largely Sunni Arabs under the Ba'th no less than under previous governmental regimes. Inclusion within a state-backed vision of nationhood proved just as starkly divided as these material inequities.

For the dominant Sunni Arabs—many of whom by the 1960s espoused an Arab nationalist agenda—Iraqi national identity was explicitly Arab and de facto Sunni. This vision of Iraqi identity, which excludes Kurds and marginalizes Shi'a, was later borne out in government policies by the Ba'th Party that sought to "Arabize" Kurdistan through an Arabization campaign and marry Iraqi identity to state-sanctioned practices of Islam in a "Faith Campaign."

Generational Histories Part II: The Revolution Generation

The goal of the Ba'th Party when it rose to power in the 1960s was nothing short of its name: the "rebirth" of a new Iraqi society through the rec-reation of the Iraqi man, woman, and family. To achieve this rebirth, it attempted to mold a generation of Iraqis who identified with the revolu-tionary visions of Arab nationalism and state socialism, and who could become the champions of the revolution. The Ba'th Party saw the mobili-zation of school- and university-age youth to be key to its success, as had the Communist and other political parties across the Middle East. Sad-dam Hussein had himself become involved in the Ba'th party as a member of a student cell in Egypt in the late 1950s and early 1960s.

Saddam Hussein would be influential in the 1968 coup, which brought the Ba'th Party back to power (after its brief ouster) under president Ahmed Hassan Al-Bakr, serving as a deputy for much of Al-Bakr's presi-dency. Saddam Hussein officially became president in 1979, but had pos-sessed a great deal of power over economic, military, and foreign policy in Iraq for some time. If Iraq's school- and university-age youth in the 1960s and 1970s were the children of the revolution, then Hussein was one of the fathers of the revolution.

The 1968 Ba'thist revolution set out to "modernize" Iraq: to sever backward ties and practices associated with the patriarchal tribal society and to replace them with values of equality and modern progress. The Ba'th attempted to instill a sense of filial responsibility in the national family—as brothers and sisters of the revolution—rather than in kin and tribe. The Ba'th utilized the "iconography of [the] familial," as many state projects have done, to this end (McClintock, Mufti, and Shohat 1997, 90).[5] Education was central to the mission, and as a result the generation of the revolution was imagined as "children of schools" (*awlad al-madaris*). To a significant degree, the revolution generation consisted of urban, middle-class young people. While the term may be used to describe those in a similar age cohort throughout the country, the state's target population in forging a revolutionary generation was made up of educated city-dwellers—many of whom were already politically engaged in the wake of competing revolutionary movements. For example, Ali's father Yaqoob was a prime target of the state's generation-making efforts. From a middle-class Baghdadi family, he was active with the Communist Party off-and-on in the 1960s, and was skeptical of the Ba'th. An aspiring college professor of political science, Yaqoob was encouraged to join the Ba'th Party in 1971 and, ultimately, was compelled to teach aspects of Ba'thist ideology in university. At a moment of profound national transition, two defining social forces became central features for Yaqoob's generation as a whole: the far reach of the Ba'th Party structure into young people's everyday lives; and the Iran-Iraq War, whose effects on Iraqi society were near total.

The Party

The Ba'th Party faced the historically difficult task of consolidating political authority—and warding off yet another revolution—by using two opposing tactics: providing access to social benefits and state employment, on the one hand, and subjecting its citizens to constant surveillance, on

---

5. See also Collins (2000) and McClintock (1993).

the other. In an era of oil-fueled opulence, the Iraqi Ba'th Party provided unprecedented levels of state benefits to its citizens, including some of the best healthcare and education in the region. Moreover, on an informal basis, Iraqis around the country found themselves to be embedded in state patronage networks that dispensed resources and favors. Charles Tripp has argued that these patron-client networks constituted a "shadow state" in Iraq.[6] As young men and women, members of the revolution generation were enmeshed in such patronage networks, which promised to allow or prevent them from attending certain universities, to delay military service or secure preferable assignments, and to find desirable work within the government. One's position within these patronage networks had much to do with youth's position vis-à-vis the Ba'th Party structure.

The Ba'th Party's prized citizens, school- and university-age young people, were affiliated with the Ba'th Party as so-called sympathizers, supporters, or full party members. At a minimum, students were generally required to affiliate with the party as a sympathizer to attend government universities and later to secure government work—the largest employer in Iraq (Sassoon 2011, 189). A sympathizer attended party meetings, lectures, and assemblies at their schools, but did not necessarily belong to a "cell." The Ba'th Party operated through an autonomous cell-based structure, in which party affiliates belonged to small groups that were the eyes and ears of the party, reporting to an authority chain about potentially "antirevolutionary" activity in designated neighborhoods, schools, or workplaces. Some students became Ba'th Party supporters under pressure or to gain access to selective academic programs and employment opportunities.[7]

---

6. Tripp writes: "There existed in Iraq a dual state. The elaborate bureaucracy of government agencies, state-run enterprises and organizations formed the public state in Iraq. They comprised the ministries, the official associations, the armed forces and the Ba'th Party. But behind this law was a 'shadow state,' formed by networks of associates, chains of patrons and clients, circles of exclusions and privilege emanating from the office and the person of the president. This was the real nexus of power" (2007, 260).

7. Joseph Sassoon provides an excellent analysis of the metamorphosis of the Ba'th from a revolutionary movement into a security state apparatus in *Saddam Hussein's Ba'th Party* (2011). For a comparison to Syria's Ba'th Party leadership, Lisa Wedeen's

Others, like Husham's father Omar, joined enthusiastically by choice and worked their way up in the party. Husham says his father was as enthusiastic as one could be about the revolution. Omar taught his son revolutionary songs, which they would sing together before praying for party leaders every night. Husham remembers his father telling him once that if he concentrated hard enough, he could see the face of Saddam Hussein on the moon. Ba'th Party supporters, as Omar was at the beginning of his career in the Ba'th Party, were considered "candidate members," who belonged to cells and served as informants.

To become a full party member meant to fully commit to the role of informant. In addition to this all-important work, another key job was the recruitment of new young people into the web of party membership and citizen surveillance. Young people were the lifeblood of the party in large part because their vital role as ground-level devotees and lookouts paved the way for their formal participation in apparatuses of the Ba'thist state later in their lives. The transformation of the revolution generation from activist students into employees of a security state exemplifies the metamorphosis of the Ba'th Party itself.

Despite the presence of a notorious state intelligence agency, party cells were indeed the street-level units of citizen surveillance under the Ba'th. Several cells, unknown to each other, belonged to a "division," which in turn belonged to a "section," "branch," and "congress." This autonomous network structure was designed to ensure a dispersed and wide-reaching party base, cultivating party compliance of member and nonmembers alike, as one did not know who in their communities was affiliated with the party and who was not. Citizens' mutual surveillance was not limited to the formal party structures. Mutual surveillance was a revolutionary form of sociality in their neighborhoods, schools, workplaces, and even homes. Thus, the party was very much a part of the daily lives of the revolution generation. Young people's encounter with the state also structured their encounters with their family and peers.

Ambiguities of Domination (1999) examines the paradoxical rhetoric of fear and familiarity under conditions of totalitarianism.

Tamara's parents were of the revolutionary generation—but not of the revolution. Growing up as a young girl in the early 1980s, she remembers her parents talking about politics in front of her; they admonished her never to repeat what she heard. She admitted to me that she felt quite torn about this. She had fleeting fears that her dad was "very bad" because he once "spit at the picture of Saddam," whom she was supposed to love. Sensing Tamara's ambivalence, her father shared with her the terrifying story of their neighbor being arrested because the neighbor's daughter told her teacher something her dad had said at home. To avoid possible betrayals, Tamara's father adopted a code when talking about politics. Similarly, Abbas remembers that his parents would frequently speak unequivocally against "Sadr," whom he would later learn was a leading oppositional politician. Abbas would learn years later that his family, who lived in the Shi'i district called Saddam City (now Sadr City), was actually lambasting Saddam when they talked about "Sadr," and praising Sadr when they said "Saddam."

While messages about "Baba Saddam" (Father Saddam) were reproduced in schools, on the street, and at home, thousands of Iraqis were losing their own fathers in international and domestic wars and through political persecution. Though Saddam Hussein did not succeed in severing all "backwards" tribal and kin-based loyalties, he did ultimately—through the wars he waged—take the lives of thousands of Iraqi soldiers,[8] unsettling the typically male-headed families and undercutting the principal social unit in Iraq at the time: patriarchal households.

The Iran-Iraq War

Rather than a departure from the "revolution," the Ba'thist government constructed the first and longest of its international wars—the Iran-Iraq War—as a continuation of the revolution. Grandiose rhetoric constructed the war to be about Arab brotherhood, revolutionary progress against religious tyrants, and regional peace and justice. The "war experience" (*tajrubat*

---

8. This does not include the staggering loss of civilian life. Altogether, up to half a million Iraqis died according to estimates (Hiro 1991).

al-harb) was seen to be central to the sensibilities of the revolution generation. Narratives about the so-called war experience solidified both the values of the revolutionary generation (as modern and secular, fighting an Islamist enemy) and the goals of the revolutionary generation (national advancement through personal advancement). Khoury shows that the government's attempts "to render the war experience as transformative of the 'revolution' generation was directed at an expanding middle- and lower-middle-class educated, largely urban population. The generation's sensibilities as articulated in outlets of public culture was above all *modern*, defined by a set of signs that distinguished it from an earlier generation. This generation's members were characterized by *social mobility*, distinct from the generations of their fathers and grandfathers who were uneducated and relatively poor" (2013, 205; emphasis added). The war experience, she concludes, was "as generational as it was brutalizing" (ibid., 11).

The Iran-Iraq War spanned eight years and took hundreds of thousands of Iraqi lives (estimates range from 250,000 to 500,000 Iraqi casualties). Members of the refugee network could list with little hesitation all their extended family members martyred in the conflict. Several, like Anwar, lost their fathers. Others lost uncles and cousins. The war began in 1980 when Iraq invaded Iran shortly after the Shi'i cleric-led Islamic Revolution in that country; it is considered one of the most brutal wars in the twentieth century along with World War I and World War II (Hiro 1991). Chemical warfare was widespread and employed against combatants and civilians on both sides. The most heinous chemical attack was the genocidal campaign by the Iraqi military in Kurdistan, putatively against the Kurdish Peshmerga forces but in fact killing approximately 182,000 people—mostly civilians.

With the exception of isolated air raids at the onset of the war and missile attacks on city centers, the Iran-Iraq War was not primarily an urban war as the subsequent wars would be. Still the war touched all Iraqis and certainly every member of the revolution generation, the generation of fighting age. The "war experience"—defined by direct lived experience as well as by shared cultural iconography and nationalism—deeply affected members of this generation. However, not all young men of fighting age experienced the costs of war equally. To a degree, middle- and upper-class

Iraqis could insulate themselves from the demands and devastations of war. Wealthy or connected Iraqi men could pay an exemption to avoid military service. Young men could also delay their military service to pursue higher degrees in medicine, law, or other academic disciplines. While many in the revolution generation fought in the Iran-Iraq War, many did not, and instead became part of the war efforts in other ways—as doctors or government workers. The uneducated poor constituted the largest part of the Iraqi fighting machine. As largely middle-class, educated, and urban young people, the parents and relatives of my interlocutors who served in the war tended to serve in higher military positions, and they were sometimes quite removed from the frontline. While there can be no doubt that these youths' families were shaken to the core by war, the picture of the Iran-Iraq War from this cross-section is distinct from that of predominantly poor, rural families. When I asked Anwar how her martyred father had died, she informed me that the army captain had not died in combat, but rather in a car accident. But his sacrifice, she tells me, is just as important as any fallen soldier's. As we will see, Anwar's assertions of relation to a heroic martyr was an important avenue to make claims of citizenship and national belonging in this period—and beyond.

The terror of the Iran-Iraq War was also not evenly distributed among Iraqi civilians. Iraqi Kurds (many of whom were accused to be allied with Iran) and Shi'a (who were associated with Iran by religious sect) made up key targets against which the Iraqi fighting machine would be aimed. Citizens' own ethnic and religious identifications became the grounds for additional surveillance, interrogation, and imprisonment. Domestic repression intensified as the lines between deserter, dissident, and traitor blurred. Still, Eric Davis claims that the war effort on both the front and back lines cut across sectarian differences within the revolutionary generation, forging strong collective and national attachments. Davis contends, "Iraqis of all ethnicities worked together under extreme duress to successfully prosecute what was by all accounts the largest and most brutal war of the twentieth century . . . the war elicited a deep sense of nationalism among all sectors of Iraqi society" (2005, 199). If nationalist narratives proved unifying, they were also inflected with sometimes divisive generational, gender, and class messages.

1. Pile of helmets at the foundation of Baghdad's Victory Arch, alleged to have belonged to fallen Iranian soldiers. Photo by author.

Khoury concludes that the "war experience" was an instrumental wartime narrative, which the state deployed to transform Iraqi society and Iraqis themselves—especially Iraqis of a certain age and gender: "The war experience and its meaning became the cornerstone of the Iraqi state's attempts to transform the Iraqi self, particularly the male self" (2013, 9).

This war narrative became a dynamic and contested feature of public discourse. So central was gender performance to national identity that the construction of gendered selves of a certain kind was seen to be necessary for the success of the nation itself. Saddam Hussein's now famous display of fallen enemy soldiers' helmets at the Victory Arch in Baghdad illustrates the degree to which nationalist messaging materialized in and through the bodies of revolutionary Iraqi men and villainous Iranian men (see illustration 1). Crucially, the transformation of young male selves into Ba'thist citizen-subjects was tied to the transformation of female Iraqi selves into their equals—and the reinvention of both as brothers and sisters of the revolutionary nation. Thus, gender performance was embedded in revisions to models of filial responsibility, in which the national family was to replace the natal or tribal family, and bespoke wider changes to Iraqi family structures.

Generational Histories Part III:
Revolutions in Gender and Family

In a 1971 speech, Saddam Hussein proclaimed: "The complete emancipation of women from the ties which held them back in the past, during the ages of despotism and ignorance, is a basic aim of the Party and the Revolution. Women make up one half of society. Our society will remain backward and in chains unless its women are liberated, enlightened and educated."[9] The conversion of the male Iraqi self into a modern militant citizen was bound to the liberation of the female Iraqi self from "backward" tribal customs, and was believed to entail the radical equality between men and women. Citizenship in revolutionary Iraq meant identifying as national brothers and sisters and prioritizing the national family above all else. Reorienting gender and filial identifications in this way required a redefinition of patriarchal family structures; for this reason Saddam saw women's empowerment as key to his political agenda.

9. Speech given by Saddam Hussein on April 17, 1971, translated by K. Kishainy in 1981, quoted in Baram (1991).

Thus, the Ba'th Party positioned women on the forefront of the revolution alongside men. Formed in 1969, the General Federation of Iraqi Women became the state voice for a broad-based women's movement, expanding social programs for women and working to make legal reforms to afford women greater rights over marriage and reproduction. (The government responded by amending Personal Status Laws on two separate occasions, in 1983 and 1985, granting women greater rights in the family.) The model of revolutionary femininity projected by the state through publications like *The Iraqi Woman* was a modern, liberated, and militant woman whose match was her equally militant and progressive "brother" (Davis 2005, 164). Throughout the 1970s, models of revolutionary masculinity grew increasingly militarized and not simply politically militant, amid ongoing wars with the Kurdish Peshmerga and the approach of the Iran-Iraq War.

State and society as a whole grew ever more militarized, with armed men becoming the symbol of the Ba'thist state. Once the Iran-Iraq War had begun, more and more women took up arms alongside men. Women joined men in the Popular Army on the frontlines, and the General Federation of Iraqi Women played an active role in national security efforts back in Baghdad. Manal Younus, the former head of the General Federation of Iraqi Women, remembered, "During Iraq's defensive battle, Iraqi women became a security service defending the revolution, defending it by serving as perfect informants for the responsible security service . . . the woman showed no signs of fatigue, she always pursued victory and progress."[10] Members of the Federation were deployed to visit and monitor the families of martyrs, to ensure that their sorrow did not evolve into political discontent or pose any threat: in other words, to ensure that their loyalty to the national family remained strong—if not stronger than before—given the losses in their natal families.[11] In this period, prevailing urban, middle-class norms of masculinity and femininity for the "revolutionary

---

10. Quoted in Achim Rohde's *State-Society Relations in Ba'thist Iraq: Facing Dictatorship* (2014, 98).

11. Women also contributed considerably to the war effort professionally. Women filled workplaces in unprecedented numbers, and women workers in both industrial and government sectors were absolutely essential to the war effort.

generation" hinged on the performance of modernity and militancy, while the valences of these differed for men and women. Performing "modern" gender and filial roles as revolutionary sisters and brothers was central to claiming belonging in the modern nation.

By the mid-1980s, the war had taken an enormous toll, and national morale was suffering. As Nadje Al-Ali has argued, the Iraqi government dramatically changed its rhetoric on revolutionary gender equality "to boost [men's] morale by stressing male heroism and strength, and female honor and dependence on men" (2007, 97). The government disseminated new gender rhetoric in which women symbolized the nation, culture, and tradition and men represented the nation's defender. At the heart of this war propaganda were constructions of Iraqi men as heroic, brave, and untiring, and constructions of Iraqi women as both literally and figuratively attached to the home—indeed a home that was under attack. Al-Ali concludes, the state "moved away from propagating images of men and women working side by side to develop a modern progressive nation to images of men protecting the land assaulted by the enemy. And the land was invariably represented as a female whose honor might be taken away" (ibid., 153). Middle Eastern feminist scholars have long studied the ways in which scripting women as bearers of the nation is embedded in patriarchal state and societal relations.[12] Suad Joseph concludes that "the imaginary of 'women' authenticating a place of 'belonging,' a community of kin, a safe haven for family, a 'home,' has animated the most powerful rhetoric of the nation" and has often become captive to state projects and policies (2000, 7). Rather than equal sisters, Iraqi women were now constructed as mothers, whose national responsibility was to reproduce the next generation of Iraqis.[13]

According to Khoury, the "war experience" narrative had all along been a variegated and contradictory discourse, in which women (and men alike) were sent mixed messages about their national roles: guardian of the

12. See, e.g., Elizabeth Thompson's *Colonial Citizens* (2000).
13. See Noga Efrati's "Productive or Reproductive? The Roles of Iraqi Women during the Iran-Iraq War" (1999).

Iraqi tradition at home or militant fighter. Khoury writes of the war experience narrative: "At its heart was the male soldier, whose manliness and honor exemplified the new Iraqi subject" (2013, 183). Women were featured in the narrative variously as "objects of the soldier's love, symbols of land, and militant fighters in the Popular Army" (ibid.). If in the early days of the Iran-Iraq War, women faced dual pressures to both uphold Iraqi cultural traditions and project the country's modern, militant future, by the end of the war such ambiguity about women's roles had been decidedly resolved. The Revolutionary Command Center (RCC) reversed the earlier progressive amendments to Personal Status Law and encouraged women to return home, whether from the workforce or the warfront, and focus on their roles as mothers, taking care of their families and reproducing the nation. This shift began a period in which urban, middle-class models of masculinity hinged on the performance of military heroism (even if not on the frontlines), and models of femininity turned on the performance of maternal attachments to home and dependence on male military heroes to protect them. Certainly, the active women's movement resisted and subverted the demands of these official and public constructs, but their widely circulating potency cannot be overstated.

In part, this public discursive shift, matched by the RCC's reversal of policy to encourage women to go home, was seen as a necessity given societal conditions. With the tremendous loss of life in the war, widows of martyrs and the wives of POWs became heads of their households. Women who had held professional positions in Iraq and had high levels of education were pressured to go home. Khoury writes, "Defeats at the front, deaths, and desertion led to a policy reversal. Women were encouraged to return home, produce more children, and *strengthen the family*" (2013, 78; emphasis added). The governmental response to what has been called a "crisis of patriarchy" in this period presaged later chapters in Ba'thist policy to come during the Gulf War and subsequent sanctions era.

If the official position vis-à-vis women's rights and roles in society was contradictory, so too were the Ba'thist practices toward family structures as a whole. Ideologically, the party favored the nuclear family and, for a time, forbade tribal affiliation and identification (Joseph 1991). Simultaneously, the government administered benefits and punishments to extended family networks based upon those very identifications. (The government collected "information banks" on citizens that explicitly placed them within kin and tribal communities.) Given the emerging crisis of patriarchy, the state also inserted itself in matters of the family as never before. The RCC "acquired unprecedented legal power over such civil matters as marriage, divorce, inheritance, and a myriad of other private rights. In particular, the state singled out regulations on women's rights to cope with the crisis afflicting the patriarchal family structure" (Khoury 2013, 174). In the absence of family-level patriarchs, the party established itself as the ultimate patriarchal authority to decide disputes that local-level civil or religious authorities had once decided. Early advances for women were sacrificed for social stability and security in an era of emergent state patriarchy.

Generational Histories Part IV: The War Generation

The next generation in Iraq, the war generation, was a product of Iraq's "crisis of patriarchy," born into and raised by families ravaged by the nearly decade-long Iran-Iraq War. The children of the revolution generation gave rise to a generation that had always known Iraq as a nation at war. They grew up mourning martyred fathers, uncles, or cousins and supporting widowed mothers or aunts. The national experience of loss was personally and deeply felt by children of the Iran-Iraq War era. Beginning only two years after the Iran-Iraq War ended, the Gulf War was a turning point both in the history of Iraq and in many young people's lives: a moment when historically celebrated and now woefully underpaid military heroes left their posts; a period when resistance movements rose up and ultimately fell short of removing the Ba'th Party from power; a point after which the government would decline in power and popular support; and the long months that began an even longer decade of economically debilitating international sanctions.

Coming of age in this milieu, this generation was structured by a "war experience" narrative, as their parents' generation had been, but one whose content focused on victimization at the hands of foreign powers rather than military heroism: "The defining features of the new war experience in the wake of the Gulf War and during the embargo were survival, steadfastness, and victimhood. Mass media outlets portrayed women and children as heroes of the realties of a new kind of war" (Khoury 2013, 217). The heroic victim—best exemplified by the war widow, rather than the brave fighter—became the defining figure and icon of the new war narrative associated with the generation. The feminized heroic victim required male protection, just as the female emblem of culture and home had in the Iran-Iraq War's propaganda. However, in this iteration of public war narratives, the frontlines of male protection could be found in the domestic sphere, saving the country's female-headed households, rather than on the battlefields. Further, in the context of economic crisis, the primary, and ever more urgent, assertion of filial identification revolved around kin and tribal networks of support rather than the national family.

The Gulf War

"We had a few sweet years between the wars. But then, just like that, it was wartime again," Hiba remembers, "and you couldn't even remember the sweet years. Life went on. I was 14." Hiba met her future husband, Tariq, during the first air offensive of Operation Desert Storm, when his family temporarily moved in with hers. His family lived in Baghdad and hers outside of Basrah. Cousins, Tariq's family had moved to Hiba's family home in Basrah to wait out the American airstrikes on Baghdad. At age eighteen, he had paid an exemption to avoid military service, but not all of their family was so fortunate. They shared a cousin who had been deployed to Kuwait during Saddam Hussein's attempted annexation on the bordering country. The short war—lasting from August 1990 until January 1991—resulted in the intervention of the United States and several other states. Operation Desert Storm ended in a US military victory. Hiba and Tariq's cousin, Yoseph, was among tens of thousands of Iraqi soldiers who deserted their posts during the war.

Yoseph, like many in his generation, did not support Saddam Hussein's invasion of Kuwait. For several of my interlocutors, this decisive moment congealed their critique of the Iraqi government. It was equally as important a moment in the formation of Iraqis' critique of US militarism—the first instance in which many young people saw US policies directly impacting them. Especially after a brutal war with Iran and a brief taste of peace during what Hiba called the "sweet years," many Iraqis did not view Hussein's invasion of Kuwait—nor the US counterattack on Iraq—to take civilian life into account.[14]

Given the Iraqi military's loss in what was to be "the mother of all battles," average Iraqis' support of the government wavered. The government had exhausted so many of its resources and was in such a state of disarray that it could not afford to bring its soldiers home from the front (Simpson 1992). According to Davis, the government's rhetoric "was less self-confident in outlook and tone, more reactive than proactive, and lacking in focus" as compared to the rhetoric of the 1970s and 1980s (2005, 241). The official war narrative constructed Iraqis as victims of foreign aggression—steadfast and loyal survivors in the face of difficulty. The steadfast loyalty of Iraqi citizens, however, was up for question.

Iraqi civilians capitalized on the Iraqi government's disorganization after the war. With the support of the (banned) Shi'i Dawa Party and the Supreme Council for the Islamic Revolution in Iraq, residents of Southern Iraq rose up in what is called the "Sha'aban intifada" (uprising). Many of the participants were Iraqi soldiers who deserted their posts during the war; Hiba's cousin Yoseph was among them. Simultaneously, in the north, Kurds mounted widespread uprisings. In the north, the military aspect of the uprising was matched by political demonstrations for Kurdish independence, democracy, and freedom. While the southern unrest failed to oust Saddam, and ultimately led to a widespread retaliation upon Shi'a populations in the south, the northern uprisings were a partial success, though one that came at great cost. In response to aerial bombardment of civilians during the intifada, the UN coalition imposed a no-fly zone over the north to ensure the protection of civilians, which aided in the eventual formation of an autonomous Kurdish government.

14. Only a few Iraqis that I spoke to felt the war was necessary as a response to Kuwaiti "economic warfare," which they called Kuwait's excessive oil production (over agreed-upon OPEC levels) and extraction of Iraqi oil from a reserve bordering Kuwait.

Alleged perpetrators of the intifadas were tried and sometimes killed as traitors. Fearing for their lives, Iraqis involved in the uprising appealed to the US government. The United States airlifted hundreds of Iraqis, including Hiba and Tariq's cousin, Yoseph, to US bases in Saudi Arabia. From there, these Iraqis were granted refugee status in the United States, alongside hundreds of others who found their way out of Iraq, in what was the first major Iraqi refugee migration into the United States. Yoseph, who I would later meet in Boston, considered refugee resettlement an insufficient "gesture," in place of an effective military and political strategy on the part of US leaders to support Iraqis' popular uprisings in the early 1990s.

The fact that these intifadas had support among broad cross-sections of the population and that their suppression was far from certain—indeed, they were hardly fought—speaks to the significant decline in state power by this time. While the Ba'th Party and Saddam Hussein remained in power, their command over the state-sanctioned war narratives was increasingly contested by Iraqis' counternarratives. Iraqis' war narratives focused on their steadfast survival in the face of a weakening and erratic state, in addition to or instead of foreign powers, as the state would have it. Max remembers, "The government talked about us as victims, we talk the same way, but it meant something different. We meant that we didn't have enough food while Saddam is building new palaces."

Sanctions

Though aimed at the government, international sanctions hurt the citizens of Iraq the most. Exports were limited to oil, which was exchanged for basic foodstuffs, medicine, and necessities of life in the UN-brokered Oil-for-Food program. It was common for members of the refugee network to describe this period using the idiom of the "dark years." This descriptor rang true on multiple levels: the outside world felt increasingly blacked-out due to decreasing commercial or media interaction and, most profoundly, sanctions were an intensely challenging—dark—period. The generation of war was defined by their steadfast endurance of these conditions—but as Max suggests, perhaps not in the way that the state-sanctioned narratives would have it. Khoury writes, "According to the new narratives . . . the Iraqi nation was united by victimization. Its citizens were defined by their steadfastness (*sumud*), a term used by the government to describe the essence of Iraqi national traits as well as a new generation of Iraqis who had grown up under UN sanctions" (2013, 220). In reality, growing numbers of youth felt they needed to remain steadfast in the face of a declining state in addition to internationally imposed isolation.

In a country where a large sector of the population was employed by the government, a dramatic reduction in government funds meant a life-altering reduction in household incomes. Public health services, education, pensions, and stipends to martyrs were cut dramatically. The private sector was equally hard-hit, with the elimination of trade. Elite government officials who hoarded Oil-for-Food funds and some merchants working in the black market continued to live in relative comfort, while many in the country lived in or near poverty.

Ali spoke of the sanctions era as the period in which "things were sold." His father was once a shop owner, allowing them one of the better-appointed homes in a middle-class neighborhood. Ali recalls that after all the goods in the store had been sold, they began selling personal items. First they sold their car, then the household appliances and electronics, then the rugs and furniture, and then the gold. Finally, even the mundane household goods like pencils and pens felt like treasures. His father moved abroad (to Jordan and Egypt), as many Iraqis did, to find work where he could.

Facing similar circumstances in his family, Max recounts growing ever more suspicious of the government in the wake of the failed intifadas and international sanctions. In his words: "We lived our lives suspicious of almost everything we were told by the government. Everything it tells you is true proves to be wrong. We have been lied to a lot in our lives. During the uprisings, a patriot is shown on the news, he may prevail for two, three, four years. All of the sudden he's found to be a traitor and he's killed. And vice versa. We are told the country has been robbed by America, we have no money, and then we learn about Uday's parties." Max describes social conditions born out of dictatorship and economic destitution. His critique of the Ba'thist government was not incompatible with a searing critique of the international sanctions regime, which was ultimately responsible for the country's impoverishment and had, furthermore, turned a blind eye to the misallocation of Oil-for-Food funds.

The economic devastation of the embargo fell particularly hard on Iraq's many female-headed households. Young women were compelled to marry just to survive (and unable to leave dangerous marriages). Nadje Al-Ali demonstrates that "economic hardship pushed an increasing number of women into prostitution—a trend that caused much anguish in a society where a 'woman's honor' is perceived as a reflection of the family's honor" (2007, 201). Further, tribal codes of honor were increasingly drawn into the fabric of national discourse (Marr 2010, 29). The most impressive indication was the legalization of so-called honor killings. In a move that has been variously interpreted as a product of its increasing conservative ideology or a strategy to appease potentially rival authorities, the Ba'thist government ceded more power to local tribal and religious authorities. This radical departure from early Ba'thist ideologies had tremendous impacts on the lives of men and women, structures of the family, and norms of femininity and masculinity.

Generational Histories Part V: Gender and Family in the "Dark Years"

During the Gulf War and ensuing sanctions, women were valorized as heroic war widows and patrolled as potential prostitutes and traitors. The crucible of national honor fell on women's sexuality and men's "protection" of it. A combination of "war experience" narratives and bleak material realities created two disciplinary female figures: the steadfast victim and the irresolute prostitute. By 2003 before the US invasion, female-headed households were normative in some parts of the country. For example, a UNICEF study found that over 60 percent of households in Basrah were female-headed. The dire circumstances of many of these families resulted in a significant portion of young and middle-aged women turning to prostitution for survival. Al-Ali observes, "On the level of the government discourse as well as within society, Iraqi women became the bearers of honor of the whole country. They became 'potential prostitutes.' Vulnerable to temptation, gossip and a tarnished reputation, they needed to be protected and shielded. Teenage girls and young women in their 20s and 30s frequently referred to changes in patterns of socializing, family ties, and relations between neighbors and friends" (2007, 201). The desperate turn to prostitution by impoverished women had profound impacts for Iraqi women in general.[15] A government "fidelity campaign" was accompanied by a wave of social conservatism across Iraq throughout the 1990s and early 2000s.

The emergence of new protections for women resulted in the expansion of veiling across Iraq and the resurgence of domestic seclusion. Polygamy became more common, especially as a means of supporting war widows. Saddam Hussein made selective changes to the penal code to allow for conservative interpretations of Islamic law. Most profoundly, in 1990, the government amended the penal code 111 to make honor killings not punishable by law.[16]

While at the end of the Iran-Iraq War the government reformed Personal Status Laws by positioning itself as the ultimate patriarchal authority on matters of marriage and reproduction, during the sanctions era the government made another wave of reforms, this time effectively granting local-level tribal and religious authorities greater control. This move was part of a larger move that diverted power from certain civil and party officials to local leaders. Faleh Jabar noted: "Whatever the exact nature of the arrangement, de facto, the state has devolved power to local leaders because previous mechanisms are either gone or too weak to function" (2000, 31). Society as a whole underwent a retribalization by which "tribal lineages . . . were integrated into the state to enhance the power of the fragile elite" (ibid., 28). Tribal "gangsterism" became pervasive in rural areas and even increasingly present in urban spaces, where tribal leaders were coming to hold more power than party officials in some cases. Given the emergent hierarchy, some young men even decided to invent their

15. For an elaboration of the gendered effects of sanctions, see Yasmin Al-Jawaheri (2008) and Buck, Gallant, and Nossal (1998).

16. For more on the overturn of penal code 111 and "honor killings" in Iraq, see Spatz (1991), Omar (1994), and Romano and Brown (2006).

own tribes to enter into the structures of power. When the Iraqi government reauthorized tribal structures, it essentially created another "shadow state," to adopt Tripp's phrase, where the nexus of power sat increasingly with local-level tribal and religious authorities in addition to the party. In the absence of a reliable state, scholars observed that the sanctions era only strengthened the "kin contract," or the responsibility to provide and protect kin networks (Joseph 2008). In some cases, family networks had been so fragmented that those most disempowered by the resurgence of traditional tribal structures—youth and women—felt compelled to accept local-level authorities in exchange for basic support to meet their needs. Some have argued that the economic devastation of sanctions led to a "nuclearization" of family units—meaning a dispersal of extended family in Iraq (Ismael 2004). Even if not especially in these cases, the "kin contract" may have compelled Iraqis to accept existing tribal connections all the more. Indeed, in this context, members of the war generation began to monitor one another's family responsibility, and policing the honorability of their actions, as representations of "family."

Models of masculinity governing the generation was ever more tied to the protection of women, now constructed in terms of reappropriated tribal values of honor and along familial rather than military lines. Models of femininity revolved around the disciplinary figures of the victim, heroic in her steadfast commitment to her family, and the irresolute prostitute. Filial responsibility resurged as a key facet of identification—now expressed in terms of kin networks. Hiba explains that it was in this period that her family pressured her to delay college to help the family at home (also insisting that she wear the 'abāya and minimize her time outside the home). Max remembers that in this period he began to see himself as "the man of the house," with the duty to take care of his family. As a "perpetually present past," Khoury concludes, gendered tropes about the victimization of women—and their heroic devotion to the family nonetheless—pervades "public discourse and shapes the claims that Iraqis make to their rights as citizens" in the wake of Iraq's wars (2013, 252). Quite similarly, both military and domestic/familial iterations of male protection tropes continue to shape young Iraqis' practices of claim-making and their practices of policing national belonging. In the 1990s and 2000s, young Iraqis were suspicious of the state-sanctioned war narratives and responded to them with counternarratives of their own, reappropriating the meanings of "victimhood" and "protection," which they also used to monitor each other's behavior.

Generational Histories Part VI: Postscripts

Alexi Yurchek's *Everything Was Forever until It Was No More* provides a keen theorization of liminal generations in the context of dramatic governmental change. In the midst of perestroika in the Soviet Union, Yurchek argues that young adults could in one instance view a political regime as inevitable—and all they have ever known—and in the next instance negotiate that regime's downfall with an equal sense of historical inevitability. This paradox aptly describes the situation of Iraq's war generation, the last Ba'thist generation. This generation quickly transformed into the generation of young adults to be wrangled into the social, economic, political, and military battles associated with occupation and "rebuilding" a new Iraq.[17] Young Iraqis' individual paths into such national battles were far from clear, linear, or easy, which made their suspicion of one another's every step along the path even greater.

The lead-up to the US invasion was met with a mix of dread and planning. During the protracted search for and international discussion about Iraq's alleged weapons of mass destruction, many among my interlocutors believed it was just a matter of time before yet another war struck Iraq. Their family members liquefied what assets they could, updated passports, and then waited, watching and listening to a mix of state and international media. State television declared Iraq's victory certain. Those who could afford and mane it watched international news on (banned) satellite

---

17. Some Iraqi scholars have observed that the generation of war morphed into a "thumb generation": "In the 'thumb generation' young people [were] obsessed with staying connected through mobile apparatuses. . . . Using these tools and strategies . . . can be political and provocative without being didactic or polarizing. This is a particularly valid approach for a country or people in a conflict zone or under occupation" (Bilal quoted in Al-Ali and Al-Najjar 2013, 95).

television channels, reporting on UN proceedings and the developments among the rogue UN states—the so-called coalition of the willing—that promised "preemptive" war with or without UN support.

Members of the refugee network recounted feeling a range of eerie premonitions and déjà-vu leading up to the US invasion on March 20, 2003, and the battle for Baghdad during April 3–12, 2003. From the beginning of the war, their feelings about the war were, understandably, mixed. They used words ranging from "fear" to "terror" when recounting the beginning of the so-called shock-and-awe campaign and similar words to describe their first sighting of a US tank or troop. They all recall exactly where they were. Frank had moved with his mother and sisters to the outskirts of Baghdad—further from possible targets. Tamara was watching from Amman with her mom and dad. Mikhaeil was with his cousins and their newborn baby in Mosul. Meena was in her own living room at home in Baghdad, listening, looking, waiting.

Far from dancing in the streets, almost none of these soon-to-be American allies wanted to pursue work on behalf of US Forces at the outset of the war. Only two young people whom I would meet—one middle-class Baghdadi woman with strong family connections to the Shi'i Dawa Party and one lower-class Moslawi Christian man—report knowing from "day one" that they would work for the American occupation. Their stories were unusual. Anwar recalled that during the campaign on Baghdad, her mother flew an American flag out of her window. But, neither she nor her mother—who lived in Europe for much of her adult life—supported the subsequent handling of the war by the United States, and her view on the conflict grew much more ambivalent in the years following. By 2006, she and her mother were harassed and threatened by local militias, who appeared to have free rein in their neighborhood.

If explicit political views inspired a very few of my interlocutors to work with US Forces, for others it was a desire to help reinstate basic law and order in their neighborhoods that inspired them. For a majority, it was a decision made out of perceived necessity—"it was not really a choice," recalled Meena. She, like a surprising portion of former interpreters I met—more than half—worked for US Forces though they expressed being personally opposed to the US war. In an economic climate where an already weak Iraqi economy was once again turned on its head, some young professionals felt they had little choice but to sell their marketable skill of English. That is not to say, however, that they did not have strong misgivings, doubts, and second thoughts.

They did. As my interlocutors frequently reiterated, their work as interpreters was not just a job. It meant a way of life, a way of thinking, a way of being. It carried implications for their families and their futures. And their job presented pressing questions—some practical, others existential—about their identity and loyalty. The situation of interpreters, while unique, speaks to broader questions of identification that affected all Iraqis in postinvasion Iraq. Quandaries of belonging in the new Iraq draw in part from the period of wars and sanctions before the US invasion.

Forming and Performing National Identity

Tropes of filial duty, female victimization, and male protection were products of a "perpetually present past" by which Iraqis continue to lay claim to national belonging and cultural citizenship. These tropes are as dynamic as they are enduring. Far from simple outgrowths of cultural values or taken-for-granted state propaganda, "victimization" and "protection" narratives are responses to the realities of war and state nationalism, which have grown over the course of decades into multifaceted public discourses that were actively policed. As such, these gendered tropes might best be theorized as meaningful—and not merely instrumental—strategies of national identification vis-à-vis the state, national community, and family.

National identity, in Iraq as elsewhere, encompasses a range of identification practices at home, in the public sphere, and beyond. The practice of national identity is a product of a dialectical relationship between state-sanctioned or publicly authoritative and personal or family-mediated identifications. While school, media, and individual experiences were powerful in shaping young Iraqis' ideas about the country, especially under the Ba'th Party dictatorship, many Iraqis will tell you that they "learned Iraq" from their families through shared stories, poems, memories, songs, and legends.

Under Saddam Hussein, the focal point of official nationalism shifted, though throughout the country's conflicts, the identification of unpatriotic citizens was one consistent feature of nationhood. To ward off these suspicions, filial identifications—first as brothers and sisters of the revolution, then as heroic mother-victims or protective patriarchs—proved indispensable strategies. Family losses—deaths, disappearances, and imprisonments—alienated many Iraqis from the Ba'th Party, in turn fostering counternationalisms and positions of resistance. For example, a Shi'i Iraqi may attach to her vision of Iraq an image of the Shi'a majority's oppression under unjust government, while an Assyrian Christian may understand national identity in terms of the region's ancient history, and a Kurd may not identify with the nation of Iraq at all. Similarly, many Iraqis who identified first and foremost with a region or tribe may only selectively engage with images and discourses of the nation.

To the extent that Iraqis belong to multiple overlapping communities of belonging—tribal, religious, linguistic, and ethnic, as well as regional, class, and political—the war generation forged national identities within the plural and overlapping modes of collective identification. Iraqis thus do not reckon the nation through "ethno-sectarian" or other affiliations in any singular way, although these facets of identification—including their suppression and their politicization—are important in grasping the complex dynamics of nationhood in Iraq.[18] What is clear from this historical analysis, however, is that the war generation's performance and policing of gendered and filial roles served as common platforms for these diverse Iraqis to lay claim to national belonging.

18. When understood in the context of their wider biographies, these facets of identification may also be helpful in understanding why certain members of this generation joined the US war effort. To assert the importance of ethnic, religious, and tribal identification to the performance of national identities in Iraq is not to reduce national identity to ethnicity, religion, or tribe as some political projects would have it. Nor is it to reduce ethnic, religious, and tribal identities to simple communitarian logics. Instead, I aim to underscore the complex and situated role that these dimensions of identification play vis-à-vis other intersecting facets of identification.

2

Life and Work as a Military Terp

Perhaps the single most important of interpreters' wartime responsibilities was to serve as cultural translators. The military paradigm of "weaponized" culture hinged on the view that Iraqi culture was an isolable, masterable asset or threat on the battlefield; thus the US military utilized interpreters to navigate the so-called human terrain of Iraq, harnessing cultural assets or subduing cultural threats. The role of cultural translator is far from new; it is a recent iteration of a longstanding orientalist tradition, which seeks to master the culture of the "other" to serve imperial projects. Moira Inghilleri has discussed how interpreters in armed conflicts can subtly and powerfully influence the course of war, arguing that Iraqi interpreters, in particular, must be seen as "embodied conduits" of US power as well as powerful agents unto themselves (Inghilleri 2010, 175).[1]

In response to this weaponization of culture, interpreters have developed personal theories of translation by which they make sense of their role in the war and grapple with the power and limits they inhabited during their work. In their discussions of the war in the diaspora, members of the refugee network like Mohammed and Max struggle to identify the spaces and moments of agency, strategy, and even subversion that they carved out. Former interpreters contended with the problem of their agency no less while in the diaspora than during their day-to-day work in Iraq. While Max, who worked at the Abu-Ghraib military hospital, considered himself a "tongue," Mohammed, who worked with the Marines in

---

1. Wartime interpreters have also been shown to be "brokers" among combatants and "lifelines" between combatants and civilians (Takeda 2009).

Western Iraq, thought of his job as being a "bridge." Each man's theory of translation illuminates the configurations of agency they inhabited and their self-construction as agents.

Building on the work of Cristiana Giordano and Talal Asad, this chapter investigates the work of cultural translation as a process by which "difference is translated and recognized in . . . political context" (Giordano 2014, 6). Using the concept of *subject formation in translation*, I consider how interpreters' everyday work shaped new ways of being, dilemmas of identification, and new iterations of historically rooted identification strategies. As Giordano reveals, translation can be considered both "the process through which one language is rendered into another," as well as a "metaphor through which to think about difference," (Giordano 2014, 15). I discuss the interpreters' work in the Iraq War on two intertwined levels: firstly, on the level of language fields (i.e., Arabic or English) and the "cultures" to which those languages are imagined to cohere under occupation; and, secondly, on the level of historically governing cultural discourses—grids of difference—dynamically on the move in the interpretive encounter.[2]

Weaponized Culture

After undertaking a "shock-and-awe" invasion that killed thousands of civilians and decimated large swaths of Iraqi cities, US occupying forces experimented with a method of combat that sought out greater "understanding" of local culture and context.[3] A deft summation of the culturally reductive "understandings" that came from such US military efforts is captured by anthropologist Keith Brown in an article by the same name:

2. Note that Arabic and English were the principal languages in which interpreters worked. For the most part, Arabic was the first language of research participants; English was generally a second or third language. A minority of the interpreters I met spoke Kurdish or Aramaic (Chaldean or Syriac dialects) as a first language and Arabic as a second language.

3. Oxfam estimates that over 6,000 Iraqis died in the opening days of Operation Iraqi Freedom, particularly in the shock-and-awe bombing campaign.

2. A view from a Green Zone watchtower into the so-called Red Zone. Photo by author.

"all they understand is force" (2008). Patricia Owens (2010) and Patrick Porter (2009) have termed the incorporation of "culture" into US Armed Forces operations "military orientalism."

It would be a mistake to view US efforts at cultural understanding as merely lip service. Cultural understanding—and the view that culture was a field of threat or opportunity—was a guiding framework of the war in Iraq. Once the war was underway, US service members received training on "Iraqi culture" in simulation camps—with Iraqi refugees often serving as civilians—in the deserts of Arizona and California. Soldiers were taught a handful of Arabic words, phrases, and greetings. While gaining cultural skills to win the trust of Iraqi civilians, these measures also reinforced military constructs of the violent Arab other. In an "us-versus-them" framework, Iraqi civilians who were not immediately perceived as agreeable to the US occupation became thinkable to US service members as threatening "others" motivated by cultural traditionalism and religiosity. A most telling illustration of us-versus-them thinking could be found in the language used to describe the International Zone in Baghdad, dubbed the "Green Zone," and the Iraqi Zones of the city, dubbed the "Red Zone" (see illustration 2). Some interpreters traversed this physical boundary-marker daily, underscoring the sharp discursive divides across which they existed.

The preoccupation with understanding culture as a field of battle culminated in the military approach known as the "Human Terrain System," a program rolled out in 2007 in which American social scientists were consulted on military planning and operations.[4] Long before this program's inception, local Iraqis were the frontline cultural experts in military operations. Much like previous wars—as in Vietnam—but on a new scale and with new emphasis, local interpreters were relied upon to provide a ground's-eye view of situations, to liaise with civilians, and to provide broader cultural advice and guidance.

Hired as participants in a war against "terror," whose rhetoric was as sharp as its target was amorphous, interpreters' compulsion to distinguish "us" from "them," good guys from bad guys, and victims from villains hung over their cultural translations.[5] In addition to serving as a justification for the war, terror rhetoric—and its adjacent cultural formulations such as "all they understand is force"—represented the rubrics within which the war was carried out on the ground. Mohammed recollects one of the primary techniques that US Forces adopted to operationalize this understanding of Iraqi "culture": a caricaturized view of gender in Iraqi culture. While women were assumed to be innocent—even to a fault ("ignorant")—men were assumed to be devious and disposed to violence. Mohammed and I joked that US service members wore "gender goggles." If, as Erika King and Robert Wells argue, "Bush presented his vision of a nation . . . under siege by 'men without conscience'" (2009, 147), then the

---

4. For summaries of the military policies surrounding the Human Terrain Systems, see also Gonzalez (2008, 2010). For more on the role of anthropologists in Human Terrain Systems, see Forte (2011) and Gonzalez (2009).

5. Talal Asad's *On Suicide Bombing* (2007) outlines the far-reaching implications of terror discourses on subjectivity, which I elaborate further in chapter 3.

nation under attack was represented by women without agency. The US imperial feminist mission of "liberation" was blindingly reminiscent of Gayatri Spivak's formulation of "white men saving brown women from brown men" (1988) about which many preeminent feminist scholars, such as Cynthia Enloe (2000, 2007), have written.[6] Paradoxically, as Mohammed pointed out while discussing service members' "gender goggles," Iraqi interpreters contributed to the prevailing gender caricatures. As both subjects and authors of discourses about Iraqi culture, interpreters participated in gender work through their translations of historically situated tropes about patriarchal protection and female victimization that, in their translation, were unmoored from their historical context.[7]

Interpreters were reflexive and critical in their discussions of Iraqi culture or "custom" (*eurif*), while still subject to the regulatory power of their own perfomative representations of it. Several Terps, like Mohammed, told me that the "culture card" was the most powerful one he had to play in his job interpreting for the Marines; he used that card sometimes to mock or resist Marines' views of Iraqis, and at other times to advocate for changes to unjust military actions. He shared stories in which he had "guys spinning around in circles believing they were performing a ritual," and he played similar "cards" with me in jest. (For example, after eating a fish dinner with him one evening, Mohammed said to me, "You know, after eating fish, we Iraqis say *Al-hamdulillah* [praise be to god] and then we rub our bellies with our hands, like this," and he pantomimed rubbing his belly. I could tell by his smirk that he was trying to get me to rub my filthy hands on my blouse. I smiled and said that I had never heard that before. He paused and then said, "That used to

6. Mahmood and Hirschkind (2002); Razack (2005); and Abu-Lughod (2002) provide valuable critiques of the so-called liberation mission of the war on terror.

7. More on the gendered paradigms that inform military operations during the war on terror can be found in Sjoberg's "Gendering the Empire's Soldiers: Gender Ideologies, the US Military, and the 'War on Terror'" (2010). For discussions about the media circulation of those paradigms, see Khalid (2011) and Jiwani (2011). Patricia Owens offers a provocative investigation into the role of orientalist gender paradigms played in sexual torture during the Iraq War in "Torture, Sex, and Military Orientalism" (2010).

work with the Marines!" We both laughed. His joke had appealed to me as a quotidian form of resistance to being exoticized. More commonly, he deployed the construct of Iraqi culture earnestly to achieve a specific aim—such as fair treatment for a detainee. For example, he recounted that when a Marine tied two detainees to a pole on base and left them there overnight, Mohammed told them, "Peeing yourself is a great shame in our culture. Please this could have big consequences if the people hear about it." He explained to me that "peeing yourself" is probably no more shameful in Iraqi culture than in any other culture, but he cast the issue as a cultural one to achieve the outcome he thought was fair—a place for the detainees to sleep indoors with a toilet. The Marines, he recalled, were very concerned with being—or at least appearing—sensitive to Iraqi culture. That their concern about sensitivity tended to objectify and exoticize Iraqi culture was clear from Mohammed's account. I once asked if he believed the Marines achieved any measure of their objective of "sensitivity." He answered by saying that he did not know what it meant to be sensitive when you are in uniform, carrying a gun. Still, interpreters like Mohammed worked squarely within the military concept of culture that their units employed.

This discourse of "terror" that structured the Iraq War and the operationalized concepts of Iraqi culture that accompanied it on the ground and in the media represent what some have called an "Iraq War culture." Iraq War culture—characterized by a weaponization of culture both abroad and at home—has had enduring impacts on the lives of Iraqi and American citizens alike. Fuchs and Lockard write, "The Iraq War, in other words, persists, as do the cultures that both structure and emerge from it" (2009, x). Perhaps one of the most compelling artifacts of Iraq War culture—forged at the intersection of terror discourses and attempts at intercultural "understanding"—were the varied materials that Iraqi interpreters wore during the course of their work to conceal their faces. Whether a scarf (*keffiyeh*) or military-issued helmet and goggles, these materials symbolized the orders they followed as contracted employees of the US military to conceal their identities and the real threats they encountered. Above all, these artifacts represent the dilemmas of identification that they faced on the treacherous terrain of weaponized culture.

Behind the Mask

Iraqi men and women who were hired as military interpreters spent months and sometimes years of their lives behind what many described as a "mask." Interpreters in the early years of the occupation (2003–6) frequently wore *keffiyeh* to conceal their identities. Alternatively, others wore ski masks. Some scholars document that interpreters even wore brown bags over their heads to travel on and off base (Brown and Lutz 2007). In the later years of the occupation (from 2007 on), interpreters dressed in military uniforms, helmets, and goggles. The Arabic verb "to mask or veil" (*yehjib*) was widely used by interpreters to describe wearing a scarf, a ski mask, or a military uniform. The same verb is used to describe the generalized postinvasion necessity to conceal, lie, and evade for survival in the complex sociopolitical landscape under occupation. Masking—in both senses of the word—was central to the life of an interpreter. While many people in postinvasion Iraq faced imperatives to conceal their identities (at militia checkpoints, for example), what distinguished the act of masking for interpreters was the confusion that came from the uniform and uniformed repetition of a simulacrum. Each time interpreters "put on a mask," the reality of the mask became ever more a part of subjects' bodily reality. Yet, the felt sense that the mask was "fake"—distinct from a real identity behind the mask—also grew, and became all the more burdensome each time one put it on or took it off. Several interpreters said that masking, rather than the danger they faced or the distance they felt from family, was the single worst thing about their work as an interpreter.

As much as the mask weighed on interpreters, they tended to agree that it was absolutely essential—and not least for safety. Masks were crucial to guard their anonymity but also, more fundamentally, to create the possibility for authoritative speech—a space for the utterance of words from which they felt they could dissociate themselves. It was the scratchy ski mask or military uniform that enabled young Iraqi men and women to enter into the embattled terrain of official military discourse. The degree to which interpreters relied on the "fakeness" of a mask reflects the precarious physical and linguistic spaces that they occupied, at the collision of an occupier's signifying systems and local idioms: between regionalized and classed iterations of their mother tongue, and a hegemonic "yes, sir!" iteration of English military-speak.

Working behind a mask as an interpreter involved both the presence and absence of bodily experiences. Interpretation involved the felt sense of a staged performance—of playing a character. As Mohammed told me: "In Sunni areas I was Omar. In Shi'a areas I was Mahdi. I played different characters." The idea that one's interpreting self was a character to be played allowed for the belief that one maintained a "real" or true identity behind the performed "fake" identity—a self, apart from the words being spoken. Yet, in the back and forth between the "real" and the "fake," the edges of these identities moved, frayed, and at times dissolved.

This preoccupation with masking points to—just as it attempts to conceal—more considerable performances in process: the performative formation of subjects within the discourses into which they are interpellated (Althusser 1970). The discursive performances that I track here do not correspond to the presence or absence of a physical mask—this, despite the fact that talk about "masking" was a cannily suggestive signal of a performative process underway. Quite unlike a "front stage"/"back stage" approach to performance (e.g., Goffman 1959), the performances that interest me here are not self-authored or even discrete events; nor are subjects duped into "acting as if." Alexi Yurchak has usefully distinguished a theory of performativity from a view in which a performance is equated to play or "wearing a mask." He writes: "This view of . . . speech acts as constitutive of the person is different from the view of these acts as divided between mask (acting "as if") and reality, truth and lie. In the mask/truth models the person is first posited and then is involved in the act of wearing masks or revealing truths. By contrast most performative theories do not posit the person completely in advance, before the acts. . . . There is no performative person before the person wearing a mask" (Yurchak 2005, 22). Subjects are always performing—even when we are performing the "real." This is by no means to say that social life, or accounts of it collected here, is frivolous wordplay. As Yurchak suggests, we exist in and through our citational performances, which are themselves material conditions of social life.

Al Suqut

US troops recruited university-age, English-speaking Iraqis within days of what is called *al suqut*—the toppling. An American translation company first known as Titan Communications Corp.—and later known by two successive subcontractors' names, GLS and L3—received the Department of Defense contract for most translation in Iraq. Titan was responsible for hiring "local national interpreters," or "Terps." Other interpreters in Iraq during the war included Category 2 (CAT 2) interpreters, who were US citizens or legal permanent residents and 09 Limas, who were linguistic specialists in the US military. Terps were, however, by all accounts the most important interpreters in the day-to-day conduct of the war.[8]

While scholarly analyses of Titan as a feature of the Iraq War's vast defense contracting industry are lacking, media accounts of Titan and the fate of its interpreters in general have abounded. For example, a joint *L.A. Times*–Pro-Publica report found that in the earliest days of the war Titan hired over 8,000 interpreters, who each received on average only $12,000/year in compensation to do what an Associated Press report called "one of the most dangerous civilian jobs in one of the world's most dangerous countries: translating Arabic for the US military in Iraq."[9] The same *L.A. Times*–Pro-Publica report estimated that over 1,200 local interpreters were severely injured and 360 interpreters were killed between the beginning of the war and the so-called surge, when Iraqi interpreters were hired on an even wider basis. The figure of 360 interpreter deaths constitutes nearly half of all defense contractors in Iraq and exceeds the figure for casualties of non-American coalition forces in the same period (317).[10]

8. After immigrating to the United States, some local national interpreters returned to Iraq as CAT 2 interpreters or as military 09 Limas.

9. Christian Miller, "Foreign Interpreters Hurt in Battle Find US Insurance Benefits Wanting," *L.A. Times*, December 18, 2009; and "Translators Dying by the Dozens in Iraq," Associated Press, May 21, 2005.

10. Christian Miller, "Foreign Interpreters Hurt in Battle Find US Insurance Benefits Wanting," *L.A. Times*, December 18, 2009.

Initially, Titan's method of recruiting Terps was informal, relying on word-of-mouth references or even door-knocking in commercial or university neighborhoods, where English-speakers were expected to be found. Minimal testing and background checks were required in the early years of the occupation.[11] According to the interpreters with whom I spoke, this informality reflected the relatively safe "security situation" at the beginning of the war. Technically, interpreters were required to conceal their identities with pseudonyms and masks to protect themselves from each other as well as from the Iraqi civilians whom they met. But as Max told me: "In the beginning we did walking patrols without anything on our faces sometimes. The soldiers didn't always carry guns. We even used to stop for lunch at a *shawarma* [sandwich] shop together. No guns, no masks, nothing." Only after the Battles of Falluja in 2004 (the apex of the insurgency) and the bombing of Samarra in early 2006 (an event sparking widespread sectarian violence) did these security measures come to be seen as a necessity. The relative safety and increasing scarcity of professional employment attracted recruits from a variety of fields in the beginning. Some recruits, having studied English in medical or engineering school, were near fluency; others had learned English only from grade school and had very limited proficiency. (These interpreters were referred to by some as "good morning, sir" interpreters, as this was reputedly the only English phrase they knew.) By mid-2006, work as an interpreter was generally pursued quietly if not covertly, often without the knowledge of family or friends. By 2006 and 2007, many early interpreters left their jobs—and sometimes the country. At the same time, interpreters were more and more in demand: new positions were created to accommodate the surge. New recruits, many of them having exhausted other options, just graduated, or acquired enough English to meet the standard of fluency, filled these spots.

Whether one was an interpreter during the early or later years of the US occupation, the question of where one worked mattered a great deal.

---

11. Given the lacuna of scholarly work on the role of translators in Iraq, the primary data presented here reflect my observations on US military bases, interviews with over fifty former interpreters, and surveys with US service members.

Interpreting on base—for governmental meetings and US-led training of the Iraqi police or military, for example—entailed a high degree of technical vocabulary, some prestige, and relatively little imminent danger. Interpreting for military units on patrols or checkpoints involved more gear, longer hours, less predictability, and much greater danger. Working on patrols or at checkpoints could require interpreters to effectively join the military unit in combat; interpreters in these cases wore the military uniform of their units. From 2007 to 2009, some interpreters on missions carried weapons. The assignment of Terps to different posts was also gendered: while male interpreters were assigned to combat missions as well as routine procedures on military bases, female Terps were almost exclusively assigned to noncombat assignments on military bases.

Bases

On base, interpreters translated in a range of capacities, from high-level meetings to interrogations (euphemistically called "interviews"). Interpreters were also responsible for assisting in joint Iraqi-US intelligence and training operations, for example, in training the new Iraqi military or police. Finally, interpreters worked as the personal interpreters to top US military officials, traveling from the base as needed. Though favored over combat missions by most, work on base brought its own challenges, especially the sense of confinement living on a US military post.

Work on base could be construed as prestigious—with the chance to meet "VIPs" and to attend high-level meetings. (A couple of interpreters had met Donald Rumsfeld and Dick Cheney, for example.) For young men, being selected to work on base was a sign of achievement after having worked on missions. Though one's work on a military base was sometimes described as monotonous, an assignment to a base could be welcome relief for young men who no longer had to "gear up" for long and dangerous missions and could instead focus on more "professional" work. Both men and women tended to agree that women received the harder of the two assignments by working almost exclusively on base, which involved the mastery of more extensive and technical vocabulary. Meena thought this was "ironic." The view that some female Terps lacked adequate English to do their jobs—and were hired by US companies for other purposes, namely to "satisfy men," as Meena put it, rather than for their English skills—was pervasive among both men and women.

Missions

A "mission" was the general term used to describe any movement—routine or emergency—off a US military base. Therefore, a mission could refer to a routine "convoy assist"—accompanying a convoy of supplies from point to point—or to a midnight raid. Interpreters assigned to active combat units were effectively on call twenty-four hours a day: they may be awakened at 3:00 a.m. with orders to "gear up." If working on base was a goal for some, for others "it was all about the missions," as Abbas told me. He explained, "When you are an interpreter, your life is about your missions. You are living for those hours and you need to be on." By contrast, Husham says, "I hated it. I hated being woken up. I hated being in that Humvee. I hated seeing accidents, the bodies. But once I started working on base, I missed it. I missed the excitement. It's weird to say that because I didn't agree with the war, but it was exciting." Husham saw many "accidents" as a Terp. He had helped a soldier escape from a burning Humvee after a nearby explosion. He saw his reporting officer killed right in front of him. He was on a raid where women were killed, and he found himself negotiating with his superiors for the release of an elderly couple.

War Life

In the early days of the occupation interpreters commuted to US bases for their shifts. Occasionally, a late-night mission could keep an interpreter on base overnight, but this was unusual. When it became increasingly dangerous for interpreters to commute to work, interpreters began living on base. Some Terps maintained a working schedule of five days on base, with two days off to visit their families. Others lived and worked on base for three weeks at a time, leaving the base for only seven days a month. A few interpreters reported staying on base for as long as three months at a time. As the security situation worsened, the treatment and benefits interpreters received on base improved. By 2006, interpreters carried badges that allowed them to eat at the US military dining facility and utilize some recreational and social facilities. Sleeping accommodations differed by base: in most Baghdad-area bases, interpreters slept in single-sex air-conditioned trailers, though in the southern and western parts of the country, interpreters frequently slept in large tents that sometimes housed both men and women.

Former interpreters described the work as frequently tedious—full of many long, hot, and sometimes banal days. At other times the work could be exhilarating—and just as distressing. A handful of the interpreters I met had a single assignment with set posts for the entirety of their work as Terps. For example, Max worked exclusively at the hospital compound at Abu Ghraib, interpreting for US Forces, doctors, and patient-inmates. However, the majority recounted being frequently reassigned from military unit to military unit and, once assigned to a military unit, from post to post. As a result, their work demanded that they perform a wide range of duties.

Working in very close quarters with US Forces, certain Iraqi interpreters formed friendships with US service members. Some interpreters also formed close relationships with fellow interpreters. Because of the veil of anonymity that governed work as an interpreter, however, most former Terps recall feeling a degree of mistrust toward the other Iraqis they encountered on US bases, including Iraqi colleagues at Titan. Interpreters explained that mutual suspicion among Iraqi civilians in the orbit of the US military was rampant, especially given that background security checks were minimal during the height of the insurgency and sectarian violence in Iraq. Terms like "sectarian violence" (*al 'anf atāfi*), which became commonplace in both English and Arabic, are products of the governing discourses of the occupation that code and ramify the suspicion interpreters describe feeling toward one another.

The Bridge and the Tongue

The manner in which interpreters represent the personal and political significance of their work with US Forces can vary as much as the work itself. On one afternoon, Max described his job as a "calling" and his work as an interpreter as being "a tongue . . . loyal to two languages." A short drive away on another day, Mohammed considered interpretation as "a bridge . . . between different worlds." These two representations, succinctly captured by the metaphors of "the bridge" and "the tongue," shed light on how wartime interpreters reckon with their work both by asserting themselves as embattled agents and selectively downplaying their agency while working as agents of the occupation.

The Bridge

Mohammed, a thirty-year-old cell-phone vendor from Basrah, quit his job working with the Marines multiple times. Every time that he returned to the job, the goal of building a "bridge" of understanding was one of his leading motivations. He recounts:

> The Americans and the Iraqis come from different worlds. Even if they spoke the same language, they would not be able to understand. I was the bridge. Once in the West of Iraq, my unit was collecting personal weapons, and my officer was speaking to a sheik. He wanted me to translate something like, "Sir, you must turn in all your weapons to US Forces. You have no right to possess private weapons. I will come to your house tomorrow and retrieve all firearms from your residence." I knew this would go badly. Owning weapons is a traditional thing in Western Iraq—saying that this sheik has "no right" to weapons is insulting. The men had no relationship. So, for the safety of my whole unit, I translated something else. I said: "I am new in this town. I would like to pay my respects to you and your family tomorrow. Could I ask your advice on this issue of illegal weapons in the village?" The sheik extended his hand to the officer and said, "Welcome. Yes, illegal weapons are a problem. I will welcome you tomorrow." The next day at tea, the men talked for two hours. By the end, the sheik had identified two possible weapons storehouses near the village and voluntarily gave up some of his old weapons to the officer. See, you have to listen to the intention behind the words.

Mohammed describes how he listened to the "intention behind the words," explaining how he altered words and manipulated meanings to

achieve communication across distinct cultures so distant that he identifies them as different worlds. Mohammed's view of translation is somewhat reminiscent of Walter Benjamin's theory of translation, as outlined
in "The Task of the Translator" (1968). Benjamin writes: "Language is in
every case not only communication of the communicable but also, at the
same time, a symbol of the noncommunicable. . . . All translation is only a
somewhat provisional way of coming to terms with the foreignness of languages" (Benjamin 1968, 74–75). Mohammed shares stories of mistrans-
lating as a badge of his commitment to mutual understanding between
Iraqis and Americans. Here, brokering an understanding between the
officer and the sheik requires Mohammed's production of purposeful
misunderstanding between those for whom he is interpreting. Mohammed credits his mistranslation with potentially saving lives—both Iraqi
and American. Wearing a US military uniform, carrying a firearm, and
participating in raids and patrols alongside US Forces, Mohammed refers
to the Marines with whom he worked as his brothers. At the same time,
he often used the same phrase—my brothers (*ikhwani*)—to refer to the
Iraqi civilians for whom he spoke on patrol. Mohammed's subjectivity is
dynamically shaped in these translations. A subject in translation, he finds
the subject position as a "bridge" in and through his experience of discursive disjunctions.

As a bridge between his American and Iraqi brothers, Mohammed
explained that he both understood the US mission of reconstruction in
Iraq and "Iraqi traditions." Though he critiqued many aspects of the war,
he believed that Iraqi desires for basic security and the US vision of reconstruction were more similar than different. Hired as a broker between
Iraqi "traditions" and the US mission, Mohammed is positioned as a particular kind of cultured Iraqi subject: one who can, as he says, "work with
Iraqi traditions" but who can also broker deals as a rational and recognizable ally to American military forces.

Mohammed recounts that "when I put on that uniform, my first priority was my unit's safety. But believe me I never stopped thinking about the
Iraqi civilians." The principal goal of his translation was, in this sense, to
reduce threats and maintain security—both for the safety of his US colleagues and for the safety of Iraqi civilians. He attempted to humanize

Iraqis for his American colleagues by teaching them local jokes to recite to children and encouraging the Marines to follow his lead in exchanging greetings with men they met on patrol, whom he identified as "good guys." If Mohammed was able to humanize Iraqis to the Marines, he was also disciplined to join in systems of knowledge that viewed culture as a potential threat and divided Iraqis into "good guys" and "bad guys."

Mohammed conceptualizes his agency as a broker between cultural worlds—a bridge. He quit his job several times when he felt that he had failed as a broker, and when he believed that the harm he was doing outweighed the good. The conditions for his agency were his subjectivation as a uniformed combatant, who could "work with Iraqi traditions" and divide his countrymen into good guys and bad guys alongside his American colleagues. Formed in translation, the subject position of "the bridge" is one that enables recognition in and through alienation.

The Tongue

While Mohammed believed in the possibility or even necessity of mutual understanding between Iraqis and Americans under occupation, and sought to broker it through his purposeful mistranslations, Max believed that understanding across languages and cultures—especially under occupation—was partial at best. Max saw his role as constrained by the conditions of war—he was a "hired tongue"—but, as such, he felt that the stakes for doing the job right were tremendous. Max reflected: "I was a tongue. Of course translations were not word-for-word. If I translated what the civilians said many times it would not make any sense to officers. There is not always the right word. It is about culture, not always about the right word. You read people and situations. Terps find the word that will work without starting a firefight. Sometimes I didn't even know what I was saying, I was reading and speaking, reading and speaking. . . . My job was to hear words, put them into other words that make sense to another ear." Max is a twenty-nine-year-old Baghdadi, whose first language was Kurdish, second language was Arabic, and third language was English. Taking on a language, he says, means taking on new anatomy: new tongues, new ears.

He imagined himself as an analyst, reading and speaking, reading and speaking. However, Max understood that which he analyzed to be not only linguistic but also cultural scripts. He says, "It is about culture, not always about the right word." Max describes reading "people and situations" as texts of sorts, in much the same way he would read words on a page. As a cultural expert—a hired tongue—he was hired to do just this: to translate dynamic social situations into predictable articulations of culture. Rather than facilitating understanding, Max's primary goal was to give translations that were faithful to the meaning of the texts he read.

For nearly all of the time he worked with US Forces, Max worked at the military hospital at Abu Ghraib "reading" inmates, as he puts it: he was asked to speculate about inmates' background, decipher their mental state, and assess their credibility. He was charged with analyzing Iraqi inmates as foreign texts, translating their complex lives—now confined to a jail cell—into English categories such as "insanity" or "insurgent." He says: "I got good at reading people at Abu Ghraib. I had to. I worked with the American doctors that were trying to figure out who was crazy, who was not. The doctors would always ask me: 'What's your opinion about this guy?' There would be a man in a cage, and he's naked, and I had to form an opinion about him. They put you in that position, what are you going to do? You have to judge them. Is he pretending to be crazy, is he not. Is he a schizophrenic, is he a terrorist, is he Sunni or Shi'i. . . . I tried to be faithful to what I heard. But, I saw just like that, life could get twisted just by the words we use." Face to face with detainees, and in a position to "give his opinion" about them, Max grappled with the power of his words as a tongue. In the same instance, Max minimizes his agency by saying: "They put you in that situation, what are you going to do?"

Max, unlike Mohammed, does not claim full authorship for the translations he produces, but instead tries to offer translations that "work." In this way, Max's view is evocative of Jacque Derrida's theory of signification (1988), which Umberto Eco has aptly summarized this way: "The power of language [is] to say more than it literally pretends to say . . . and that every signifier is related to another signifier so that there is nothing outside the significant chain, which goes on ad infinitum" (1992, 33). The signifying chain takes on a life of its own outside and apart from the author. While relinquishing authorship of his translations, he acknowledges the power that his words wield, commenting on how "life could get twisted just by the words we use."

Despite and because Max struggled with the arbitrariness and the finality of words, he locates the power of his agency in his capacity to deliver translations that "work," where the principal work of his translations was to give voice to those most marginalized by the occupation. Max felt that by providing detainees with a committed and fair interpreter, he was using his agency to confront the injustices he saw on an everyday basis at Abu Ghraib. Max made clear that even and especially in the face of injustice, he tried to read people faithfully. It was precisely those faithful readings that sometimes subverted the hegemonic framework within which he was hired as a tongue. For example, he recalls the American doctors' chief concern was that men might pretend to be "crazy" to receive better treatment and reduced punishment. Max met detainee after detainee who had been mistreated and tortured; and then he was asked his "opinion" of the guy—namely whether he believed the detainee was "really crazy." On one occasion, he remembers answering: "The man is naked in a cage. In our culture, he has been stripped of his dignity. I don't know what his state was before, but I would say this is a normal response to torture, sir." He cast such matters as "cultural" to his superiors—this was the framework in which he was hired—though he would later explain to me that he wondered whether these were matters of Iraqi culture, or basic human dignity.

Formed in translation, the subject-position of the tongue entails distinct processes of recognition and alienation from that of the bridge. Max understands his agency as the analyst and voice for linguistic, cultural, and human texts. He is subjectivated as a cultural expert and the rational subject who might speak for Iraqis as textual others. Max makes sense of his wartime role by asserting his agency as a faithful translator for marginalized people, but at the same time, he selectively undermines his agency by calling himself just a "tongue," rather than the author of texts. He de-centers his own self-presence, saying: "Sometimes I didn't even know what I was saying, I was reading and speaking, reading and speaking." Unlike Mohammed, Max's self-described resistance comes in the form of faithful interpretations, rather than mistranslation. He continually returns to the limits of his agency, however, saying, "they put you in that situation, what are you going to do?" Despite his feelings of powerlessness, Max's case also clearly demonstrates how, in the first and last instance, his power as a tongue serves the purposes of US power. If he understood his agency to reside in his faithful translations, he demonstrated agency not only when he was resisting US power but also when he was exercising and reinforcing it.

The use of Iraqi interpreters as cultural translators—and the larger weaponization of culture of which their work was a part—grew out of an orientalist theory of cultural translation in which "culture" can be deciphered, decoded, and deployed in the interests of power. Mohammed and Max's emic theories of translation are both products of and responses to this weaponization of culture in the Iraq War. Through these theories, they attempt to reckon with their power and limitations as agents—agents of US power and agents of resistance. Mohammed figures his agency as a bridge, and willfully authors mistranslations in an effort to cultivate understanding. Max, by contrast, minimizes his agency and considers himself a "tongue"—though he highlights the fact that through his faithful translations, he was able to give a voice to many who had been silenced by a repressive occupation. In both the constructions of the bridge and the tongue, Mohammed and Max present themselves as embattled agents, profoundly limited by the systems of knowledge and power in which they worked.

Both men also became subjects of the words they translated and of the systems of power in which they held meaning: the tongue and the bridge represent subject-positions carved out of processes of subject formation in translation. When Mohammed put on the US Marines uniform, and when Max described "not knowing what he was saying" as he read inmates at Abu Ghraib, both men describe this process of subjectivation. Their subjectivation was also the condition for their situated agency. Interpreters' liminality and embattled positions cannot be mistaken for a lack of critical reflection and agency. Clearly, their agency not only resists power but also can reinforce it. In the first and last instance, they acquire their speaking positions as a bridge and as a tongue in and through working as agents of the occupation.

Interpreting the Other

In the context of occupied Iraq, interpretation was not a process between two equal languages or "cultures" but instead was an unequal process of change brought about by the encounter between a "strong" language and a "weak" language, to use Talal Asad's terminology. To hear Max tell it, "We spoke a lot more to the Iraqis than to the Americans." In other words, American rhetoric and discourses—crystallized in the wording of rules or criminal charges—were translated into Arabic far more than questions, concerns, or explanations were translated into English. Asad observes that interpretation across unequal languages implicitly entails the "change from 'worse' ways of living to those that are 'better'" (1995, 330).

Frantz Fanon observed that a subject's access to the language-world of an occupying power affords great power. Fanon illuminates issues of language, power, and betrayal in the context of French colonialism. In *Black Skin, White Masks*, he writes: "To speak means to be in a position to use a certain syntax, to grasp the morphology of this or that language, but it means above all to assume a culture, to support the weight of a civilization. . . . A man who has a language consequently possesses the world expressed and implied by that language. What we are getting at becomes plain: Mastery of language affords remarkable power" (1967, 18–19). Reflecting on the situation of Africans serving as interpreters for the colonial French Army (as well as those who had left Africa for France), Fanon continues: "He betrays himself in his speech. . . . What is the source of this new way of being? Every dialect is a way of thinking" (ibid., 24–25). Here the word "betray" conveys dual meanings. Because "every dialect is a way of thinking," for Fanon "a man who has a language" gives himself away in his speech.

Some have written about the practice of translation as a form of betrayal itself.[12] Here, Fanon is making a different point about the betrayal involved in leaving a mother tongue (as a migrant in France) or in objectifying your mother tongue for an occupying power (as a colonial

12. See, e.g., Crapanzano (1997).

interpreter). On one level this betrayal appears inherent to the very act of speech. On another level, however, Fanon's betrayal appears to unfold at the level of a subject's desire for recognition: in taking on the language of the occupation, the subject finds recognition and a certain degree of freedom. In the vein of subaltern studies, we could say that by taking on an occupying power's language, a subject takes on the ability for legible speech itself (Spivak 1988). She asks to be considered; she asks for selfhood; she asks to no longer be the other. Navigating the translation encounter thus raises questions of loyalty and identity on multiple registers for wartime interpreters: not only at the level of perceived political allegiances but also at the personal level of subjective recognition and interpellation into the dominant discourses of the occupier.

In the American-led occupation of Iraq, English was a crucial medium for interpreters' recognition. However, English-language discourses and concepts also contained the frameworks under which Terps rendered Iraqi culture and history as texts for US Forces—an exercise in alienation. Through processes of subject formation in translation, interpreters translated and mistranslated into English, forging subject-positions such as "the bridge" and "the tongue." Mohammed and Max's subjectivities were dynamically shaped in the act of translation, whilst being translated themselves into military grids of understanding and into institutional channels of simultaneous recognition and alienation. The intellectual tradition of reducing dynamic cultures to flat texts has a long history in European and American orientalism.

Abiding orientalist legacies in the Middle East raise concerns about any study of the Middle East by a Western scholar, including myself. By making Iraqi interpreters the subject of this research, I do not eliminate the troublesome role for myself, the ethnographer, as the final interpreter/analyst. The danger is to perpetuate what Edward Said explains is a largely "textualized"—that is, dematerialized, dehistoricized—reading of the Middle East as "other." Said contends that: "The Orient is [the West's] deepest and most recurring images of the Other. . . . Orientalism is a style of thought based upon an ontological and epistemological distinction made between 'the Orient' and (most of the time) 'the Occident.' . . . Orientalism [is] a Western style for dominating, restructuring, and having authority over the Orient" (2000 [1979], 68–69). The cunning of this mode of thought is the burden and authority it affords the "Occident" to understand, protect, and save the "Orient." The work of the scholar has been key to those efforts. As James Clifford writes in his introduction to *Writing Culture*, the orientalist scholar's authority is to bring "lovingly to light" the complex depths of the Orient (1986, 12). The power dynamic in this arrangement allows "the observer with a standpoint from which to see without being seen, to read without interruption" (ibid.).

This approach is predicated on the view that the Orient is occult, requiring a keen interpreter. Talal Asad reminds us that anthropologists have long served as the "cultural translators" responsible for interpreting the Orient in a range of capacities: providing the scientific justification for colonization of "uncivilized" peoples; accompanying and advising colonists on their adventures; and, now, serving with military units in the war on terror to provide insight into the "human terrain." In keeping with a long history or orientalism, Terps were hired to read Iraqi culture and render it as a legible text for US Forces—sometimes alongside anthropologists hired under the mantle of the Human Terrain System. Yet, as Talal Asad concludes: "Society is not a text that communicates to the skilled reader" (1995, 155). Working as the US military's "skilled readers" afforded young men and women some degree of freedom, but it also positioned them as focal subjects of the textualized constructs of culture they were interpreting and, to some degree, produced a subjective disjunction between their experiences of membership in dynamic societies and their positionalities as skilled readers—above and apart from it. Processes of subject formation in translation proved also to be the conditions for the formation of interpreters' strategies upon the fraught discursive terrain they traversed.

3

Honor and Terror on Loyalty Base

A "duck and cover" drill sounded as soon as the plane full of government officials deplaned in the airfield at Camp Victory in Baghdad. I ran toward the nearest building—an airplane hangar—not knowing exactly what to do because I had not yet attended any sort of security briefing. We waited for several silent minutes in the heat of that August afternoon.[1] When the all-clear came, I followed others who had just arrived to collect our luggage and report to the private security personnel whom I later learned work for the defense contractor called Xe, formerly Blackwater, whose job it was to confirm the plane's manifest. As I approached the contractor—who wore wraparound sunglasses and all khaki—he slapped the small of my back and nonchalantly let his hand slide down further. "Welcome to Baghdad," he said. The next day I attended the security briefing at a brand-new US Embassy compound, situated on some of the most desirable real estate in Baghdad's so-called Green Zone. A State Department security officer asked the women in the briefing to stay a few minutes extra. His message to us in that pristine, overly air-conditioned boardroom was simple: "At this point in the Iraq conflict, your greatest day-to-day danger here is other Americans. American men to be specific. We've had several reported incidents. Be aware."

Working as a refugee officer on Prosperity Base located on the border between the "Green" and "Red" zones, I encountered a kaleidoscope of

---

1. I arrived in Baghdad two months after the United States withdrew troops from most Iraqi cities and just days before one of the deadliest coordinated attacks to hit Baghdad's Green Zone, which occurred on August 19, 2009.

differently colored ID badges for this cast of governmental, private, "local national," and "foreign national" workers, which corresponded to a hierarchy of effective privileges on base. At the hierarchy's apex were direct employees of the US federal government or armed services, though this set of employees was itself highly differentiated and ranked. At the bottom were the "foreign national contractors": non-American and non-Iraqi service and security workers from Asia, Africa, and South America contracted by KBR-Halliburton. Those at the top of the hierarchy had greatest access to facilities on base and greater mobility both on and off base; those at the bottom typically had restricted rights, range of movement, and recourse for grievances.

In theory, the interpreters I encountered on Forward Operation Base (FOB) Prosperity held a privileged position in the base hierarchy. Terps were able to eat and sleep in US military facilities, rather than in non-secured trailers elsewhere in the Green Zone; they had the theoretical right, and sometimes the professional expectation, to access much of the base and navigate the Green Zone. For some interpreters these rights were realities. While decisive, these badges did not tell the full story. The US military bases also contained inescapable gender hierarchies, which intersected with labor hierarchies in ways that marginalized contracted female employees most of all. As the State Department official had hinted (indeed he had never specified what "incidents" had been reported), the Green Zone and surrounding bases was a male-dominated space and was not always safe for women. Rajiv Chandrasekaran, author of *Imperial Life in the Emerald City*, observed that the gender ratio was "overwhelmingly skewed toward men—something like 10-1 men to women. . . . The environment in the Green Zone really did verge, in many cases, on rampant sexual harassment."[2] Female interpreters were among the most visible— and vulnerable—women on base and in the Green Zone as a whole. In spite of their theoretical right to access the base, female Terps faced the greatest challenges moving around these male-dominated spaces; they

2. Chandrasekaran quoted in PBS *Frontline*'s "Inside the Green Zone," October 17, 2006.

endured everyday harassment. In one of the most widely publicized cases, a contractor named Christopher Kirchmeier—whose job it was to issue the important identity badges on Prosperity Base—was accused of sexually harassing at least five female interpreters (who like many of my interlocutors went by self-chosen "American" names): Linda, Susan, Kathy, Mary, and Angel.[3] While female service workers were bussed en masse to and from work and trailers on the periphery of the Green Zone, female Terps had the right to sleep on base and move around the Green Zone independently. This right became a liability when women faced all-too-common harassment and abuse around the Green Zone—especially at night.

The Green Zone transformed in the evening. A party atmosphere pervaded the bases, surrounding cafes, trailer and apartment complexes, international embassies, and UN compounds in the Green Zone. Chandrasekaran described the "emerald city" this way: "Life in the Green Zone is thoroughly disconnected from the reality around. . . . Inside the Green Zone, it was like a different planet inside those 17-foot-high walls."[4] A visitor could not miss the Cuban cigars and alcohol for sale in markets on or near US bases. Throughout the Green Zone, one found hookah cafés and bars—such as the "Baghdad Country Club."[5] The bar and nightclub in the Al-Rashid Hotel, with a long history of international press and political clients, was one of the most notorious (see Illustration 3). Entering Al-Rashid was eerie, with Ba'th Party seals on ballroom floors, Americans visiting hotel gift shops as if on vacation, and evidence of incoming mortar on the surrounding walls. Thomas Ricks reflected: "Walled off from the rest of Iraq . . . a bunch of bars open up. . . . The al-Rashid Hotel becomes a kind of weird scene. A lot of alcohol is flowing. . . . US soldiers would come in from these dusty, dirty bases elsewhere, and they come

3. See "Iraqi Interpreters Seek Punishment for Contractor They Say Sexually Harassed Them," Jeff Stein, *Washington Post*, April 22, 2011.

4. Ibid.

5. For more on the Baghdad Country Club, see Joshuah Bearman's book by the same name; or the *Atlantic* article based on the book, "What It Takes to Open a Bar in Baghdad," *Atlantic*, December 20, 2011.

3. The lobby bar of Al-Rashid Hotel showing evidence of shelling. Photo by author.

into the Green Zone for some sort of meeting, and their jaws would drop. They feel like, 'Wow, this is Sodom and Gomorrah, man.' They haven't seen a woman in months. They certainly aren't drinking alcohol out there, those commanders. They come in here, and it's Friday night at the Al-Rashid; it's the disco scene. It was sort of 'Wow, this is a whole other world.'"[6] Prostitution was pervasive in these spaces. Independent journalist Debra McNutt studied the sex websites tailored to service members and defense contractors. One post she analyzed advertised, "for one dollar you can get a prostitute for one hour."[7] The bar in the US Embassy itself, called "Baghdaddy's" and open to contractors, badged Iraqis, and certain representatives of other embassies, was where I witnessed the most severe sexual harassment of all.[8]

Local and international contractors joined in drinking and dancing alongside government employees and military personnel. As Chandrasekaran and others observed, the majority of Iraqis that Americans "interfaced with" were young English-speaking interpreters.[9] Officially, after contractors, officials, or service members had arrived at the location of a get-together—whether the popular Al-Rashid Hotel, a hookah café, or an embassy—they were required to hide their IDs, usually worn around the neck on a lanyard. Toward the end of the occupation, US service members and defense contractors ventured even further off base to nearby Al-Nawas Street, outside of the Green Zone, to party. Journalist Sudarsan Raghavan reported on one Baghdad nightclub on Al-Nawas Street, which was opened with a $10,000 grant from the US military to foster goodwill and economic development. He writes: "The American soldier stepped out of the Baghdad nightclub. In one hand, he clutched his weapon. In the other, a green can of Tuborg beer. He took a sip and walked over to two comrades. . . . Inside the club Thursday night, US soldiers of the 82nd

6. Ricks quoted in PBS *Frontline*'s "Inside the Green Zone," October 17, 2006.

7. The post is attributed to US Army Reservist Patrick Lackatt in McNutt's "Privatizing Women," *CounterPunch*, July 11, 2007.

8. Embassies frequently threw raucous parties—often "invite only" in their bars. The gatherings that I witnessed at the Italian and Dutch embassies resembled raves with loud music, strobe lights, and water hoses aimed at women in particular. For a more subdued evening, one could visit the pools in one of Saddam Hussein's former palaces.

9. Chandrasekaran quoted in PBS *Frontline*'s "Inside the Green Zone," October 17, 2006.

Airborne Division ogled young Iraqi women who appeared to be prostitutes gyrating to Arabic pop music."[10]

With badges off, contractors, government officials, and military personnel approached partying as a great equalizer in a sense. Yet, the stakes were clearly not equal for men and women. Women were sexually harassed by men whether or not a woman was herself "partying." As I learned through personal experiences of harassment at Baghdaddy's, women working in the Green Zone—whether married or not—were often referred to as "Baghdad single" and were considered "fair game." Some women's harassment amounted to abuse and rape.[11] Certainly, not all workers in the Green Zone "partied," but a culture of partying was widespread and, from my observations, had extremely harmful effects for Iraqi women's lives on base.

Female interpreters had a difficult time being taken seriously by some American superiors and Iraqi colleagues. Whether or not a woman "partied" or participated in sexual encounters on base (and whether or not she had participated in them willingly), female interpreters were widely suspected of sexual involvement with Americans by fellow interpreters and sometimes by friends and family. The matter was not helped by the fact that, as the former interpreter Meena told me in Boston: "Titan was hiring female Terps who don't speak English. . . . They would send young women just to satisfy the men on base. . . . And then throw them away if they spoke up." While the prevalence of prostitution in the Green Zone is now widely acknowledged, the degree to which female interpreters engaged in sex for money—if at all—with US service members or contractors is

10. Sudarsan Raghavan, "An End to Baghdad's Dark Era," *Washington Post*, February 28, 2009.

11. Though difficult to measure due to a lack of reporting and systematic suppression of data, a 2008 Amnesty International document reports on multiple cases of US soldiers on trial for raping Iraqi women and girls, such as fourteen-year-old Abeer Qasim Hamza Al-Janabi. The number of cases that go undocumented and untried certainly far outnumber those in which legal action has been taken. See Amnesty International, *Amnesty International Report 2008—Iraq*, May 28, 2008.

unclear. Regardless, the rumor was widespread because of female inter-preters' visible presence in the Green Zone and their professional intimacy with US Forces. As a result, female interpreters like Meena, as well as her Boston roommate Tamara, found themselves at the center of gossip on and off base. In response to sexism and sexual harassment on base, in addition to suspicion of sexual misdeeds circulating around and beyond the base, female Terps developed inventive responses. Here I will focus specifically on the strategies of one woman, Meena, whose story is indica-tive of a broader trend. In her account of her time on base and in the diaspora, Meena identifies within a symbolic binary of women, in which sacrificial, even victimized daughters stand in opposition to prodigal bad girls, whose sexual danger may bespeak even more sinister intentions.

This binary evokes distinct histories and has surprising futures, as young women like Meena continue to call upon it, situating themselves as devoted filial subjects along the global route they follow to New England. On the one hand, this regime of femininity keyed upon gender ideals that emerged in "war experience" narratives in sanction-era Iraq, which pre-sented women as heroic victims as well as corruptible sites of danger. On the other hand, this model of femininity calls up American discourses that figure Iraqi women as dangerously duped, which emerge in the con-text of the war on terror—a war that was justified as a liberation mission but that came to suspect all social agents as possible threats.

As Meena performatively calls upon the figure of the good Iraqi girl/heroic victim, she also unsettles this construct in several important respects. Firstly, just as she moves to downplay her agency and choice (in working for US Forces, for example), she demonstrates the degree to which she makes these moves agentively and strategically. Secondly, while she strategically positions herself as a victim, she ultimately identifies herself as a woman who does not require either an Iraqi or an American man's protection. Indeed, it was *by* Iraqi and American men that Meena articu-lates herself as having been victimized. Thus, thirdly, she deploys the fig-ure of the "good Iraqi girl," in direct resistance to both Iraqi patriarchy and American imperial feminism.

In what follows, I first provide a vignette in which the figural charac-ters of the "bad Iraqi girl" and "good Iraqi girl" emerge. In a discussion of a YouTube clip, "Sexy Female Interpreters!," we find that figures of fidelity and infidelity are not only used to regulate women's behavior but also used to guard the boundaries of acceptability and betrayal among men, raising the stakes even higher for women. Next, I contextualize the good girl/bad girl binary within a brief cultural history of the multiple discourses from which that dichotomy has been drawn. Then, I turn to Meena's story as it unfolds on Loyalty Base, comparing it to the story of female interpreter "Linda," one of Christopher Kirchmeier's accusers. I conclude by considering how a regulatory binary for women—measuring the boundaries of innocence and danger, loyalty and betrayal—has traveled and translated in the US-based diaspora, at once leaving the figure of the good Iraqi girl unbound and leaving women like Meena all the more squeezed.

"Sexy Female Interpreters!"

A former interpreter named Abbas was the first of several Iraqis I met in the Boston area to show me the YouTube video "Sexy Female Interpreters!" (In the video, two young women dance seductively to Arabic music for men in American military uniforms. The women look directly at the camera. The men are laughing and clapping.) I met Abbas at a midweek Ramadan *iftar* (feast) with a mutual Iraqi acquaintance, Husham, for whom Abbas had served as a sponsor. After dinner and a game of *taqshiish* (a group punning game), Abbas took a phone call from his mother in Baghdad, where it was early morning. When he hung up, he sighed somewhat remorsefully, and began recounting his mother's summary of the meal she and Abbas's sisters—still living at home—had enjoyed the night before. Abbas had not seen his family in two years, he told us. He continued to explain how the war had changed everything for his family. At first, I expected that he was sharing these stories because I, a researcher, was there; I assumed that Husham would have already heard them. I was wrong.

It turned out that Abbas and Husham had not seen each other in months, and there was tension between them. The evening unfolded with playful and acerbic accusations between the two men—that the other person had not called, visited, shared a lead on a job as promised, and so on. Abbas dealt with this tension by telling story after story about his work with the US Army, the subtexts of which I would only make sense of later. From a large family, led by his mother after the death of his father, Abbas felt responsible to provide for his mother and sisters. At the same time, he felt a great deal of guilt about leaving home to work on US bases five days out of seven. Who was going to operate the generator at home? Take care of the water tank? Drive his mother to her doctors' appointments? Abbas joined up with Titan Communications alongside two college friends. Beyond this intimate group of friends, Abbas was uncertain about the intentions of other interpreters he met. He knew what had motivated him to join: Abbas had observed a deadly miscommunication between US troops and Iraqi civilians shortly after the fall of Baghdad near his home in Sadr city—a miscommunication that took the lives of two women and could have been avoided with competent interpretation. After witnessing this, he began volunteering as an interpreter at a local police station that the US Forces had made a neighborhood command center. As the months went on, more and more interpreters were being hired. Abbas had a growing sense that many of them were working for the wrong reasons: just for money or to use their position to gather information for various "groups."

He could, however, understand these things, because: "Every man had to make a choice. Either they were with the Americans, the militias, the insurgents. Whatever, but he had to pick a side." Abbas had a much harder time accepting the interpreters, especially the women, who appeared to join up just for "an adventure or a party." While most men had to "choose a side," he felt that the women did not always need to and, much of the time, were just looking for fun. Worse, Abbas feared, they could be selling their bodies or working as "agents" for causes they didn't fully understand. He found female Terps to be two-sided in appearance and demeanor. Off base, they were soft-spoken "nice Iraqi girls," wearing ʻabāya, but on base they would wear seductive, tight clothes.

One young woman stood out to Abbas. He spoke of a Terp who went by the pseudonym Celina: "Many of the girls, like this girl Celina I used to work with, they used to change clothes when she came on base. She came in wearing ʻabāya and then would change into tight jeans and tee-shirts when we were off duty on the base. She'd go from one person to someone else. This means you really can't trust her. Why does she have to change? What kind of girl is she? She should be the same person all the time. This was hard for me to deal with." Abbas asserts that Celina, and women more broadly, should be the same person all the time. His description of the precautions he himself took traveling on and off base, provided moments earlier, seemed like a wholly different conversation. He had explained carefully to me how he wore different clothes, baseball hats, and sunglasses going to and from work, and how he took different bus and taxi routes. Following up on his account of Celina, I inquired: "Didn't you do something like this yourself? How is it different?" He responded, earnestly: "I was doing what I had to do to take care of my mother and sisters. She was having fun, playing around." I asked him to explain the difference to me further. He said urgently: "Do you think I like to hide and lie? No, I hate it. Do you think I liked being called by fake names? No, I hated telling stories, like, 'Oh, I work at a candy factory.' But I had to. It was not a joke for me."

As I grew to know Abbas better, I learned that most people from his extended family and friend group in Sadr City do not know he is in the United States. They believe he is in Malaysia. He says this eats at him. He tells me that many in Iraq believe that all Iraqis in the United States had some affiliation with US Forces; if people knew he were here, they would know he worked with the United States in Iraq, which would put his family at risk. Further, Abbas is afraid that people would "get the wrong idea," as many in Iraq believe that Iraqis come to America for the "American life" of dating and partying. "You can see it here in Boston, many people do go for that life. I live just the way I lived in Baghdad. I hate to say it, but it's the girls who are changing the most after moving to America. The guys are pretty much the same." He attributed this change in Iraqi women's behavior in the United States to a loss of family "support" for women in the United States and even back in Iraq, and he says this makes him fear that "we are losing Iraq." Abbas was one of many former interpreters to express this view, showing me YouTube videos, as others had, to make this point visually. After showing me "Sexy Female Interpreters!," Abbas closed up the laptop on the kitchen table and looked at me, visibly affected by the video, and said, "See what I mean now?"

I later heard from Husham that he perceived Abbas's story as a coded message for him directly. Husham had started dating an Iraqi woman—living apart from her family—about whom little was known. Husham felt that Abbas was communicating his apprehension about him dating a single Iraqi "girl" through the messages embedded in his stories. The central message in Abbas's story surrounded a woman needing to "be the same person" all the time.

Many members of the Iraqi diaspora articulated a similar position that while men could be expected to "mask"—an idiom interpreters used for concealing or changing one's identities—women could not be trusted to do so. Those women who did mask could not be trusted. Abbas names his sisters as the type of "girls" who are who they say they are: "They know some English, but they would never consider being Terps because of all the lying and hiding."

Iraqi women certainly did "mask" under the US occupation. Women changed clothes and routes when they traveled outside the home; they covered for family members and friends; and they, like men, carried multiple ID cards with different identities for the various neighborhood checkpoints. The widely circulating assertion that Iraqi women could not mask themselves as ably as men is a product of the unique historical moment and social space that liminal subjects like Abbas occupy. I am therefore more interested in this assertion as an index of regulatory discourses at work in that time-space rather than as an indication of any discernible sociological pattern. This assertion about how women and men cope with war represents the challenge for women to maintain an illusory innocence for men to guard. Gender ideals about women's innocence unfold at the junction of distinct projects and histories, to which we now briefly turn in order to contextualize the sociocultural imperative to present themselves as "good girls" that young women like Meena encounter in their lives on base and in the diaspora.

Honor, Terror, Gender

On the one hand, the good girl/bad girl binary emerged out of recently reauthorized discourses and practices about the protection of women's "honor" in Iraq. Just as Abbas attributes Iraqi women's loss of innocence in the United States to a lack of family support, the view that families must protect a woman's honor resurfaced on a national scale in the wake of the Gulf War after two decades of progressive gender politics, sparked by a robust women's movement and early Ba'thist revolutionary goals. In the late 1980s, 1990s, and early 2000s, tribal codes of family honor were integrated into national policy and ideology as a result of the government's "fidelity campaign" and increasingly conservative reforms in family law. This ushered in an era of heightened conservatism, in which the protection of women's honor justified increased domestic seclusion and even honor killings. On the other hand, this good girl/bad girl binary emerges out of the specific context of a war on "terror." Authoritative discourses on terrorism have figured women as non-agential victims or dangerously duped agents for someone else's plots (Naaman 2007, 132). In the day-to-day operations of the war on terror, nearly all non-American agents were possible threats. As a result of orientalist biases that paradoxically echo Iraqi formulations of "honor" as timeless values, Iraqi women were widely assumed in advance to be *non*-agential, placing the burden of danger on all women who exerted recognizable shows of agency.

Honor on Loyalty Base

While some posit that defending women's "honor," *sharaf,* is an essential cultural value in Iraq, the way in which honor has been deployed ideologically and politically is historically and socially situated. A striking example of the kind of essentializing account that has been co-opted by Western orientalist projects can be found in Sana Al-Khayyat's book *Honour and Shame: Women in Modern Iraq.* She asserts: "To understand how behavior is regulated and conduct controlled in Iraqi society, one must understand the Arab concept of honor, which is generally linked to the sexual conduct of women. . . . The phenomenon of 'honor and shame' bears a direct relation to family ties, and to the complex interrelation of social organization and conduct in Arab society. Once a woman breaks the rules, the whole family will be drawn into a sea of shame. An Iraqi proverb states, *al-bin tala ala-umha,* which means, 'The daughter takes after her mother morally.' In other words, the purity of the daughter reflects that of her mother" (1990, 21–22). Al-Khayyat asserts the centrality of honor and shame to Iraqi social organization by establishing each as essential-ized cultural quantities.[12] This account hinges in particular on the notion that *al-bin tala ala-umha*, "the daughter takes after her mother morally." In this formulation, a mother is the symbol of the family honor and her daughter is the clearest danger to that honor. The sexual behavior of the daughter reflects upon her mother, which in turn reflects upon the whole family—especially its patriarchal leader. Rather than a cultural essence, I conceptualize this configuration of honor as a historical product of ideol-ogy that was reinvigorated in recent decades and in prevailing models of masculinity and femininity, which have circulated in official and public discourses since the sanctions era. The ideological regime of honor, dis-tinguishing pure and dangerous women, sometimes takes its power from the perception of timelessness; however, a historical perspective shows that notions of honor have been developed and deployed to diverse ends at various historical moments (Jowkar 1986).

By the sanctions era in the wake of the Gulf War, the specific out-line of the good girl/bad girl binary emerged around the figures of the war widow and the prodigal prostitute. Following an era in which gender equality was made a revolutionary goal, in the latter half of the Iran-Iraq War the government began to circulate gendered rhetoric in which Iraqi women represented the stricken motherland, and men represented their defenders. Women who were left widowed by the war became symbols of

---

12. Michael Herzfeld (1980) and Unni Wikan (1984), among others, have challenged the notion that ideas of "honor" or "shame" as such correspond to emic categories in the Mediterranean or Middle East, respectively, suggesting that these concepts may instead be reductive analytical glosses. Lila Abu-Lughod has worked to situate specific discourses around shame ('eb and 'ar in Arabic) and honor (*sharaf*) in the Middle East, examining "honor" and "shame" as products of ideology rather than as products of a cultural essence (Abu-Lughod 1986, 129); while some, such as Amanda Weidman (2003), have aimed to "move beyond" the categories of honor and shame in the Mediterranean. This move, though welcomed and perhaps necessary at a level of themed discussion among scholars, should not sideline our attention to the empirical life of these categories in the world.

the country's purity and sacrifice. As a consequence of extreme economic hardship during the sanctions period, a significant portion of women turned to prostitution for survival. In response to this widespread development, Nadje Al-Ali reflects: "On the level of the government discourse as well as within society, Iraqi women became the bearers of honor of the whole country. They became 'potential prostitutes'" (2007, 201). Now, not only did women's sexuality reflect the honor of the family; it also reflected that of the nation as a whole. The crucible of honor has remained at the feet of women like Celina, whose actions signal to Abbas that "we are losing Iraq." Models of feminine national identity began to hinge on the performance of victimhood.

The most dramatic indication of increasingly conservative gender codes in Iraq came in the early 1990s when "honor killings" were sanctioned by the government (Spatz 1991). More broadly, legal matters relating to the family—such as marriage, divorce, and inheritance—became the domain of local-level familial, tribal, and religious leaders. Tribal codes of "honor" were integrated into Iraqi ideologies and identities at the national scale (Marr 2010). Alongside them, new, highly restricted gender ideals took shape.

As cultural translators in the Iraq War, both male and female interpreters evoked constructs of honor—translating tropes of patriarchal protection and female victimization—to clarify the cultural context of Iraq for US Forces. Abbas told me that he was constantly reminding his American supervisors that Iraq was a very "traditional" place: "Social roles matter a lot here. We believe that a man's role is to protect his wife and family. Honor is everything, I explained. I am sorry to say but women are treated differently. So I told them when they talk to the people, address the men." Abbas, who had shared the story of Celina with me earlier, told me that he gave advice to soldiers to "watch out for some of the Iraqi girls on base." He explained his reasoning this way: "If they are playing around with you, I guarantee they come from a bad family. If they come from a bad family, you don't know what they could do." Abbas implies that "bad girls" are not only sexually dangerous but possibly dangerous in other ways as well, which he leaves undefined. At the same time, he asserts that women have it hard in Iraq. He attributes this to the lack of "support" for women.

He admits—and "is sorry to say"—that the picture of Iraqi tradition he paints contains a double standard for men and women. While he articulates elements of sanctions-era public discourse, he appears to evoke them as timeless cultural truths. Tamara also addressed double standards in Iraq, saying: "Now, Iraq is not like a Syria or an Egypt. Iraq is a very strict place for women. Okay, people in Arab countries will tell you that family is everything, but in Iraq it's something different. People watch everything you do and are free to interfere in your life. The smallest thing can be understood as disrespectful and ruin a whole family." While talking to Max about "honor" over dinner at a Syrian restaurant, he told me: "For example, see these young Syrian women, they are sitting there eating and chatting. One of them has her foot resting on a chair opposite her. In Iraq, I swear, this would be shameful. It's crazy, but it's true." Even as they aim to garner greater understanding on the part of Americans, several interpreters voiced opinions like Max's that elements of Iraq's preoccupation with honor were "crazy." These self-orientalizing sentiments tapped into and reinforced American views of Iraq as backward and perhaps in need of liberation, perhaps having the opposite effect than intended.

US rhetoric exploited the conservative turn in Iraq as proof that Iraqi women needed "liberation," but, at the same time, American rhetoric deployed similar gender constructs to those found in Iraqi discourses about women's honor. Paradoxically, US projects of liberation and discourses of terrorism call upon and reproduce similarly restrictive and binarized roles for women. Discourses of terrorism and liberation were not merely wielded in rhetorical battles about US military intervention, but also shaped on-the-ground military operations with profoundly gendered impacts.

Terror on Loyalty Base

Because of the hegemony of the term "terrorism" and the slipperiness of its logic, it permeated many aspects of day-to-day military operations—as a framework for understanding any and all antioccupation violence and as a justification for "unconventional" military tactics. In surveys conducted with US Forces online, I found that "terrorism," "terrorist activity," and "terrorists" were principal idioms through which US Forces understood their adversary as well as the object and rationale for their operations. The surveys indicated that the expansive term "terrorist" could stand for an old-guard Ba'thist commander involved in the insurgency in Anbar or a young militiaman working for Jaish al-Mahdi in Basrah, but in almost every case this term stood for an Iraqi man who was a threat to Iraqi innocents. If men were read as possible combatants, Iraqi women in this formulation were victims rather than perpetrators of terrorism, and they were in need of US Forces' protection. The widespread perception that women did not participate in combat—a perception that I observed in women's differential treatment in passing through US checkpoints, in security vetting for US employees, and in immigration proceedings—mirrors the US military's internal policies during the Iraq War. Military policy excluded females in the armed services from participating in active combat (and similarly limited female interpreters' ability to participate in combat missions). It should be noted that such a pacific view of Iraqi women contrasts sharply with the view of women as possible combatants elsewhere in the Middle East, such as in the Israeli-Palestinian conflict, where, since the first intifada, Palestinian women have been treated by the Israeli military as potential participants in the conflict.[13]

To a striking degree, operational approaches in the war echoed orientalist gender stereotypes, sanctioned by the war on terror's liberation rationales, which circulated in political discourse and media.[14] Women were presumed to be less-than-agential: to the extent that a woman was discovered "harboring" someone or something in her home, collecting information, or participating in violence herself, she might be understood as an agent for someone else's plot but not a self-possessed actor herself. Interpreters described the disheartening work of rounding up anyone on a raid who was not forthcoming with information about the location of weapons or people of interest. But, after separating women and children

13. See Victor (2003) and Hasso (2005). For a broader discussion of women as participants in "terrorism," see Sjoberg and Gentry (2008, 2011).

14. For a discussion of media coverage see Jiwani (2008) and Khalidi (2011).

from men, it was almost always only the men who would be taken in for questioning. Women, in the instance of a raid, did not count as "anyone." A notable exception to this rule was the case of female relatives of "terrorism" suspects being detained in efforts to apply pressure on the male suspects to turn themselves in.

As Talal Asad has noted, the belief that social actors are either willfully agential or passive victims is foundational to the liberal humanist tradition. Immanent to the liberal tradition from which the very idea of "terrorism"—that is, politically motivated nonstate violent action—became thinkable, is a persistent problem of individual agency. Asad writes, "There is a secular viewpoint held by many . . . that would have one accept that in the final analysis there are only two mutually exclusive options available: either an agent (representing and asserting himself or herself) or a victim (the passive object of chance or cruelty)" (2007, 79). The bifurcation between victim and agent that Asad describes appears to subjects of terrorism discourses as an imperative to distinguish victim, in need of foreign liberation, from possible villain, in need of justice. This was an acutely gendered division and the one with the most immediate implications of war on terror discourses on interpreters' everyday lives. Chris Coulter has observed that "discourse[s] of 'victimhood' . . . creates a certain kind of subject" (2009, 149). Male subjects struggled to construct their agency as nonthreatening. Female subjects, imaginable as double victims—first of a tyrannical regime and now of senseless terrorism—faced an imperative to construe themselves as unknowing and nonagential vis-à-vis US power.

Closely related to the discursive regimes of terrorism is the project of liberation.[15] At the level of rhetoric, liberation has to do with the movement—sometimes forcefully—of someone from the state of perceived victimhood to the state of imagined agency. On the ground in a war on

15. For discussion of the ill effects of liberation orientations in "reconstruction" efforts in Iraq, Deniz Kandioyti's "Political Fiction Meets Gender Myth: Post-Conflict Reconstruction, 'Democratization,' Women's Rights" provides an adept analysis (2007). See also Al-Ali and Pratt (2009); and Efrati (2013).

terror, where all non-American agents were potentially dangerous, liberation presented a double bind for women. Within military grids of intelligibility a "liberated woman"—became a potentially dangerous woman.

According to Meena, the prevailing option for women who were directly subject to such authoritative formulations given their work for US Forces was to appear passive, say "I don't know" whenever possible, thus presenting themselves as one-dimensional social actors whose only purpose was to work. Yet, female Terps also faced pressures to party, which for many felt like a contradictory imperative. Participating in "fun," or reciprocating soldiers' advances, could result in a woman being maligned by fellow Iraqis on base and "thrown away" by US Forces. Meena told me: "It was all about the chase for US soldiers. . . . If you actually do what they want you to do, they use you and throw you away." Even if not especially in the sexual realm, female Terps felt the need to appear passive, despite countervailing pressures to "have fun." Women's self-construction as passive sometimes meant resigning themselves to being harassed. For Meena, putting up with "minor" harassment was preferable to being "thrown away" if she actually participated in fun. (For her the harassment remained "minor" so long as it was nonphysical. Her assessment changed when she was physically harassed.) Indeed, sexual harassment was not always, if ever, minor.

It turns out that a woman's passivity could also make her the target of gossip—either because it was seen to "invite" American men's advances, or because it raised speculation about what sinister intentions (if not "fun") motivated her to work with US Forces. Because some like Abbas assumed that most women on base were seeking fun (sowing suspicion of women's sexual promiscuity), a woman who shows herself not to be fun-seeking may be viewed by fellow Iraqis as "too good," sparking concern about her possible involvement in violent activity. Meena explains that someone who is too good is "just another kind of bad girl"—and all the more dangerous.

A frequently discussed example of a "dangerous" Iraqi woman in US military and media conversations is the female suicide bomber. After the 2008 suicide bombing by Hasna Maryi, this figure powerfully took hold in the midst of the war.[16] Though occasional bombings carried out by women had been reported in Iraq since 2005, the rate of female suicide bombing tripled in 2008 according to journalist Mona Eltahawy (2008). Maryi, who is reported to have never opened a Koran, infamously gave her brassiere to a jihadi group to fit her for an explosive belt. In the video capturing her spoken suicide note and the detonation of her belt in downtown Baghdad, she is giddy and unveiled. After her death, the cameraman, an acquaintance of Maryi, says: "The silly woman did it!" The increase of female suicide bombing did not radically alter the gendered policies on patrol and raids or increase the rate of female imprisonment. To the contrary, one senior military official I met in Iraq used the example of female suicide bombers as proof of the need to provide better educational opportunities and greater "empowerment" among Iraqi women—implicitly assuming that women engage in these activities because of a lack of education or choice.

Indeed, a common way for the US military and media to make sense of a female suicide bomber—just like the cameraman taping Maryi's death— was to imagine her as a duped, ignorant, "silly" victim of patriarchy, but a potentially dangerous one nonetheless. In this way, even she is less than a full social actor because she does not grasp her own agency. Colleagues on base—or acquaintances off base—might speculate about a woman's possible connections to "groups" when her motivations were unclear for taking such a weighty and improbable step as leaving her family to work for US Forces. The specter of terrorist associations raised the stakes even more for women like Meena to construct themselves as passive victims who worked with US Forces for lack of better options to support their families in an era of female breadwinners. Simultaneously, it was sometimes a woman's passivity or refusal to participate in "fun"—to guard herself from accusations of sexual danger—that led to rumors about her potentially violent danger.

Here we can return to the widely publicized case of "Linda," whose experiences as a female interpreter are strikingly similar to Meena's.

---

16. This figure has multiple contemporary and historical analogies, as Sjoberg and Gentry show in their 2008 article "Reduced to Bad Sex." See also Claudia Brunner's review of related debates in "Occidentalism Meets the Female Suicide Bomber" (2007).

Linda was considered one of the best interpreters in her unit and was well respected by high-level officials like Major David Underwood, who became the staunchest advocate on her behalf. She, among four other women, accused an American contractor named Christopher Kirchmeier of repeated sexual harassment. According to a *Washington Post* investigative article: "Although Kirchmeier's relations with several Iraqi women drew notice, it was his treatment of an interpreter known as Linda, who had worked with US combat units for nearly six years, that provoked particular anger. . . . After she resisted Kirchmeier's 'advances,' [Major] Underwood wrote, the contractor 'had her fired and kicked off' the forward operating base" (Stein 2011). The rationale for these actions was framed as a matter of "security": Linda was believed to pose security concerns that were not clearly specified or prosecuted. After it became evident that she would not get her job back, Major Underwood attempted to help her resettle in the United States through the State Department's Special Immigrant Visa program. She was refused admission, again on the grounds of security concerns. According to the *Post* article, "Nomi Seltzer, the US Embassy's Immigrant Visa Unit chief, told him in a May 2010 e-mail that there was 'a plethora of information regarding [Linda] to which you are not privy'" (ibid.). Major Underwood found the alleged security concerns baseless: "She was honest, loyal, and courageous. In the five years I have known her she has always been loyal to the US. Why isn't she in prison? Why wasn't she detained for whatever it was that was so bad?" (ibid.). Linda herself appealed for help from the position of a victimized woman at risk: "I faced death threat many times. . . . They said because I worked with the Americans, I betrayed my country . . . and I should be dead for that" (ibid.). She constructs her work as "sacrifice" rather than betrayal. Yet, her sacrifice was honored by neither her countrymen—who considered her a traitor—nor the US government, who came to consider her a security threat in the process of her reporting sexual crimes on US bases. Linda herself believes that if she had accepted Kirchmeier's advances, she might have been fired ("thrown away," in Meena's words), but she would not have been flagged as a problem. She told the *Post*: "Trust me, if I said yes to Chris and had a relationship with him, I wouldn't be [kept] out of the States now" (ibid.).

Gender on Loyalty Base

As young women on military bases, Linda and Meena participated in processes of subjectivation in which they were either the purest sacrificial models to Iraq nationhood or the gravest danger to it, either passive victims in need of American protection or threats to peace. The configuration of gender in Iraqi narratives relating to "honor" and American wars fought against "terror" are quite distinct in their social logics and histories, yet they are strikingly similar in their representations of women within a binary frame of purity and danger. At the junction between those histories, women like Meena performatively reconfigure the governing binaries for women, asserting and reshaping the lines of a "good Iraqi girl," much like Nadine Naber has found Arab American women to do in the San Francisco-based diaspora (2006; 2012).

Meena is acutely aware of the pressures women face to construct themselves as passive at the risk of being seen as dangerous—either sexually or otherwise. Yet, Meena personally saw how men on base took advantage of that perceived passivity to pursue women—adding a new layer to Iraqi women's actual victimization on US bases. Paradoxically, those women like Meena who rejected such advances could be seen as "too good," arousing curiosity about other, more sinister motivations she might have. On base, at the junction of honor and terror discourses and in the presence of widespread sexual harassment, the figures of the good Iraqi girl and the victimized Iraqi woman are unbound. When Meena was "too good" sexually, questions began to emerge about her potentially dangerous agency.

Meena: The Perfect *Bint Iraqiya*

Over tea and dolma, Meena tells me and our mutual Iraqi friend in Boston—Tamara—that she "did it all for her [mom]." I would later learn that this conversation was the first and last time that Meena would speak directly of her work for US Forces with Tamara. "I did it all for her," Meena repeated; Tamara nodded knowingly. After graduating from college in Baghdad with an English degree, her dream had been to teach, but this changed with the financial strains that came with the war. Her father had been an officer in the Iraqi military and had passed away of a heart attack during the Iran-Iraq War; her brother had left Iraq for Jordan after the Gulf War. Meena was in middle school during the Gulf War, and she recalls that afterward her extended family was left scrambling. Most of Meena's relatives (aside from distant cousins) ended up leaving Iraq in the years following the Gulf War due to participation by one of her maternal uncles in the illegal Da'wa Party, which put everyone in his immediate family at risk from the government. After the US invasion, Meena's mother fell into a depression. She did not feel safe in Iraq, but she could not imagine leaving the house in which she and her husband raised their kids. Their neighborhood, Adhamiyah, began to be dominated by Sunni militias; Shi'a residents were leaving their homes for surrounding areas. From a mixed religious background, Meena and her mother thought it was a matter of time before someone knocked on their door. Somehow, they were spared (Meena speculates that it may have been her father's high rank in the Iraqi military that saved them from the Sunni militias who had allegiances to the old regime). Around the same time, Meena heard about linguist positions with US Forces. She recalls how, in her job interview, she described her living situation as "two women alone." When she was hired, her boss allowed her to keep a cell phone, strictly forbidden for interpreters, to check on her mother in Adhamiyah.

At the beginning of her work for Titan, Meena worked with US military units all over Iraq. Her supervisors told her that she was one of the best Terps they had seen, and yet she was frequently passed over in favor of male interpreters for highest-level meetings on base. Frequently the first up in the morning and the last to go to sleep at night, she attempted to prove her seriousness. She also found that she liked the work; it was not only better than sitting in the girls' dorm with little to do, she felt that she was good at it.

Once she had earned a reputation with Titan, she requested to stay in Baghdad in order to be close to her mother. Eventually, she was sent to work with the US Army unit working with the Iraqi military Transition Team based on Loyalty Base. She describes her routine on Loyalty Base as grueling. The gear—especially the Kevlar bulletproof vest—that she wore on routine trips off base for meetings gave her acute back pain. Her schedule of working four days on base and three days at home off base, every week, demanded that she perform dual personas—she went by "Rim" at home and "Meena" at work—which was as heavy a burden as the vest. She explains: "At work, I wore a uniform, ACUs. Some girls took off their uniforms off duty and relaxed in jeans, but I always kept it on unless I was in the girls' dorm. When I left the base to go home, I wore black ʿabāya and hijab. It's a big difference. No one would think I'm the same person. When I wear a uniform, I am young and American. When I am in ʿabāya, I am middle-aged and Iraqi."

Meena guarded Rim carefully. For five years, Meena lived as two people. She spoke to very few people on base or, for that matter, off base. She told us, looking at Tamara with a smile: "I read a lot in those years. Jane Austen is my favorite." It was an escape. She read whatever she could find on base, and even braved carrying English-language books on and off base when she traveled back home across town. When she left the base, she found she left some parts of herself there: "Even when I left, my mind was on base. I would go to the market and speak English. Imagine this woman in ʿabāya speaking English to strangers. I had to tell people a few different times: 'Oh, I'm a private English tutor, I've been with students all day.'" Meena says that her life revolved around her mom, a retired schoolteacher in her sixties, suffering from diabetes. By asserting her filial duty Meena both clarifies her rationale for working with US Forces and identifies with a model of femininity, hinging on sacrifice and victimization, which her mother represents. "I did everything for her because she gave everything to me. I worked so that she could finally enjoy an easy life. I cooked for her. I cleaned. I even bathed her. For that reason I am thirty and unmarried. I'm the good Iraqi girl, the perfect bint Iraqiya, but, see, that's what makes people suspicious."

Though she worked out of a sense of duty to her mother, Meena explains that it felt like a betrayal every time she left her mom for Loyalty Base, like she was "breaking a piece of her heart." According to Meena, her mother would sometimes not eat or sleep when she left. But still her mother told her adamantly: "Go, go!" Meena felt sick leaving her alone—with only cousins to occasionally check in on her. She had tried to talk her mother into leaving Iraq with her to join her brother in Jordan; her mom refused to leave her home. Meena asked her military supervisor, a captain from South Carolina, to help her mom. She asked if he could share any information about upcoming military operations in her neighborhood to warn her mom about. Instead, he gave her the advice that her mother should leave. I told him, "This is her country." Meena looked up from her tea, straight into my eyes, "See all that I had to do? Who would want to do it? What choice did I have, really? My mother had no sons or brothers left in Iraq. We could have survived off of our cousins' charity. But, my mom has medical bills. She needs working generators, a comfortable house. And she will not leave that home. She wants to die in Iraq. . . . I kept working until I couldn't anymore. . . . I was stuck. . . . I wish she would join me here in Boston. My cousin tells me she goes days without eating. I know I broke a piece of her heart. She wants me with her in Iraq. But she knows I did it all for her."

Tamara and I were equally rapt by Meena's account. What had struck me was how Meena's depiction of her mother's level of devotion to Iraq sounded like both fulsome qualities and visceral bodily conditions. When represented as the backbone of the nation in the postcolonial Middle East, mothers are generally symbols of strength and motherhood, a matter of cultivation. Meena depicts her mother's connection to Iraq— and her desire to have her Meena beside her there—as strong enough to be something like an ailment: a "broken heart" shown in a refusal to eat or sleep. Her mother's devotion to her daughter and her country was also the source of her suffering. That devotion—the basis for her intertwined national and gender identities—*was* her victimhood. Meena herself accesses the positionality of "victim," carved out in contradistinction from the positionality of a fun-seeking girl, by claiming that she "did it all" for her mother. The available models of femininity and national identity that she emulated required her to reiterate that she was "stuck" and "had no choice" but to work for US Forces. Paradoxically, it was her fulfillment of her filial duty that most devastated her mom.

Meena says, "The problem is that the people, they don't like women working with the US Army. They shoot her without asking a question." Meena knew that it was not only her safety that concerned her mother.

It was also her life after the US military left. Meena's mom did not disapprove of Meena's work—and she recognized Meena's sincere motivation in taking the job—but she knew what people said about women like Meena who worked with the US Army. She had hoped for Meena to marry, if not for love, at least for stability. Both mother and daughter knew that the longer Meena worked for US Forces, the more difficult it would be for her to marry. Meena and her mother told neighbors and acquaintances that Meena worked for an engineering company as a translator, but anyone who wanted to uncover the nature of Meena's work could do so easily.

The danger to her immediate safety and her long-term marriage options gave Meena pause. (She took two month-long breaks—one over Ramadan one year, and the other when her mom was having medical problems. Each time she had real doubts about returning to Loyalty Base.) And the gravity of her sacrifices made Meena all the more apprehensive about the other young women with whom she worked who appeared to take the job lightly: "Some of the girls and guys weren't there for their families. They were there for fun. Unfortunately, Titan hires those people. You would think they [Titan] needed interpreters, right? But they were sending interpreters who don't speak English. I swear to god. Excuse my language, they would send young girls to the male soldiers just to satisfy them. How can you go to a Transition Team meeting if you don't know what 'Transition Team' means? For them, FOB [Forward Operating Base] Loyalty was a big party. Not me." Meena recounts that several young women had "boyfriends" among US Forces. Others, she had reason to believe, were having sex with men for money. She noticed quickly that these "girls" were let go as easily as they were hired, leading her to suspect that the American troops did not care to have women around after they had sexual relations. Just as soon as she offered this observation, she added: "Of course, you could be fired for *not* dating one of the guys too." In other words, there was a great deal of turnover among female interpreters.

Meena said she went to one social gathering in her five years as an interpreter. "It was not for me," she said, and she never went to a party again. She was, however, aggressively pursued by a couple of US soldiers. She shielded herself from the two men's advances by wearing her ACUs at all times on base and befriending her supervisor, the captain, whom she trusted and even sat with during meals. Meena did not report the soldiers' behavior until it became physical. She recounted: "Two guys kept telling me things. I wasn't used to people telling me, 'You are so hot,' 'You are sexy.' They told me, 'This is the American way.' I ignored it. But then, one solider invited me to see a movie . . . this is the ambush, I learned: Come and see a movie. I told him, 'OK, I want to see the movie, give me the DVD and I can watch it at my trailer.' I didn't know it's like a fish getting the food. The solider said, 'What? I'm inviting you to my room.' I said, 'What kind of movie is this that I can only watch in your room? A special movie?' I began to walk away and he grabbed me by the arm and pulled me near him, too close to him, and said, 'Don't you like me?' I told him, 'I am not here for fun, I am here for my family. Please get off of me.'"

There was a long pause after Meena told Tamara and me about this incident. From her silence and body language, I understood that Meena did not wish to share any more details about the incident, but also sensed that there were more details to share. After taking several sips of tea, Meena continued cautiously by saying that she reported the incident to the captain, who disciplined the young man and did the unusual thing of speaking to the entire unit about sexual conduct. As a result of the captain's help, rumors began to spread that Meena was having a relationship with him—and was even pregnant with the captain's child. Other rumors surfaced that there was something "wrong" with Meena. She was "too good." Perhaps she had something darker and more sinister than a pregnancy to hide. Why *was* she so close to the captain? Other Terps began to ask uncomfortable questions about her family: about where her brother was and who he "worked for." She believed that they suspected her of "working for a group." Her reticence now became a red flag; when the good girl is "too good," Meena explains, she arrives dangerously close to the bad girl.

In the end, it was not the potential peril to her life that her work posed or her concern for her mother that made her quit the job. It was this incident of sexual harassment and the period of gossip that followed. The captain recommended that she apply for refugee resettlement, and began the paperwork for her and her mother. She was ambivalent about that prospect. To Meena's surprise, her mother did not oppose the idea. But her mom also clarified that she would not be joining Meena. Again she said:

"Go, go!" Meena never told her mom about her problems on base, but she felt that her mother implicitly understood that life had become untenable for her in Iraq. She seemed to grasp that there was "nothing left for me."

Meena ultimately made up her mind one day, sitting at home with her mom, when she closed her eyes and tried to imagine what her life would be like in Iraq. Would she marry? Would she start a family? Did she want to? She tried to imagine a life in the United States. Did she know anyone there? Could she go back to school? Could she become a teacher? She discovered that she could more easily imagine a future in an unknown country than in her home country. Now, several years after resettling in the Boston suburb of Chelsea, Meena has one foot in Iraq and one foot in the United States. She spends about half the year in Boston to maintain her green card, renting a simple room and finding work through a temp agency when she can. She spends the rest of the year in Baghdad with her mom. She is still contemplating her next step: she could acquire her US citizenship and permanently move back to Iraq, or she might finally persuade her mom to move to the United States.

In some respects, little has fundamentally changed in her life. She still maintains two personas—Rim at home with her mom, Meena in Boston. She continues to keep to herself, not seeing many people in either Boston or Baghdad. She remains torn between family and the work she does to serve her family (though she gave up on sending much money home within months of arriving in the United States). In other respects, her life has drastically changed. Now Rim and Meena live thousands of miles apart. Now, she has all but decided that she does not want to marry. She explains that she felt like she got on a track that she cannot reverse—a track whose destination she does not know. Her mother remains the single most important thing in her life, but knows she cannot be the "good girl" that she is expected to be. Neither can she be a fun-loving, carefree girl.

Over the course of her work with US Forces and resettlement in the United States, Meena discovered the impossibility of being a good Iraqi girl. In her effort to provide for her mom, Meena discovered what felt to her like the outer limits of loyalty. Meena knows that her mom accepts her past choices; she even understands why Meena felt that she had "no choice" but to then leave for the United States. On base her life was unworkable. In the end, her discreetness did not insulate her from sexual advances and gossip; it invited them. When she did not accept soldiers' sexual advances, and in fact reported them to the captain, she believed that other people on base suspected her of being "too good"—perhaps participating in more sinister activities. After getting on that seemingly irreversible track as an Iraqi woman working with US Forces, she found "nothing left" for her in Iraq.

The Good Iraqi Girl Unbound

In the United States, Meena arrived into a refugee network of former interpreters, within which gossip and rumors continued. She sees Iraqis through her work at the temp agency (arranged by the refugee resettlement agency). She says that people seem "fascinated" by single women in the United States: "I tell them I am here to protect my future and my family's future." After going to a salsa dance class once with Tamara, she says that they somehow became Boston's worst "bad girls." She says with frustration, "It was not exactly a night club! It was a dance studio in the middle of the day." Now, she avoids Iraqis except for Tamara as much as possible. Even with Tamara, she shares very little personal information. When she does see Iraqis, she answers their questions politely and continues to assert herself as a devoted daughter working for her mother much as she had done on base. Yet, as she calls upon the figure of the good Iraqi girl, she challenges the regulatory discourses out of which that figure emerges. She says, "I know my heart, and my mom knows my heart. If they want to call me a bad girl, let them. I am a bad girl. I believe it tells you more about what is in their hearts than mine. I know what kind of Iraqis they are." She challenges the authority of those who would call her a "bad girl." When I asked Meena if she could imagine ever saying that aloud to other Iraqis, she responded animatedly: "I *have* said that to Iraqis at work." Although she had appealed to various men's "help" in the past, she ultimately rejects the idea that a man's protection is necessary. Meena's decision not to marry underscores this rebuke.

As the three of us talked over lunch, Meena told Tamara and me that it was the first time she had spoken about her work with the US military to anyone—ever. In talking about the tragedies of war, she draws analogies between her conditions of being stuck with her mother's conditions of isolation. She calls upon her mom's story of being left alone in a house surrounded by "terrorists"—many of whom she feels the United States actually armed. She identifies with the figure of her mother, the heroic victim physically stuck in a house, to illuminate her experience of stuckness and to reveal the real impacts of the war. Meena positions her mother as a victim of the US-led war whose "liberation" amounted to house arrest and depression. By juxtaposing her mother's sacrifice to her own—working for US Forces, being harassed and fondled by soldiers, and becoming the subject of gossip, all of which put her dangerously close to the "bad girl"—she challenges the binary between innocent victims and dangerous villains. She also positions the United States as the entity most responsible for their victimization, directly challenging the "liberation" rationale for the US war.

Nadine Naber has explored the regulatory power of a similar binarized construct for women in Arab America: the good Arab girl versus the Americanized whore, which has emerged amid shifting cultural politics of belonging in the Arab diaspora (2006, 2012). She outlines the ways in which subjects resist this with reference to authoritative religious texts and through activist channels. Meena and other young female interpreters have resisted the construct of the good Iraqi girl on the very same discursive terrain that produced the good girl/bad girl binary: US war on terror discourses and dynamic Iraqi narratives of honor.

Being "too good"—too innocent—was a "red flag" in Meena's experience. She spoke up against harassment, refused to be silenced, and, as a result, grew to be seen as suspicious. When pushed and questioned by other Iraqis in Boston, she has responded by saying, "Call me a bad girl"—powerfully rebuking the pressures to uphold female honor or the perception of more sinister danger. The figure of the good Iraqi girl reaches its limit on base where, juxtaposed, the contradictions and paradoxes of terrorism and honor discourses are laid bare. Female interpreters like Meena arrive at the unattainability of the models of femininity they call upon at the collision of terror and honor discourses. Yet, they continue to performatively call upon them, somewhat subversively, destabilizing the regulatory regimes that produce the elusive figure of the good Iraqi girl.

Meena's strategic rebuke of the "good girl" and her subversive acceptance of a "red flag" comes with some measure of unease; she selectively embraces and distances herself from a model of feminine national identity that her mom represents, she fears she is in fact growing more and more distant from her mother. Young men confront a similar experience of disorientation as a function of their physical distance from family (whose job it is to "protect") and their historically rooted models of gendered national identity surrounding patriarchal protection.

4

Reconstructing Patriarchy on Patrol

I met Joe in the lobby of a five-star Boston hotel where he worked as a doorman. Over coffee in the lobby bar, he told me that this was his last week at the hotel; he would be shipping off to basic training in less than two weeks' time. As an interpreter with the US Army's 101st Airborne Division, he had heard from soldiers about opportunities for engineers like himself to advance their careers faster in the Army than in private industry. After immigrating to the United States, he found it nearly impossible to find a job in his field with an Iraqi degree.[1] He began studying for the ASVAB—the Armed Services Vocational Aptitude Battery—and working overtime at the hotel to save money for his mom back in Iraq. She, I would learn, knew nothing of Joe's decision to enlist in the army. Joe did not tell her "for her own safety," much as he had not told her when insurgents in the west of Iraq briefly held him hostage. (He had his ransom negotiated through his uncle—telling his mom only months later.)

Joe is ambivalent about US military policy and outspoken in his opposition to many aspects of the US-led war in Iraq—in particular the dissolution of the Iraqi military in which his father had served. Still, he believes in the importance of the US military to help people in moments of crisis. Joe points to the Army Corps of Engineers as one of the most "obvious" humanitarian-driven divisions of the military. While Joe met some service members back in Iraq whom he described as "ignorant" and war-hungry (and shared compelling stories of his attempts to humanize Iraq for these soldiers), he was impressed by several soldiers' integrity. He

---

1. Joe has a master's degree in civil engineering from Baghdad University.

was surprised that so many of them really "cared" about what they were doing in Iraq.

Joe says that he daydreams about his distant relatives and old friends back in Iraq discovering his new life and speculates on their responses: a range from surprise to shock and outrage, he suspects. He believes that his closest college friends would support his decisions, but he could not risk telling them his news. Joe has not spoken to them in several years. He tells me that he has had to "start fresh" in the United States. His new life not only involved his enlistment in the US military but also entailed "coming out as a gay guy." He did not publicize it, he says, but he also did not hide it from his friends—whom he says are mainly "Spanish" (Hispanic) immigrants who also worked at the hotel. Joe avoids Iraqis, but occasionally sees some Syrian acquaintances to watch soccer. His closest friends, he says, remain a handful of soldiers he met in the army's 101st Airborne Division, whom he stays in touch with over the phone and by email. They have helped him through the ASVAB and had even come to visit him in Boston. "We became like brothers," Joe explains. He tells me that he has not "come out" to his army friends, but he believes they know because they did not tease him about women the way they teased other people. He paused briefly, looking out the window, and then said, "A gay Iraqi in the US military!"

Joe's story was unique and his telling of it especially poignant. Yet, his description of brotherhood with US Forces was broadly resonant with accounts of other young men I met in Boston who, like him, had worked alongside US troops. In important respects, it was precisely the paternalistic mission and rhetoric of "helping" and "reconstruction"—meaning variously security and counterterrorism efforts, institution building and training, and infrastructure development—that forged a filial bond between Joe and soldiers while he was a Terp. The use of such rhetoric was not insincere; it represented an identification strategy to which young men turned to cope with rampant suspicion by US military personnel and contractors. In an adjacent strategy, male subjects constructed themselves as would-be patriarchal leaders, warding off—or attempting to ward off—suspicion from fellow Iraqis.

Joe told me that after basic training he hoped to be deployed to Iraq, because he was particularly committed to that mission succeeding. Joe's personal mission of helping Iraqis mirrored accounts I received from US service members in surveys. Ideas of "helping" and "rebuilding" had varied meanings, evoking divergent histories for US service members and Iraqi interpreters. While many service members positioned themselves as defenders of Iraqi civilians against insurgency or terrorism, Terps like Joe found a productive slippage by which they could identify themselves as defenders of civilians from terrorism—and, on occasion, from US Forces themselves.

As interpreters on patrol alongside US soldiers, young men (and it was almost exclusively young men that accompanied such missions) jointly occupied the position of an Iraqi authority, when speaking to or on behalf of Iraqis, and the position of an American ally. They found themselves promising to help Iraqi civilians in their everyday challenges under occupation and simultaneously shared in the American mission's promise of rebuilding a new Iraq. Young men like Joe traversed the liminal spaces of American patrols strategically. He, among others, identified selectively as a brother to Americans and as an Iraqi leader—a patriarch-to-be—looking after the people. In all cases, Joe positioned himself as protecting Iraqis. But, while in certain instances he does so within the US military logic, at others he identifies as a protector of Iraqis to directly challenge US militarism. Responding to dual imperatives—to appear nonthreatening in the US Forces' gendered rubric of danger and to confront ubiquitous accusations of collaborating with the enemy—young men called up dynamic narratives of male protection that run through both Iraqi and US public discourses. They would use similar strategies of identification to those they developed on patrol while en route to the US-based diaspora.

Young men's performed identities are situated within American discourses of military humanitarianism and formulations of patriarchy in Iraq that surround men's military and domestic protection of women. Successive iterations of "war experience" narratives pinned manliness to the protection of women on the war front and home front, respectively.[2]

2. For more on Iraqi narratives of masculinity during and after wartime see Sagieh (2000) and Rohde (2006).

Under the US-led occupation, rhetoric around reconstruction empowered foreign forces to "protect" Iraqi women. In response, Iraqi male interpreters deftly alternated between positionalities as foreign and local, exploiting the overlap and the divergences between projects of American military reconstruction and shifting Iraqi prescriptions of patriarchal protection. Here I follow the stories of two men: Mohammed, a former Terp now in Providence, Rhode Island, and Tariq, who, after working as a Terp and migrating to the United States, enlisted in the US military and deployed to Iraq as a US soldier. The chapter considers: How do young interpreters identify with constructs of an Iraqi patriarch-to-be or an American brother? How do young men use these constructs to secure recognition by US power while also talking back to US militarism? How do they modify and even subvert gendered models of national identity—and configurations of patriarchal authority—in calling upon them?

In what follows, we first rejoin Joe in the hotel lobby, where he fleshes out his vision of his generation as a generation without "models"—patriarchs-to-be without fathers of their own. Then, I briefly sketch a history of patriarchal shifts in Iraq and recent legacies of American military humanitarianism and reconstruction efforts. Finally, I turn to the stories of Mohammed and Tariq before considering how male subjects continue to grapple with and reconstruct patriarchy in the diaspora.

A Generation without a Model

Over coffee, Joe told me that he learned what it meant to be a man on his own. His father passed away when he was a young boy. Many of his friends had lost their fathers to war. Joe described how a whole generation of young men in Iraq had grown up "without a model." Boys like him had to assume adult family responsibilities from a young age. Sometimes, Joe says, this can be a point of strength and even pride: young men could learn a great deal about family and duty by growing up fast. For his part, Joe attributes the deep commitment he feels toward helping others to the responsibility he shouldered as a boy.

On the other hand, Joe suggests, young men without a model could become "lost." He shared the story of a friend: "When we grow up without a model, without a person who can be a model—a father—we are missing something essential. For example, I had a friend, Omar, who lost his father in the Iraq-Iran War. He went through a lot of searching. He turned to uncles, on both his father's and mother's sides, he turned to a teacher, but it's not the same. He grew lost. . . . He later joined the insurgency during the war. I don't know if he's still alive." Joe explains that even Omar—like the young men who held him captive for eight days—may think he is "helping" the people by participating in the insurgency. Indeed, "help"—a versatile and multivalent construct—emerges as a key thread of Joe's formulation of being a man. This configuration of masculinity is both an artifact of years of war and directly challenged by the effects of war, namely by the loss of fatherly models. As Joe indicates, young men like Omar who grow up on their own may follow their commitment to "help" as far as engaging in insurgent violence. Cultural translations about a generation of "lost" young men gained traction among US military efforts. The US military supported a "Sons of Iraq" campaign, most impressively, which partnered with local tribal leaders in an attempt to harness young men's inclination to defend their communities to support rather than oppose the US occupation.[3]

Enumerating the reasons that the father's role was matchless, Max told me, "When you lose your father you lose your mother too." He elaborated: "Look at our current situation. There is a huge price to pay for broken families: We have widows who must turn to prostitution to sustain their children. They sacrifice everything for the kids. But this also affects the kids. With so many widows and orphans, it's hard to say we have a complete society. Generation after generation, this accumulates. The question now is whether it's possible for our generation to rebuild Iraq with a model." In this statement, Joe indicates that it is not only children but also women who become lost without the presence of a patriarch. Without their husbands' support and protection, women purportedly turn to such

---

3. Many members of the Sons of Iraq would later become founding members of the so-called Islamic State.

desperate measures as prostitution to provide for their families. At the same time, Joe resists elements of the patriarchal model he flags, commenting that "these are traditions not laws. They can change." He himself challenges the model of masculinity in his sexual orientation. "For this reason, I'll never be that traditional Iraqi man." Still he continues to performatively evoke that model.

Joe's formulation of Iraqi masculinity takes on new intonations as a former Terp soon to join the US Army. A model of masculinity hinging on male protection and defense of innocents resonates with militarized constructs of male heroism in American popular discourse. Even more striking than generic images of military heroism writ large, which have broad histories, is the specific way in which discourse about men-as-protectors calls upon recent images of American soldiers as the world's peacemakers since the early 1990s.[4] The role of the US military as humanitarian-driven defenders of peace has infused the rhetoric and identities surrounding the US Armed Services more broadly since the 1990s era.[5]

Joe himself strategically deploys this rhetoric in his discussion of why he decided to join the US Army. He told me he wants to someday become an engineer in the Army Corps of Engineers so that he can assist people during crises and rebuild after tragedies. The dynamic model of masculinity that Joe posits calls upon both histories of patriarchy in Iraq and militarized nationalism in the United States. In using them, Joe and other young men are also in the midst of reconstructing patriarchy and resisting elements of US militarism. As a "gay Iraqi in the US military," Joe considers himself an unusual candidate for an Iraqi patriarchal authority and

4. Notable examples of this include the Balkans; see Brown (2009). For broader discussions of militarism and masculinity in peacekeeping missions see Whitworth (2004). For a discussion of sex trafficking during peacekeeping missions in the Balkans, see Mendleson (2005).

5. Take, for example, the new motto of the US Navy, "A Global Force For Good," launched in 2009.

yet, in his own self-accounts, he is just that. In assuming that identity, he also resists the very underpinnings of the construct.

Iraqi Fathers, American Brothers

Young men's strategies of identifying selectively as Iraqi patriarchs-to-be and brothers-to-Americans come in response to the gendered rubric of danger by which they must construct themselves as devoted Iraqis and trusted American allies. They also draw upon American projects of military humanitarianism, best symbolized by "reconstruction" efforts, and Iraqi histories of fluctuating and even faltering patriarchy. As Nadje Al-Ali and Nicola Pratt (2009), among many others, have discussed at length with reference to Iraq, American reconstruction agendas emerge out of a paternalistic and imperial logic. What concerns me in particular are the constructs of men as the armed protectors of civilians as opposed to the broader tropes about heroic warriors. Such "protection" and reconstruction agendas form a common discursive terrain for US service members and young male interpreters.

For Terps, protective, paternalistic rhetoric also evokes a recent history of shifting patriarchal authority in Iraq. Saddam Hussein's regime can be divided into two epochs: a period of state patriarchy (1979–91) and a period of reauthorized, kin-based patriarchy (1991–2003). During the period of state patriarchy, Saddam attempted to undermine traditional extended family structures and establish himself as the national patriarch. The Revolutionary Command Council, the heart of state power, became the ultimate judge of personal status issues relating to reproduction and marriage—matters that had just years before been civil matters and, before that, were seen as distinctly familial matters. In the subsequent period of kin-based patriarchy, Saddam reauthorized local-level patriarchal networks, with contradictory outcomes. While local-level patriarchal authorities had greater authority over familial, tribal, and religious affairs, back-to-back wars had taken many men's lives, undermining the male-headed household. Interpreters dynamically call upon the embattled figure of the familial patriarchal authority that reemerged in the waning days of Saddam Hussein's regime.

Iraqi Fathers

State patriarchy under "Baba Saddam" meant, among other things, that Iraqis found themselves part of extensive formal and informal patronage networks beholden to a supreme fatherlike figure. Formal patronage networks hinged on the allotment of jobs in an expansive government, while informal patronage networks doled out privileges according to personal ties. A leading way that the Ba'th regime secured its legitimacy was to hire a large portion of the country as employees—transforming citizens into workers.[6] According to Joseph Sassoon, the Iraqi state became the single biggest employer in the country, ushering in a system of economic patronage in which "decisions were made not on economic grounds, but to reward or punish certain groups" (2011, 189). Additionally the Iraqi Ba'th Party provided extensive social benefits, such as health and education, to citizens. In the Ba'th Party's early years, educational and health outcomes improved dramatically. Informally, Iraqis around the country participated in patronage networks, making up a "shadow state" in Iraq (Tripp 2007, 260).

Wishing to realign citizens' sense of filial duty to the national family, the party's rhetoric mirrored its policies of state patronage. The Ba'th came to earn the name "family party" in the 1990s, as power grew more tightly concentrated among Saddam's family network in a climate of national unrest. Especially in the 1990s era, but throughout the Ba'th Party's reign, paternalistic rhetoric was matched by violence, as the now-controversial social critic Kanan Makiya observed.[7] Saddam's leadership was total and unchecked. Messages and signs stating that "Saddam is Iraq, Iraq is Saddam" were ubiquitous.[8] Makiya suggests that a condition of "statelessness

---

6. Other Arab nationalist regimes such as Abdel Nasser in Egypt similarly sought legitimacy by bankrolling citizens in recently nationalized industries; see Posusney (1997).

7. Makiya, a political exile of Saddam's Iraq, came out in support of the 2003 US-led invasion of Iraq, sparking controversy among exiled Iraqi academics. See Rohde 2010 for a reappraisal of Makiya's seminal work *Republic of Fear*.

8. See an article by Post and Baram of the same name (2002).

is . . . the outer limit of the everyday quality of citizenship in Ba'athist Iraq. . . . [For example,] a perfectly valid document can be withdrawn from any individual without warning" (1989, 137). In this way, to live under the authority of the Ba'th was to live in a state of rule that was profoundly unstable but absolute.

This instability grew all the more acute after the Gulf War. Under sanctions, the state maintained putative authority, but its genuine base of support through employment and patronage was undermined. The economy had "shattered" (Sassoon 2010, 190). While the majority of Iraqis suffered deeply, the most wealthy and connected continued to prosper from the Oil-for-Food arrangement. According to Tripp, "These were the people whose privileged access to the hoarded resources of the Iraqi state and to the various oil and commodity-smuggling enterprises set up by Saddam Husain to evade sanctions largely insulated them from the effects of those sanctions—and thereby marked them off from the vast majority of the Iraqi population" (2007, 259–60). While the elite prospered, the government could no longer pay some of its most valued employees, its armed men. Iraqis turned toward kin networks for the services that the state once provided. These networks, however, were being dismantled as a result of war and sanctions.

Given its weakness in the 1990s and early 2000s, the Iraqi government formally and informally reauthorized familial and tribal networks it had once sought to undermine. This government strategy reintroduced tribal honor to state rhetoric and policy as a means of officially authorizing unofficial support systems for citizens that the government was unable to provide and, equally importantly, controlling the power of tribal leaders.[9] Included in this neotribalism was a wave of conservative legal reforms, effectively empowering local-level patriarchs to make decisions about matters relating to the family.

Over the same period of time, the very fabric of family networks was being demolished in and by the actions of the state and international

9. For more on neotribalism in Iraq, see Baram (1997) and Al-Jabbār and Dawod (2003).

sanctions. During the Iran-Iraq War, the following Gulf War, and ongoing political repression (as well as military campaigns in Kurdistan), female-headed households became widespread. Many families were also torn asunder by economic migration and displacement.

In the period of reauthorized kin-based patriarchy that ensued under sanctions, family structures were challenged by the loss of life and displacement, making the authority of assumptive leaders all the more urgent and commanding. In this period of increased "protections" for women—evidenced in the resurgence of domestic seclusion and in the rise of honor killings—the disjunction between the gendered rhetoric of protection and the reality for women was stark. Such a disjunction, a product of shifting patriarchal structures, would also be seen in later US efforts of reconstruction.

American Brothers

Military, commercial, and "expert" circles posit reconstruction in Iraq as a project of democratization and development that requires external assistance. In keeping with David Mosse and David Lewis's observations of development projects (2006), the view that prevailed on the military bases I visited was that reconstruction was a largely technical project. Reconstruction discourses—unified around a putatively universal goal for peace and stability—positioned those working for the occupation as forces "helping" the local population in a cunningly depoliticized vein.

As scholars like Timothy Mitchell (2002) have observed, such a view presumes that what rebuilding government ministries and bridges alike require is, above all else, expertise. The experts on such projects are, by and large, American.[10] In this way, reconstruction was widely figured as an infusion of resources and "help" in Iraq by non-Iraqis. Iraqi interpreters represented an important exception: Terps occupied a singular position as both local and expert. Though it was their localness

---

10. Further discussion of the Human Terrain System (HTS) can be found in Gonzalez (2008, 2009, 2010).

that garnered them their expertise, male Terps could strategically shift between identifying themselves as Iraqi locals and assuming the voice of global experts.

In a series of surveys I conducted, I found that many US service members and interpreters expressed a common goal for the US mission in Iraq: "reconstruction" or "rebuilding Iraq." In response to the question, "What impressions of local national interpreters will stay with you after this tour of duty?," a US army colonel with over thirty years of service wrote: "Their understanding of why we do this, which is to reconstruct Iraq, and their investment in the same goal. Figuring out our similar desires for Iraq was very impressive to me. Whatever their background, I find for the most part that local Terps really believe in the mission of reconstruction. They accept our presence in their country for this purpose." Not only was this colonel struck by interpreters' understanding of the mission, he found Iraqi interpreters themselves invested in the mission of US-led reconstruction in Iraq.

This common investment constituted something of a bond between Iraqi interpreters and US service members, which the colonel describes as quite distinct from soldiers' relationships to local nationals in other combat situations he had seen, such as in Afghanistan, where there is a greater "breach." Many interpreters I surveyed in Iraq echoed service members' narratives about the US mission. A thirty-three-year-old professional who left his successful business to work as an interpreter wrote: "From the first day of Operation Iraqi Freedom, I hoped to participate with America in building the new Iraq. I participated in the mission in order to reconstruct my country. My goal is only to live in peace and prosperity in my country." In response to the question, "What impressions of US service-members will stay with you after you complete your work as an interpreter?," the same individual wrote this: "Our brotherhood. We are in the same boat trying to rebuild this country but also suffering from bombs and shooting. I will always remember how much the Army tried to do in Iraq. I can't forget how they took care of me when we were under fire. I won't forget how the sergeant threw himself on top of me to provide cover for me when the terrorists were shooting at us and I had no vest. I worked with them for more than eight years and every day there is a memory."

The mission of reconstruction—as well as the dangers that such a mission entails—forged a "brotherhood" between interpreters and US service members in this account. The language of reconstruction is clearly masculinized; Terps' evocation of it represents a form of Iraqi masculine national identity triangulated through US militarism. In reconstruction narratives, women are generally objects of aid rather than "sisters."

While the rhetoric of reconstruction was bridge-building between certain Iraqis and Americans, the business of reconstruction was anything but inclusive; it was almost exclusively an American-led effort. Reconstruction contracts in Iraq were granted to a handful of American companies almost exclusively. Large corporations like Bechtel and KBR (Kellogg, Brown, and Root), a subsidiary of Halliburton, received billions in contracts to reconstruct Iraq's infrastructure and oil industry, respectively, with limited competition in the bidding process.[11] A lack of accountability in the federal disbursement of money and oversight of contracts in Iraq was widely documented. In 2007, for example, it came to light that the US federal government had shipped 363 tons of shrink-wrapped cash on pallets to pay its contractors and subcontractors in Iraq.[12] Several interpreters confirmed that such money and resources flowed with little oversight. Husham, for example, mentioned to me how contractors on his base would bury or hide air conditioners and other equipment, claiming that they were lost or broken, in order to receive new equipment and sell the old equipment on the black market. Some interpreters, such as Husham, took cases like this to indicate corruption or bad faith on the part of their American "brothers." But even while Husham thought that reconstruction had more to do with Americans getting rich than with Iraqis getting their country back, he nonetheless employed rhetoric about rebuilding his country—if sometimes with a cynical inflection.

---

11. See, for example, Brown University's ongoing "Cost of War" project, which reports on the cost of the Iraq War. Additionally, see the 2004 report by the Project on Government Oversight "Federal Contracting and Iraqi Reconstruction," http://www.pogo.org/our-work/reports/2004/co-irc-20040311.html.

12. Rajiv Chandrasekaran, "Democrats, Bremer Spar over Iraq Spending," *Washington Post*, February 7, 2007.

As Al-Ali and Pratt powerfully demonstrate in *What Kind of Liberation?: Women and the Occupation of Iraq* (2009), the "reconstruction of Iraq" was more rhetoric than reality. In reality, reconstruction efforts in Iraq did not serve the interests of everyday Iraqis as much as they served foreign governments and contractors. The occupation of Iraq left millions without access to basic infrastructure and the necessities of life. For many Iraqis, "reconstruction" meant waiting in danger. Despite the gendered rhetoric of "protecting the nation," the lack of security in Iraq combined with the absence of essential goods and services imperiled women the most. In the absence of a reliable state, conservative religious movements and militias took hold throughout Iraq, resulting in disorder, violence, and a conservative social backlash. Al-Ali and Pratt write: "The failure to invest in reconstruction and effective general security at an early stage helped to create conditions for the reconstruction of a 'hyperpatriarchy'" (2009, 81). This form of hyperpatriarchy translated into a diminished public role for women in Iraq and a woman's ongoing fear of being harassed or even having acid thrown on her face if she appeared in public without a veil, for example.

While they deployed "reconstruction" rhetoric in their strategies of identification, interpreters such as Husham were also keenly aware of the failures of US reconstruction efforts, and young male interpreters frequently used their unique positions to speak back to US military policy. As they called up patriarchal structure and paternalistic rhetoric in their strategies of identification on patrol and in the diaspora, young men like Mohammed and Tariq also challenged both the axioms reconstructing patriarchy in inventive ways.

Mohammed: Antiwar American Ally

The ambivalence Mohammed felt working as an interpreter for US Forces was not a function of his moral uncertainty. Actually, it stemmed from deep moral conviction. Everyday Mohammed (or "Mo" as he came to call himself during the war) weighed the good he was doing against the possible harm. On the one hand, he was an effective communicator on behalf of Iraqi civilians—a "bridge" in potentially volatile situations. On

the other hand, he had no choice but to participate in missions and interrogations that he found deeply problematic and to follow orders he found
abhorrent. Mohammed quit the job on three different occasions. He
rejoined each time because he believed the people needed an ally, someone in an American uniform to "look after their interests." The Americans had tanks and planes and weapons; the least he could do was to give
the Iraqi people a voice.

Mohammed, a thirty-year-old former cell-phone vendor from Basrah,
showed me the daily journal he kept from 2004 to 2008 when we met in
Providence several years later. He had chronicled his duties and the notable
events for each day he worked with the Marines. He showed me pictures to
match. And he recounted many, many stories from those years, a few surrounding instances of American folly or injustice, and others concerning
episodes when he had taken matters into his own hands to make things
right.[13] Though he had strongly opposed the US-led war in the beginning,
he found in the course of his work that he had become personally invested
in elements of the US mission in Iraq—namely in rebuilding a stable Iraq.
He found also that he had forged a bond with certain US service members
in the Marines with whom he worked side-by-side. Yet, as he recounted to
me in his new home in Providence, "I felt sometimes that it wasn't worth
it. I was trying to help the people and meanwhile they don't accept me. . . .
It means so much when someone said 'thank you.' I remember meeting a
boy on patrol—he was really badly burned. His dad was carrying him in
his arms. I took them to the American medic, and afterward he thanked
me, said a prayer for me. I felt so honored." Mohammed assumed a position of authority, in which he could "look after" Iraqis within a complex
landscape containing few reliable leaders. Mohammed viewed his job as
an interpreter as one to build communication between Iraqis and Americans, often through deliberately manufactured misunderstandings—as in

13. See chapter 2, in which Mohammed describes deliberately cultivating a linguistic
misunderstanding so that a sheik and US Forces might come to a practical understanding
about the removal of the sheik's weapons.

the case of his mediation of a sheik's disarmament. He tells me that most of the time, however, he failed. It is the failures more than the successes that he remembers.

One afternoon when I arrived for lunch, Mohammed had queued up a series of YouTube videos to show me. The first few videos in the queue contained footage of what he called the "tragedies" of the Iraq War: videos of US soldiers firing into a crowd unprovoked; footage of an air raid in Baghdad that was later found to have murdered dozens of Iraqi civilians. Then, to my surprise, after these videos of tragedy, there was a video of American soldiers at an Iraqi wedding, singing and clapping along with the music, cheered on by the Iraqi guests. "I will never forgive the Americans for many of the things I saw. But they were not all bad. Really. I just wish I could have done more," he said earnestly. Mohammed continued:

> During my time as an interpreter, I didn't do anything wrong toward the people. . . . But it was complicated. . . . I saw behavior from Marines that I didn't like. One time we were delivering food from the FOB [Forward Operating Base] to Babil province. There was a stupid guy driving the tank I was in. I knew I didn't like him, but I had a job to do. Anyway, sometimes the Iraqis got confused about what to do when a US convoy was coming, so there were cars that didn't pull over like they were supposed to. So this guy was driving really fast, going straight into oncoming traffic, trying to hit the civilians' cars just to "show them a lesson." He hit a car and he was laughing. I don't know if anyone was hurt, we just kept driving. The sergeant was laughing. The gunner was laughing. I was screaming. That was *bullshit*. I was yelling, "Stop!" but they didn't hear me because they were wearing headsets. I was about to jump out and quit. Even if it meant the people would kill me because I was wearing an American uniform.

Mohammed stopped the story abruptly. After several minutes, he looked at me and repeated: "I can't forgive America. But Iraq was in a critical state; I needed to help my people however I could." We sat for several more minutes in silence, before I asked in Arabic "What ever happened with the driver? Did you report it?" He nodded and continued to speak in English.

I settled down and decided I needed to talk to someone. So when we returned to the FOB, I approached the sergeant. You know what the sergeant told me? He said, "It's no big deal. No one was hurt." I said, "Sir, this is not a game, sergeant sir. These are lives. There were children in that car. By doing this, you are making the people hate you." He apologized and said the driver would be punished. But those were just words, I know. So it was difficult to know what to do, to know which side you are on, you know. . . . It was a very complicated situation. There are always going to be good people and bad people—in the US military it is no different. There were times when I was helping the people who I know were hurting my people. But what am I going to do? I also helped a lot of Iraqi people too—if you make their time with the Americans a little bit easier, I think you are helping.

Mohammed powerfully captured the quandaries involved in assuming a role as a spokesperson and leader for Iraqis while wearing a US uniform. His complex thoughts and emotions were visible on his face, in his body, in the wringing of his hands; it felt that he was reliving the story as if it were yesterday.

We took a break from the conversation to look at the new fish he had added to his home aquarium. He told me he would like to have "real" pets, but that his work schedules—at an industrial laundry facility and a security firm—would make it hard. I asked him if he grew up with pets, and as he answered, I realized he almost never spoke explicitly about his family back in Iraq—although he often spoke abstractly about his family responsibilities. He answered my question curtly, saying yes, he had a dog that lived outside because his mom was afraid of dogs. I asked casually how and where his mom was now. He said only, "At home in Basrah with my sisters and brother. Thank god." In the many times we met, he never initiated conversation about his family. Later, after we had known each other for a couple of years, I asked him why he rarely spoke of his family. He told me, "It's too hard. Sometimes I feel like I left my family for good. I don't want you to think that [laughter]. I'm the 'bad son.' I know my family doesn't, but it's just really hard." That he readily evokes patriarchal idioms about protecting the people, broadly defined, and would later speak of Americans as his figurative brothers, made the absence of talk about his own family (as well as the usually unspoken remorse he felt about leaving his family) all the more striking. After the talk about pets and home, he quickly segued into another story.

> I remember another time in Ramadi, my brigade was assigned to work with a unit from the Iraqi Army at a coalition checkpoint. We saw a big fuel truck coming very fast. The Iraqi soldiers said, "Stop," but the truck didn't stop. He slowed down but did not come to a complete stop. The American commander was getting very nervous and shot at one of the back tires. When the truck finally stopped down the road, we approached the passenger side and found a young boy—maybe six years old—and his father was driving. I asked the guy why he didn't stop and he said his brakes were failing. I said, "Are you stupid driving a fuel truck without brakes?" He said he had no choice; it was his only chance to make a living. The commander didn't accept it. He had both the man and the boy get out of the truck. And, you know those plastic handcuffs the coalition used? He used those to handcuff both people— even the child. I went to the commander and said, "This is not legal." I had to do it in a way he would respond to—because if I just said, "This is wrong," he wouldn't respond. I learned that. But if I play a game—if I say, "Think if people put a picture of this little kid in handcuffs on the Internet! This will be a big problem"—well, then he will listen. So he untied the child. He kept the father because he insisted that the man had a fake *gincia* [citizenship ID]. It wasn't fake but anyway, I took the child and took care of him for a while. . . . Looking back I wish I could have done more.

Mohammed grapples with his former work in story after story, identifying moments in which he helped people and prevented dangerous miscommunication in one instance and underscoring the limits of his ability to help in the next.

A handful of American servicemen with whom he worked are now among those he considers his best friends: "My best friend from the Marines, he's now in Georgia, but when we were in Iraq he'd take his pay and give it to the poor people who came to the gates of the FOB. I felt we were from the same culture. I felt we were really brothers." Particularly now when he does not feel comfortable telling his friends in Iraq where he is, Mohammed turns to his American brothers. Initially, the juxtaposition of Mohammed's stories about his "brothers" in the US Marines and those he observed abusing Iraqis was jarring. Mohammed speaks fluidly about Americans as "good guys" and "bad guys": sometimes, as shown in the YouTube videos, bad guys do the wrong thing, but other times good guys sing and cheer along with Iraqis at local weddings.

I pondered how Mohammed determined his brothers from the "bad guys" among US Marines. Asking this question left a kind of specter over the conversation; it changed the way I had understood most of what he had told me so far, from "I will never forgive America" to "my best friend in the Marines." His response was disarmingly straightforward: "They are all my brothers. I put on their uniform, right? It's like with the brothers in your family, you can give advice but they still have to make their own decisions. No one is a bad, bad guy. They are in a horrible situation. They are pawns; it is not their fault. That's why it is our job to help them do the right thing." He explained that he honed his skill for giving brotherly advice from years of attempting to help the Americans "do the right thing." He understood it as his job to teach Marines to do right by the Iraqi people. In assuming this role, he also took on the burden of responsibility for cases in which he had fallen short. The quandaries involved in assuming this sort of patriarchal authority vis-à-vis Iraqis expressed themselves in anger, frustration, and guilt. He recalls, for example:

One time, I was working with some guys at the gate of the camp in Babil. There was a civilian, an old Iraqi man, who came with a prosthetic leg. He had an appointment inside the base. You know what they did? They made him take off his prosthetic leg and searched it. The man had no rights. I told him, "Come on guys, this is wrong. He's an old man. You let in tons of people without searching them. Why do you need to search this one [this man]?" They didn't listen—again, who am I? Just an interpreter. All I have is words, no power. So he took off his leg and came in carrying his leg. This old man could have been my father. Can you imagine? . . . I left my post and didn't return until the next day. I told my friend from Georgia and he was as mad as I was.

The single "civilian" evolves over the course of Mohammed's account into Mohammed's could-be father. The regret belying Mohammed's rhetorical "Can you imagine?" arises from the fact that his brothers mistreated what "could have been my father." What most upset Mohammed was the feeling he had that US Forces were treating the man as an object and not as a fully human person. In one sense, Mohammed's resistance reaches its limits here with the prosthetic dismembering of his could-be father. That which granted Mohammed the power to witness such an encounter—his job as an interpreter—also punctuates the fact that, in the first and last instance, he came to hold that power as a conduit of the US occupation ("I put on their uniform, right?"). By the same token, he speaks back to US power on this and other occasions precisely by assuming the role of brother to US service members.

Mohammed sought to humanize himself and other Iraqis by "speaking freely" with the Marines he worked with and answering any questions they might have. He recounts how one American used to ask him if it felt "weird" to work for a country that so many Iraqis consider an enemy. He recalls: "I told them, 'Of course, sometimes. But I don't work for a country; I work for people. Do you feel weird working for the country that some Iraqis think is their enemy?' In that moment, they realize I am like them and they see all I wanted was a normal life. And maybe the same is true for all the other Iraqis—all they are looking for is a normal life." Mohammed attempts to interrupt the objectification and othering of "his people." In those moments when Mohammed identifies as being "just like them," he attests that US Forces realize "the same is true for all the other Iraqis—all they are looking for is a normal life."

Mohammed strategically identifies himself with hegemonic reconstruction discourses at the same time that he challenges certain elements of this discourse, namely the dehumanization of Iraqis. He capitalizes on a productive slippage between identifying as an Iraqi leader and as a brother to Americans—a slippage enabled by his unique subject-position. In both his identifications as an Iraqi authority and an American ally, Mohammed emerges as a patriarchal protector, although in the course of assuming this role, he fears he has been a "bad" son and brother to his own family. The paradox Mohammed faces between working as a patriarchal protector

writ large and feeling neglectful of his own immediate family duties resonates with many other male interpreters, such as Tariq.

Tariq: Returning to Iraq as an American Soldier

In a suburb of Boston, I met Tariq during his two-week R & R to visit
his new wife, Hiba. Tariq, a trained agronomist from Baghdad, began
working as an interpreter with US Forces on a part-time basis after the
Coalition Provisional Authority (CPA) disbanded his division in the Iraqi
Ministry of Science and Technology. He never imagined he would emi-
grate to the United States. Nor, once settled in the United States, would he
have considered returning to Iraq as an American soldier had it not been
for the couple's dire economic situation.

Tariq reflects contemplatively on how life decisions have become
thinkable—desirable, even—that he would have never thought possible:
becoming an American citizen, joining the US Army, deploying to Iraq,
and leaving his young wife in the United States. Tariq was not alone in
making these weighty life decisions. Hundreds of former interpreters have
found work in the US military under special programs for linguists speaking "languages of interest." Called 09 Limas, the positions offer a fast track
to citizenship and select military benefits. Almost all the young men I met
in the diaspora had considered this option, talked to a recruiter, or taken
the ASVAB exam. I met several interpreters who were currently members of the US military; several were in the process of joining. Most had
not come to the United States with the intention of joining the military
but cited an inability to find "civilian" work in the United States as the
deciding factor in enlisting. The prospect of working as an 09 Lima was
itself far from secure: 09 Limas are contracted year-to-year—and sometimes month-to-month. They hold rank, which can advance, but they may
be terminated at any break in their contract and are not eligible for pensions.[14] Given this, most young people I met did not view military service

14. Joe was the only Terp who enlisted as a private once he received his green card;
he alone will receive full military benefits as a standard enlistee in the armed services.

as a career path; instead, many hope to acquire their expedited US citizenship, leave the service, and look for work in Iraq as a Category 2 (CAT 2) interpreter—among the best-paid civilian contractors in Iraq, who were expected to be in Iraq long after the military withdrawal.[15] The remaining 09 Limas like Tariq worked for the US military in Iraq in a capacity not dissimilar from the work they did as locally contracted Terps.

Tariq has given up his Iraqi citizenship to take the position of an 09 Lima, though he shifts between calling himself "Iraqi," "American," and "Iraqi American." He tells me that he is familiar with the criticisms Iraqis in the United States have about Iraqis joining the US military. But, he adds, "The Iraqi guys in the US who don't agree with Iraqis being in the military, I guarantee these same guys have tried to join." Sitting in Hiba and Tariq's living room, I asked how he had made the decision to join. He shrugged and said, "This whole thing—from the first day I signed up as a Terp in Iraq until today—it has been like a dream. I wake up in Baghdad on an American base and I'm thinking, How did this happen?" He proceeded to tell me matter-of-factly how it had happened.

> In 2003, the Army was literally going house-to-house in my neighborhood and recruiting. What made me decide to work as a Terp? Here was an opportunity. Saddam's done. . . . It was a good chance. So I did it part-time after they closed down my division in the Ministry. Until 2004, everyone was happy to do this. Then, it [violence] began. Everyone in my family was saying quit, quit, quit. Everyone. And I stayed: for fifty-two months. Until my wife and I came here to Mass [Massachusetts], September 5, 2007. First I was with the 101st Airborne, then I moved to the Federal Police Transition Team in Baghdad. And that's where I work now, but on the other side. I'm working with the same Terps that I used to work with, but now I'm their boss. You know, the first time I landed in Baghdad as an American soldier, after many months away, I couldn't believe it. We arrived at night. I thought, "Really? I'm here again? Really?" I just wanted to go outside and see it. But I couldn't. I couldn't

---

15. So far, however, only one interpreter I met has, in fact, left the service to become a CAT 1 interpreter.

even see my family across the river. It was tough. There's no denying that. . . . But I had no other options. When I came here, I couldn't find a job. I was so close to living on welfare. So, I told my brother that I had two options: return to Iraq or enlist. He advised me to enlist.

Tariq's oldest brother served as a role model to him, after his father died in the Iran-Iraq War. As it turned out, his brother, Yaqoob, would become an officer in the new Iraqi military around the same time that Tariq joined the US Army. Remarkably, the two men were stationed in the same base in the Green Zone for several months and would attend several of the same Transition Team meetings representing the two different countries. Tariq showed me a picture of the two men, side-by-side, both with the same piercing green eyes, wearing two different military uniforms.

No one can believe we are actually brothers. Sometimes I can't believe it. Really, it is a very strange thing. . . . He is a counterterrorism expert. The American officials respect him a lot. I just hope that he is safe, you know. The vetting in the new [Iraqi] Army is not the best. . . . I wouldn't say my family was pro-American. But they are realistic. Even before '03 my brother was dealing with the Americans in a secret organization. What we call "Charlie India Alpha" [the CIA]. He wanted to get rid of something, you could say. He did not do it for money. Just like me, when I began working as a Terp. This was not a matter of money; my family was doing okay. But then I came to the US and we had nothing. . . . Eventually, the only job I could find was as a role-player with the military in El Paso. All the soldiers have to go to this training before deploying to Iraq or Afghanistan. Your convoy is hit by an IED [improvised explosive device], what do you do? How do you differentiate between good and bad people? How to meet with sheiks, imams, generals? I did it for a few months but I didn't like it because my wife stayed here and I didn't make enough money to pay the bills back in Mass and live in Texas. So I enlisted in the middle of 2008. I got my American citizenship in Iraq on July 4, 2008. Joe Biden was there. It was a big deal. Hundreds of us in Iraq got citizenship that day.

He could not visit his mother or relatives on the other side of Baghdad. But, almost every day for months, he saw his brother, Yaqoob. "There we were. Two brothers, from the same father, in different uniforms, representing two different countries. But," he adds, "uniforms are just clothes. Blood is blood."

He explained that a particularly poignant moment for him was the single time his brother organized for their mother to come on base and visit Tariq. The three of them—Tariq, Yaqoob, and their mother—sat together, looking at each other, without speaking much for the first few minutes. Then their mother turned to each of her sons in turn. First she turned to Yaqoob and said, "You take care of your brother." Then she turned to Tariq and said, "You take care of your brother." Tariq expresses conviction that he and his brother are "100 percent on the same side." He continued:

> At this point in time, the success of Iraq is the same as the success of the US mission. Iraq still needs the US and everyone knows this. Most real people in the Iraqi military and police force do not want the US to leave. We [the US military] need to maintain our presence over there. Maintaining bases in Iraq is extremely important for Iraqis. I don't especially care about US interests. But, we [Iraqis] need somebody to protect our people over there. If the military leaves, who's going to be there? Iraqis cannot protect themselves yet. Even my brother says that. Their institutions don't have enough experience. That's what units like mine are trying to do—to train Iraqis on how to build peaceful institutions. A police force not like Saddam's. I didn't want to enlist at first. But now, I have to say, I am glad I've gone back to serve both Iraq and the US as an Iraqi American. I have been able to train a lot of Iraqis. I have a special interest in the mission succeeding.

Tariq identifies with a "we" standing for the US military before shifting to identify with a "we" that stands for the Iraqi people. He clearly calls upon US reconstruction discourses and military humanitarian traditions in his discussion of "institution building" and "protecting" the people, and "training" Iraqis to help themselves. Yet, he underscores that his commitment is to Iraq. He does not care about "US interests" as much as the Iraqi people. Still, he tells me, "It is tough. I went over there [to Iraq] to help Iraqis, but I can't go around freely and mingle with them, can I? I can't even see my own family. So even though I tell myself I am doing it for the people, I sometimes feel far away from Iraq when I'm on base."

Tariq explains the deep disorientation that comes with being on an American base in Iraq. Despite or because of this fact, he took great pains to keep Iraq close—and real—not only for himself but also for the soldiers with whom he worked. He continues:

> I have tried to teach soldiers how to deal with Iraqi people. I met soldiers above my rank pointing their weapons at every Iraqi they saw. I told them, "That's not cool, guys. That Iraqi man you are pointing your gun at looks just like me, right? An Arab man. Well, you trust me, right? All right, well that man could be my brother. If he's not carrying a weapon, consider him *Tariq's brother*. Go to him, smile, shake his hand." . . . In the first two weeks I was back in Iraq, the other soldiers in my unit were so unprofessional that I went to my commander and told him I wanted to be reassigned. He told me it was my job to correct their behavior. But think about it. These soldiers receive tons of training directly or indirectly telling them that the Iraqis are *bad*. That's difficult to correct. I tried. I started talking to the soldiers a lot. I repeated to them again and again, "Look at Iraqis like you look at me." Some of them accepted this, and I felt like I really got through to them, they could see the Iraqis as people, you know. They became my bros in the army. That made it worth it. But, some of them didn't and kept acting the same.

As Tariq pleads with US soldiers to consider other Iraqis as his brothers, he also must continually remind himself that he and his own biological brother are on the same side. When Tariq says, "uniforms are just clothes," he begins to capture the arbitrariness of the divergent subject-positions that he and his brother have come to inhabit. Yet, these uniforms have their own history and social lives. Tariq's uniform, though arbitrary, cloaks his words. He states that his mission was "to train Iraqis on how to build peaceful institutions." Spoken from the subject-position of a member of the US Armed Forces, this expression of Iraqis' need for help reverberates with the US military's humanitarian sentiments that are shared by many of his American compatriots. In one instance, he strategically edges close to the positionality of the Americans, while in the next, he identifies the Iraqi people as *his* people.

Tariq indicates that educating fellow US soldiers so that "they could see the Iraqis as people" made his involvement in the war "worth it." Like Mohammed, he speaks back to US power—if only by saying "that's not cool, guys"—and sometimes soldiers altered their conduct as a result. If Mohammed was able to humanize Iraqis by identifying as a normal Iraqi guy himself, Tariq is able to disrupt that othering of Iraqis by identifying simultaneously as Iraqi *and* American (an "Iraqi American"). He says to the soldiers, "That Iraqi man you are pointing your gun at looks just like me, right? . . . Well, you trust me, right? . . . When you look at me look at them, consider them Tariq's brother." By asking soldiers to view Iraqi civilians as "Tariq's brother," Tariq strategically deploys an image of brotherly love, a felt sense of mutual interest. Tariq pleads with soldiers to respect civilians by offering an illusion of their familial commonality—an illusion that changed several soldiers' conduct and personalized the military encounter between US soldiers and Iraqi civilians. But this rhetorical move also cunningly masks the material reality of military occupation.

He speaks at length with me about those soldiers who "didn't listen" and continued to mistreat Iraqis. He says that it is mostly these soldiers who come home with Post-Traumatic Stress Disorder (PTSD) because they "know they did bad things over there." He says of the soldiers who return home traumatized by their own actions, "We can call their condition 'PTSD' or we can just call it having a conscience. . . . Even if the guys that soldiers killed over there aren't *my* brother. They are someone's brother, right?"

In Tariq's home, a medal that he earned in the US military is framed alongside his father's medals from the Iraqi military. He tells me, gesturing toward the medals with his hands, "We do not choose the parents we are born to. We don't choose much of what happens after that. But this is life: we do the best we can for our people around us. We try to do it honorably." I followed up by asking who the "we" was in that statement. Given his previous assertions of "we" (the US military) and "we" (the Iraqi people), I was expecting him to say something akin to "my brothers" (American soldiers) or, possibly, "my people" (Iraqis). Instead, he answered simply: "men."

Tariq posits a sort of transcendental male "honor," echoing strands of both US military and Iraqi constructs of social conduct.[16] One effect of deploying such a transhistorical, universal construct of honor is to reduce the justness of war to individual combatants' honorability. In perpetuating a sense of familial commonality between soldiers and civilians, Tariq strategically personalizes the structural power relations of the war and effectively redefines the morality of the occupation in terms of honorable and dishonorable conduct. The fact that later his wife, Hiba, would say he showed symptoms of PTSD, a condition that Tariq believed stemmed from moral crisis, was a poignant marker of the quandaries he would face in living "honorably." The illusion of familial commonality between US soldiers and civilians that Tariq inhabited both justified him putting on a US uniform and made wearing that uniform all the more alienating.

Hyperpatriarchy Unbound

In one reading, the social developments accompanying the "reconstruction of Iraq" can be seen to restrict Iraqi women all the more, making them beholden to new or reempowered male authorities, such as militia men or even Iraqi interpreters. "Hyperpatriarchy" is a harsh reality for many in postoccupation Iraq and also in the diaspora. In some cases, however, the conditions that gave rise to hyperpatriarchy also undermine it: for example, when would-be patriarchs, like Mohammed and Tariq, actually depart from their families to "protect" them elsewhere, leaving their family members to "protect" themselves. I became close friends with Hiba over the months and years that Tariq (her husband) was away in Iraq, and I also grew to know Tariq better over phone and Skype during his deployment. Hiba encountered a great deal of difficulty as an Iraqi woman living alone in the diaspora. She became the target of gossip: Why

---

16. For more on "honor" in American militarized models of masculinity see Hinojosa (2010) and Fancher, Knudson, and Rosen (2003).

would she decide to stay in the United States with her husband gone? She didn't work, so what did she do? Why did she not move back to Iraq to live with her family? Then matters grew only more challenging when Hiba was asked by her husband to serve as a sponsor for one of his former colleagues and close friends, Frank.

Frank would temporarily live with Hiba while Tariq was deployed in Iraq. While uncomfortable with it, Hiba agreed to having Frank live in their second bedroom "like a brother" for a few weeks. Tariq told me that he felt better knowing Frank was there to help out with anything Hiba needed. She too appreciated Frank's help with household tasks and errands. But Hiba's decision to take Frank in made her the subject of even more damaging gossip—not least of which originated from Frank's own family. After a few weeks, Frank moved out of Hiba's apartment into another unit in the four-unit complex. Frank's parents immigrated to the United States within a couple of months of his arrival, moving into his apartment in Hiba's building. That began a period of acute tension between Hiba and Frank's family, culminating in an incident in which, according to Hiba, Frank's mother called her "a terrible word for women" publicly and loudly outside the building. Hiba was shocked and devastated. She traveled to Iraq for several months (though she could not visit Tariq, who was deployed), but had to return to the United States to maintain her green card. Upon her return, Hiba found that Frank, who came from a family of property owners in Baghdad, had purchased the entire apartment building. She received a notice within the week of her return that she was being evicted.

Hiba found a new home—a small duplex in the outer suburbs—and adjusted to living alone and far away from the eyes of other Iraqis. A powerful paradox emerges in Hiba and Tariq's life histories: While Tariq frames his work with the US military as work to help and protect "his people" (broadly defined), he had to leave alone and even put at "risk" (in both Hiba and Tariq's words) his closest kin: his wife. Quite similarly to Mohammed, who felt he had abandoned his mother, Tariq has left his family to fulfill a more broadly defined patriarchal duty. Hiba came to embrace elements of life as an "American woman": driving her own car to and from a job she found as a sales clerk, mowing the lawn, and building a fence around her house. Paradoxically, as a result of Tariq's effort to protect his people—and support his family by taking the only job he could find—Hiba proved to him that she could "protect" herself despite all the gossip she has encountered living alone.

Tariq returned home within a month of the withdrawal of forces from Iraq. A little more than a month after Tariq's return, I got a call from Hiba asking me to come over as soon as possible, a request she rarely made. I could not guess what precipitated her call. I thought she may have had another run-in with Frank's family, but could not imagine why she would call me with her husband there. I arrived to a bizarre scene at the usually subdued home: Hiba was upset but composed, standing in the kitchen; Tariq was laughing awkwardly. He greeted me at the door, shook my hand, and said to me respectfully, "Your friend needs you," then served me some Arabic coffee Hiba had just made.

Hiba and I sat on the couch—under the framed case of Tariq's military medals—drinking our coffee. Tariq sat in the next room watching YouTube videos on his iPad. Hiba spoke to me in a voice audible to Tariq: "Madeline, he has a second wife. He asked me before if he could take a temporary wife while he was in Iraq.[17] I said okay, but it must be temporary and do not tell me about it. Now he is telling me he did not divorce her. I don't know anything about her. Just that she is a woman from the Green Zone. They started a relationship years ago. He swears to God he is not playing with me, but he won't even tell me her name. I told him 'it's her or me' but he says he cannot choose." I sat quietly, considering how to respond and pondering what my role was in this extremely personal matter. From the next room, Tariq said, "Do you want to hear about it from me?" I looked to Hiba for a sign of how to respond; she nodded with a shrug. So I replied to Tariq, "If you want to talk about it." He joined us in the living room, saying, "I was gone for over three years. I was over there working very hard. I was away from my wife and you know that is not easy. A man has needs. Taking a second wife is a tradition in Iraq. Hiba's

17. Hiba is referring to the permitted (though not widespread) Shi'i practice of marrying temporarily if one is traveling or working away from one's wife, called *mut'a*.

brother has two wives, Hiba's own father has had many women, but didn't marry them. This is not a big secret. . . . A lot of soldiers have girlfriends over there. I wanted to do it the right way, by marrying her. I didn't want to just leave her . . . I feel responsible for her. Hiba has to understand that."

Both Hiba and Tariq looked at me expectantly, awaiting a response. I was taken aback by their candid speech, and equally surprised by the fact that I had become a mediator in this discussion. Hiba looked at me and told me that she believed that he would not divorce "her" (I never learned her name) because they have children together. "He's spent more time with her than with me," she said. Then she turned to Tariq and responded quietly: "You think it was easy for me to be here alone? A woman has needs too. Now you are home and you go to bed at 8 o'clock without looking at me. You know, you didn't have to go. You could have found a job here. . . . Thank you, Tariq. Thank you, US Army."

I asked some basic questions about how he would manage his two marriages logistically. Would "she" stay in Iraq? If so, would he split his time between Baghdad and Boston? Could he afford two families? He said he didn't have all the answers, but that he knew they could work it out: "Don't think that I didn't ask for Hiba's permission, I did. I told her in the first year, 'I am lonely, I am lonely over here. What would you say if I had a marriage of *mut'a*?' She said, 'Oh yeah, you go enjoy yourself!' Maybe she thought that I would never do it. Maybe I thought I would never do it. But war changes you. I do not believe I was wrong to take a second wife. I know it changes things for Hiba, and I am sorry for that. But I can't leave her. That would destroy her life. I have to take care of her now." To this Hiba said simply: "What about my life? This is not what we planned. You did not even ask for our families' permission." Tariq nodded knowingly, and then a few minutes later asked Hiba to make some more coffee. She sat still. In the silence, I stood up to make the coffee, leaving the couple quiet in the living room.

The three of us sat together and talked for hours, sometimes crying, sometimes walking away, sometimes sitting in silence. Hiba asked, "So I guess this is who you have been talking to on your long phone conversations outside?" Tariq said, "Yes," and said that he would ask for Hiba's permission to call her in the future. Tariq added, "We will be okay. You will come to accept it. Believe me." Hiba responded, "You don't know that. I am a strong woman. I am used to living on my own." Tariq said, "If you are smart you will stay with me. I support you. If you are smart, you will go back to school and get your master's—or even PhD I can cover that." When I asked Tariq who among his friends and family knew about his second wife, he said, "No one except for friends in the army—and now you two." I sat with this fact for some time, contemplating the paradox that although he married his second wife to do right by her vis-à-vis Iraqi "tradition" by his account, he had told only his army colleagues about this action, not even his brother or friends in Iraq. As if anticipating what I might be thinking, he added: "Most of the guys have women over there. I married because in my culture this is more acceptable. My American friends thought it was funny. But it's basically the same thing. I wanted to do it the right way." I later asked Hiba why she believed he had not told his family, and she responded emphatically by saying: "We are cousins. Our family would kill him for doing that to me behind my back."

Tariq's self-account of his second marriage both destabilizes Iraqi discourses about the protection of women and disrupts American projects of liberation. He positions his decision to marry his second wife as an effort to protect "her." When I ask him to explain further the significance and reasoning behind his decision to marry her—especially given the fact that he had not told anyone outside of the army about his new wife—he told me he did not want to just use a woman. Instead, he took an oath to "take care of her." He added that marriage is about a commitment, so he is unable to "just leave her," suggesting that this would "destroy her life." When I cautiously pointed out that some might interpret him to have done just that— to have left her in Iraq for his current home in the United States—Tariq said, "Well, I have Hiba to take care of too. You know what people were saying about her when I was gone."[18] While Tariq emphasized his efforts to care for both of his wives on different continents, he underscored the fact that in caring for one wife he was always leaving the other alone—and so,

18. Tariq seems to be referring to the name-calling incident between his wife and neighbor.

too, leaving people to "talk" about her. He acknowledges that through his efforts to support his wives (by staying married to both of them—thousands of miles apart), he is also potentially opening them to "talk," undermining the very axioms about female protection that he calls upon.

In addition, Tariq dramatically calls into question the mission of liberation and reconstruction that set the terms for the Iraq War in the first place. At its starkest, the fact that an Iraqi American soldier might take a second wife just as his fellow American soldiers would "use" a woman reveals a less sanguine reality about the reconstruction mission. Tariq observes that his taking a second wife on his tour of duty in Iraq was "basically the same thing" as his army friends taking women in Iraq. This assertion—and the fact of soldiers' sexual relations with the women they are supposed to be "protecting"—powerfully upsets the framework of liberation and reconstruction within which the war was rhetorically fought. Here, Tariq likens his decision of taking a second wife to other American soldiers' sexual behavior, distinguishing the two courses of action only by saying that his course involved a greater commitment to the woman. The possibility that the rhetoric of "protection" may in fact belie a reality of sexual predation upon Iraqi women rather than a defense against imagined sexual exploitation emerges as a powerful alternative interpretation of the reconstruction mission in Iraq.[19]

Tariq had told me on his last R & R that many US soldiers "know they did bad things over there . . . we can call their condition 'PTSD' or we can just call it having a conscience." Months later he agrees with his wife that he may suffer from that very condition. Whether understood as a psychological condition or an outgrowth of moral crisis, PTSD is clearly a product of the US war machine. In this instance, PTSD—or "having a conscience"—also unsettles that war machinery. Soldiers returning home in moral turmoil or emotional trauma—whether because of sexual, military,

19. Paradoxically, American liberation discourses have posited polygamy—as a facet of the often sensationalized and misconstrued construct of sharia law—to be the very type of oppressive tradition ("sexual slavery") from which Muslim women need saving. See, e.g., Mamhood and Hirschkind (2002).

or any other conduct in war—bust the myths in wartime rhetoric, such as those about liberation and reconstruction.

The cases of Tariq and Mohammed reveal a broader trend of Iraqi men working for the protection of their people, all the while leaving their family behind. This development is a direct result of the US-led invasion, which made work with US Forces a necessary source of income and mode of "helping" in the new Iraq. It also reflects the reality that, once in the United States, jobs were extremely hard to find, and a military career was seen as the only option. In and through allying with US Forces, young men like Mohammed and Tariq are able to assume the role of an authority figure in Iraq. It is also this action that can physically take them away from their families—oftentimes leaving their mothers and wives to protect themselves, in the case of Mohammed and Tariq, respectively.

In these cases, young men's immediate presence as a family protector is replaced by an assumption of patriarchal authority writ large. In addition to marking a physical displacement, the assumption of patriarchal authority more broadly also represents a subjective displacement. Many young men express complex feelings of alienation as a result of their "abandonment" of certain duties (in Mohammed's words) in fulfillment of other duties and as a result of their shifting positionalities as Iraqi leaders and American brothers. This led Mohammed to question some of the assumptions of the patriarchal model he aspired to, saying to me one day: "A man's power he receives only by tradition. I can't do anything a woman can't do for herself." The project of reconstruction that called upon Iraqi men to "help" as would-be patriarchal leaders in the new Iraq also in some measure undermines "hyperpatriarchy" in the refugee network. Though Joe, Mohammed, and Tariq call upon patriarchal ideals of protection, they also destabilize the everyday structures of patriarchy and axioms of female protection in their very actions as protectors. Male interpreters call upon models of masculinity at the intersection of Iraqi war experience narratives and US militarism; yet, under conditions of displacement, those models open up to subversive resignification.

5

From American Ally to Iraqi Refugee

Standing next to Hiba in the US Citizenship and Immigration Services (USCIS) office outside of Boston, my mind flooded with memories of the hundreds of men and women I had met during my work as a refugee officer. Her hand raised alongside dozens of other soon-to-be US citizens, I recalled the hundreds of oaths I had administered to refugee applicants, and I contemplated the uncertain road between that first, solemn oath and this one—taken in the celebratory atmosphere of a naturalization ceremony. It had been many years since I left my temporary position in the US Refugee Admissions Program, and those memories remained raw. The daughter with a premonition that her case might be denied because of her father's involvement in Saddam Hussein's military, who slipped me a note pleading for help. The extra line of questioning for all middle-aged men who, like the girl's father, had served in the Iraqi military during the Iran-Iraq War. The older military officer who, proud of his service and miffed by my pro forma questions about his involvement in possible human rights abuses during the war, pointed out to me that the biggest ally of Iraq in that war had been the United States. The older widow whom I would be required to ask for her husband's death certificate to ensure that he was not alive, involved in the war, or planning to petition to join her in the United States in an ominous plot.

At Hiba's side during her naturalization ceremony, I thought about the long road she had taken from her resettlement in the United States in 2007—and about the deeply ambivalent relationship that she and others in her position occupy vis-à-vis the US state. The US government led a war effort that turned Hiba's life upside down and then, in the course of immigration, treated her and her husband alternately like possible threats

144

or naïve victims whose only hope lay with the US state. The US resettlement program had welcomed them to the United States as refugees, but
it had not provided them enough basic support to enable them to restart
their lives, leaving Tariq's only job option to join the US Army. The US
military had given her husband a job, but it returned him to her as a different man. At Hiba's naturalization ceremony, most of the other participants had large crowds cheering in a variety of languages. Hiba, who was
acquainted with very few people in the Boston area and was no longer
close to any other Iraqis, had only invited me. I had suggested that she
invite her onetime caseworker, a refugee himself who became the go-to
person for newly arriving Iraqi refugees in Boston. Mikhaeil was the one
who had picked Hiba and Tariq up from the airport. A former interpreter
(who described having a "covenant with Americans" to me), Mikhaeil is
a Chaldean Christian whose goal in Boston was to build understanding
among Iraqis here.[1] Yet Hiba would not invite him because, as she said,
the refugee agency where he worked is like "CNN for gossip." She would
not risk throwing her name into that known gossip mill for any reason—
even for a seemingly celebratory occasion. I feared that there may be more
to the story.

For interpreters, the refugee interview was one in a series of encounters with American soldiers, officials, and police that required situated
and creative responses. (After arriving in the United States, their next
encounter with the US state apparatus was with a refugee caseworker like
Mikhaeil, charged with dispensing state benefits.) After taking an oath
in that decisive refugee interview, Iraqi applicants would find that the
most defining elements of their personal biographies became potential
liabilities. In the refugee interview, identifying as a proud war veteran or
widow—even if foundational to one's national or gender identity—became
a red flag. On some occasions, the very events that led a family to apply for

---

1. Mikhaeil described feeling a deep and abiding alliance with the United States'
mission to depose Saddam Hussein. Still, over the time that I knew him, Mikhaeil grew
more and more critical of what he considered inhumane treatment by US Forces of civilians. He became an outspoken opponent of drone usage, among other things, in the
Boston area.

resettlement—for example, a kidnapping—resulted in problems, delays, or even denials in the immigration process. If the parents of a kidnapped child paid a ransom, for example, such remuneration constitutes material support to a terrorist organization, requiring a high-level review in Washington. Responding to these murky and, at times, arbitrary realities, young Iraqi men and women put to use the strategies they sharpened on base and on patrol in the immigration pipeline: to underscore their filial duties, their victimization in Iraq, or their mission to protect Iraqis alongside US brothers and sisters in recognizable ways. As interpreters recounted their strategies in the immigration process when I met them in New England, I was struck by the degree to which their self-described accounts during the refugee interviews were as coded as refugee officers' ears were selective in hearing them.

While they were approached instrumentally, these encounters with the US state had lasting impacts. Out of these encounters, Iraqis in the diaspora developed practices of cultural citizenship vis-à-vis the US nation and state, which would prove to be focal avenues in making claims for years to come. In the xenophobic climate that followed the 9/11 attacks, where state and society in effect (and in reality) "de-Americanized" many Arabs and Muslims communities, young Iraqis found that honing such strategies of identification were as urgent as during an "us-versus-them" war in Iraq—or to ward off accusations of betrayal by fellow Iraqis. Louise Cainkar suggests that "de-Americanization revolves around the notion of perpetual foreignness and an implicit lack of national loyalty. . . . It appears that Arab and Muslim Americans were de-Americanized in gendered ways: the source of their foreignness was interpreted differently depending on whether they were men or women" (2009, 232–33). If a male subject's foreignness surrounded political inclinations of violent predilections, a female subject's foreignness revolved around her attachment to "culture," represented by a headscarf, among other things.

Here I consider how former military interpreters' gendered relationships to the US state and nation unfold over the course of immigration and resettlement processes. Beginning in the refugee interview, young men tend to take an assimilationist tack and claim belonging in the United States as hyphenated Americas, whereas young women identify themselves as betwixt and between Iraqi and US-based identifications. Strikingly, single Iraqi women in the United States tend to self-identify as "refugees"—managing their "foreignness" by claiming itinerant uprootedness rather than cultural rootedness; single Iraqi men widely assert themselves as "immigrants" or "Iraqi-Americans" and demonstrate this identity through their continued work for the US military, government, or paragovernmental organizations.

After receiving citizenship, Hiba would continue to call herself an "Iraqi refugee," while her husband Tariq called himself an "Iraqi-American" from the early days of his resettlement and work for US Forces. In part, this stark divergence in identification reflects the fact that Tariq was forced to renounce his Iraqi citizenship to become a US solider. Other young men found work as Mikhaeil had—in refugee agencies working as caseworkers for newly arriving refugees. I encountered only two young women in the refugee network who worked in governmental or paragovernmental jobs, while I met dozens of young men in such positions. By and large young women relate to the US state on a more limited basis as strategic applicants for services rather than employees, adopting a more insulationist approach. Sometimes young women try to limit their encounters with the US state altogether—and with Iraqi American caseworkers in particular. Just as female Terps expressed feeling contradictory pressures on base in Iraq, young women in the diaspora recount feeling a great deal of conflicting pressure from their caseworkers: both to Americanize and become self-sufficient as neoliberal workers (exemplified by pressure to get a job and be independent right away) and to remain Iraqi and resist Americanization (exemplified by pressure to live with a "good Iraqi family"). Another compelling example surrounds the conflicting pressures young women felt to veil or "de-hijab" in the diaspora, sometimes emanating from a single figure: the Iraqi American caseworker. The peculiar relationship between single female refugees and single male refugee caseworkers encapsulates the complex gender politics of belonging, identity, and cultural citizenship in the United States. Women and men alike face discrimination on the streets and racial profiling by police in the Boston area, further complicating the refugee network's relationships to the US state and nation.

In what follows, I first sketch the contradictory history of refugee resettlement and the complex processes of immigration from the refugee interview to resettlement. Next, I turn to the stories of two members of the refugee network: Tamara, the friend and sponsor of Meena, who reflects on her immigration experience; and Hussein, who now works as a caseworker in a refugee resettlement agency serving other Iraqis in South Boston. Finally, I consider what their stories tell us about gendered formations of cultural citizenship within the US-based Iraqi diaspora.

The Contradictory Policies of Refugee Resettlement

After the refugee crisis of World War II,[2] the United Nations (UN) chartered the Convention on the Status of Refugees, outlining the definition and accordant rights for refugees worldwide. The United States signed the UN Convention on Refugees in 1967, in the midst of massive Cuban migration to the United States and as refugee displacement from the Vietnam War began to mount. After the precipitous fall of South Vietnam in 1975, the American government faced the enormous challenge of protecting the South Vietnamese who had allied with the US military. The United States airlifted thousands of South Vietnamese allies; others made their way out on commercial ships in ad hoc arrangements. This ushered in a broader refugee resettlement program for Vietnamese, Cambodian, and Laotian refugees in the late 1970s and especially in the early 1980s.

After the partial and initially improvised response to the Southeast Asian refugee crisis, the US government passed a comprehensive Refugee Act in 1980, overhauling refugee policy and outlining the procedures for US refugee admissions thereafter.[3] The Refugee Act adopted the UN defi-

---

2. In response to the massive displacement of European Jews and others during World War II, the United States demonstrated an informal and, according to many, insufficient response. In the wake of war, assistance to refugees was far from systematic and carried out largely by faith-based organizations rather than through government programs.

3. For further history of refugee policy and the 1980 Refugee Act, see Zucker and Zucker (1992). For more on Southeast Asian refugee resettlement specifically, see Rumbaut (2001).

nition of a refugee, which identified a refugee as someone who had been persecuted or feared persecution on the basis of race, religion, nationality, or political opinion. Thus began a chapter of rigorous refugee resettlement that prioritized "victims of communism" (as a monument outside of the refugee affairs division of the Department of Homeland Security in Washington designates) from Southeast Asia, Eastern Europe, and Cuba throughout the Cold War. Refugees of civil wars in Africa and Latin America, which represented proxies for the US–Soviet conflict, became top priorities for the program as well. Though considered a "humanitarian" program, the identification of priority refugee populations and the approach to refugee processing has from the beginning been a highly political matter.

Aihwa Ong's seminal work on Cambodian refugees of this period examines the contradictory experiences of cultural citizenship among resettled families in the San Francisco area (Ong 2003). Cambodian refugees' experiences of belonging in the United States reflected neoliberal economic structures that produced them as working-class individuals, on the one hand, and their interpellation into categorical racial and ethnic identifications, on the other. In Ong's assessment, refugees are schooled to become individual workers within a structure of imagined American meritocracy. At the same time, they are constructed as racialized others, outside the bounds of the "American Dream." Such "unofficial social meanings and criteria" as language, dress, or religion represent the bases for refugees' cultural citizenship, and these criteria have long been as important to refugees' lived experience in the United States as legal citizenship (Ong 2003, 70). Following Ong, I understand cultural citizenship to refer to the everyday experience of belonging or exclusion within dominant structures of social classification (relating to class, ethnicity, race, and gender).[4]

The contradictory forces that Iraqi refugees now face—which construct them as cultural beings and simultaneously discipline them as

4. For further discussions on cultural citizenship among migrant communities specifically, see Siu (2001) and Flores (2003).

neoliberal workers—are therefore far from new. The beginning of the war on terror brought with it new trials for the waves of refugees that it displaced, however. The PATRIOT Act directly impacted the way refugees were evaluated for admission to the United States. Most obviously, federal citizenship and immigration services were moved to the newly created Department of Homeland Security, bespeaking an increased focus on national security and counterterrorism that reshaped the humanitarian program of refugee resettlement.

Iraqis—and Iraqi allies in particular—became a priority population for US resettlement in 2007 after the escalation of violence in the country.[5] In the course of their immigration proceedings, these "allies" were vigorously screened for Terrorism-Related Inadmissibility Grounds. Once in the United States, however, Iraqis faced surveillance, harassment, and, in some cases, imprisonment and deportation. The contradictions between neoliberal economic ideals of meritocracy and racialized realities thus took on new valences in a post-9/11 era of a surveillance state. The PATRIOT Act gave the state ever-greater power over immigrant and non-immigrant Arab and Muslim lives, including those who had once worn a US uniform in Iraq. Louise Cainkar observes that the implementation of the PATRIOT Act's racialized policies—and the delineation of threat— was very much a matter of gender, quite like the delineation of threat functioned in Iraq. As they set foot on US soil at US embassies[6] for decisive refugee interviews, Iraqis found that the United States represented a continuation of gendered battlefield logics and discourses of threat, rather than an escape from them.[7]

---

5. By contrast, the relatively modest Afghani refugee resettlement is due in part to the logistical challenges of refugee processing in Pakistan, where most Afghani refugees have fled. The Afghani resettlement program has been generally limited to interpreters and other allies.

6. Refugee interviews take place in embassies in certain countries, while in others the interviews are carried out in the offices of the NGO that facilitates the process.

7. For excellent analyses of the impact of 9/11 on Arab and Muslim Americans, see Cainkar (2009) and Jamal and Naber (2008).

Work proved the most viable avenue to lay claim to cultural citizenship in the United States, but neither work nor citizenship came easily or without strings attached for Iraqi refugees.[8] As we will see in Tamara's case, economic participation came with a "de-hijabing" for certain Iraqi women—sometimes voluntary, at other times under pressure from peers. This aptly symbolizes the knot of economic and cultural pressures interpreters in the diaspora encountered. Especially in the wake of the economic recession beginning in 2008, the opportunities to "belong" by way of economic participation were already slim. That to pursue them also came with some degree of embedded violence was enough to compel many Iraqi youth to return to Iraq after only months or years in the United States. Indeed, the path for Iraqi refugees from the Middle East capital cities to US metropolitan areas—and in some cases back—has been harder than many refugees had ever imagined, not least for US allies who arguably have sacrificed the most.

Dislocations: From Ally to Refugee

After working as interpreters, young Iraqis decided to leave Iraq under a range of circumstances. Some interpreters were directly threatened, while others describe a more abstract fear in Iraq or a sense of opportunity in the United States as motivating their decisions. Anwar heard rumors from her neighbors that "her name was on a list," while Mikhaeil received a threat letter signed by a local militia member; others were spared these threats but feared that it was a matter of time before similar letters arrived on their doorstep.

Iraqi interpreters applied for refugee status in the United States through two principal channels: via a case-by-case UN referral program

---

8. Sunaina Maira has similarly shown that economic participation—as workers and American Dream aspirants—represented a key channel for South Asian immigrant youth to assert their cultural citizenship in the United States during the war on terror (Maira 2009).

outside of Iraq (a "Priority 1" or P1 case); or via an expedited program in Baghdad, Amman, and Cairo if one had worked directly with US Forces (a "Priority 2" or P2 case). Most interpreters took advantage of this P2 program, and many applied through "in country processing" in Baghdad.[9] The US Congress approved an aggressive Iraqi resettlement program with ambitious admission targets after the escalation of the conflict in 2006. Between 2007, when Iraqi refugee processing began, and 2012 about 150,000 Iraqi cases were interviewed, about half that number of cases was approved for resettlement, and a total of 84,902 Iraqi refugees arrived in the United States.[10] The years 2009 and 2010 were the busiest for Iraqi refugee processing as the refugee crisis widened.[11] Resettlement slowed significantly in 2011 when two recently resettled Iraqis were arrested in Kentucky on charges of terrorist activity.

In any given case—whether the case comprises an individual or a family—only one person, the principal applicant, can offer testimony. In the case of nuclear families containing a heterosexual married couple (the only type of family recognized by US Citizenship and Immigration Services), immigration officials almost always appoint the male as the "principal applicant." In this sense, men are the speaking agents, while women are often asked to leave the room during the interview. Women most often appear as the unspeaking victims in a family's "persecution story," the name given to a refugee's testimony. If the norm was a male principal applicant, refugee officers often considered the case of a single woman— in which she would necessarily be the principal applicant—the "easiest." Whereas refugee interviews with men (for whom security concerns were assumed greater) could last hours, a case with a single woman could be over in thirty minutes. Single women commonly hold special designations as "women at risk," and their admission as refugees was widely seen as a "no-brainer." While the outcome may be seen as advantageous to women,

9. In addition, the State Department conducted a much smaller "Special Immigrant Visa" program for 500 interpreters annually, which several interpreters I met had utilized.

10. See USCIS Iraqi Refugee Factsheet (2012) at www.USCIS.gov.

11. I was among dozens of refugee officers hired on a temporary basis to meet the desired targets in the Middle East during those years.

the effect of this gendered structure, based in part on caricatured views of Iraqi culture, is to silence many Iraqi women during the immigration process. This dynamic would be echoed for many women along the resettlement path, for example, with caseworkers who would "look after them" at the expense of listening to them.[12]

To resettle in the United States as refugees, Iraqi applicants had to establish that they had suffered past harm or possessed a well-founded fear of harm on the basis of their race, religion, nationality, or political opinion. These World War II–era categories were blunt tools in assessing Iraqis' lived experiences of war, violence, and apprehension about remaining in their homes. Applicants wrote a personal "persecution story" with reference to these dominant categories prior to the refugee interview, which they would then need to perform in oral testimony during the interview.[13] Given the sectarian dimensions of the conflict in Iraq, "religion" was the chief prism through which the refugee resettlement leaders that I encountered understood and appraised Iraqis' refugee claims—at least P1 cases. (P2 cases were assumed in advance to be "political opinion" or even "imputed political opinion" cases because of the applicants' affiliation with the United States.)

In other words, if someone reports that she is Sunni and is gravely afraid of her Shi'i neighbors, she establishes a refugee claim. If one reports that he is Shi'i and had credible reason to fear his Sunni neighbors, he is a refugee. If someone reports that she is Christian and fears both Sunni and Shi'i neighbors, she also meets the criteria to be considered a refugee. I recall talking to one of my refugee resettlement supervisors who, when I questioned the logic of this approach, told me: "There's no question that it's crazy. If all you have to do is claim a sect to be a refugee, should we just pave the whole country and bring all of Iraq to America?" Unsurprisingly, many Iraqi applicants quickly learned (from one another,

12. For more on the gender dynamics in refugee processing, see "I Have A Name" about East African refugees in the US resettlement process by McSpadden and Moussa (1993).

13. Compare Coulter's discussion of the imperative for war victims to perform their "war stories" to receive benefits from NGOs in postconflict Sierra Leone (2009, 177).

the UN, the NGO that organized refugee processing, or immigration officers themselves) how the US state defines a refugee. Given this, some officers accepted the fact that what we heard in the course of our short, formulaic interviews were mostly canned "camp stories," as they called the frequently repeated stories believed to be fabrications. Many officers sympathized with the applicants as they navigated a flawed and outdated refugee process. Others believed that "rules were rules," and would deny applicants with canned stories—even if the officer had reason to believe that the individual's fear in Iraq was well founded, as *any* Iraqi's fear would be presumed to be by the program's inexact sectarian logic.[14]

Officers' real job was to screen out past or future perpetrators of "terrorist activity." Terrorist activity was defined broadly as any action—willful or coerced, knowing or unknowing—that supports the efforts of a terrorist organization. A terrorist organization was defined as a group of two or more people who engaged in violent activity targeting civilians for reasons other than monetary gain. Given this definition's breadth, officers spent a large portion of interviewing exploring past political affiliations, religious views, group membership, military training, and contact with (even as the targets of) neighborhood militias or political movements. Young single men were required to give month-by-month timelines of their whereabouts and activities from 2003 until the date of the interview—sometimes the better part of a decade. The determination of Terrorism-Related Inadmissibility Grounds (TRIG) was the central objective of the refugee interview.[15] In addition to the refugee interview, refugees were subject to multiple background checks (see the fingerprinting station at the USCIS office in Baghdad in Illustration 4). Material support to terrorist organizations, even remotely or under duress, led to delays and denials for large portions of the Iraqi refugee pool.

Apart from Terrorism-Related Inadmissibility Grounds, US refugee law bars the admission of applicants who have been involved in the

14. For an elaboration on refugee law for Iraqi refugees, see Rikoski and Finer (2009).

15. Information about TRIG can be found at USCIS.gov. For a critical examination of TRIG on refugees, see the Refugee Council USA's website at rcusa.org.

4. The USCIS office in Baghdad, a former palace of Saddam Hussein, where Iraqi interpreters were interviewed for resettlement to the United States. Photo by author.

persecution of others. Refugee officers spent a great deal of time inquiring about possible persecutory acts committed by anyone in Saddam's military (most Iraqi men) or in the Ba'th Party (most Iraqi students and professionals). Because military service was mandatory for all men and Ba'th Party membership was compulsory for many students, professional groups, and government servants, applicants were required to provide detailed records of military service and party activities to ensure that they had not participated in military campaigns against civilians or the punishment of political dissidents.

Finally, refugee officers had to assess the credibility of the applicant. While the definition of a credible claim was "plausible, detailed, and consistent," credibility ultimately came down to a "gut feeling," as one supervisor told me. Nearly every officer I met admitted that "instinct" or "sense" about the applicant played a significant role in the final decision to approve or deny a case. Even if an applicant did not appear to raise any red flags relating to TRIG, an officer might deny the applicant on the grounds of being "evasive" or "uncooperative" if he had a bad "gut feeling." The assignment of a case to an officer is the first of multiple rounds of roulette for Iraqi refugees in the process of resettlement.

After the refugee interview, applicants waited for weeks or months for processing of their fingerprints, background checks, and, if they worked with US Forces, verification of their employment. Though theoretically an "expedited" process, the P2 program for contractors of US Forces was sometimes delayed well over a year due to the need for employment verification. This was a common complaint of interpreters. Though often slow, the approval rate for P2 cases—US allies—was extremely high. If a case was approved, the applicants would be informed of their travel date and destination, and would attend a "cultural orientation" that aimed to equip them for life in the United States. If a case was denied, applicants might petition the decision, though this rarely resulted in a reversal of the adjudication.

Dislocations: From Refugee to Sponsor

If the first round of roulette decides the officer to whom a refugee is assigned for the refugee interview, the second round of roulette decides where in the United States he or she will be resettled. After a case has been approved, several refugee agencies, which have offices in different cities across the United States, "bid" against each other to receive the case—and the government funding that comes with it. Those agencies, sometimes referred to as "volags" (short for voluntary agencies), are paragovernmental service agencies. Some volags, such as Catholic Charities and Lutheran Social Services, are religiously affiliated though their funding, guidelines, and procedures for refugee resettlement are drawn from the state and federal government.

In theory, volags "win" bids on refugee families based on their demonstrated ability to provide the services for a refugee's unique needs—whether linguistic, psychological, or educational—though many refugees will tell you this is often not the case. For their part, many volags point fingers at the diminishing amount of federal and state support for refugee assistance. Funding for resettled refugees has been steadily stripped away over the past decade, just as Iraqi refugee resettlement has ramped up.

The effective refugee assistance that families see is not uniform across the country or even in a single city. Depending on existing local programs and state budgets, volags' budgets vary—as do their access to supplemental programs and discretionary funds for any given refugee. The states with the best-funded Offices of Refugee Resettlement—such as Massachusetts—tend to also be the costliest places to live, making them challenging places for refugees to actually remain.[16] Because of this, access to supplemental programs (such as heat assistance in the winter) or discretionary monies within the agency is a prized right of caseworkers to disperse.

As of 2013, approximately 2,700 Iraqi refugees had resettled in Massachusetts. Substantially fewer—on the order of hundreds rather than thousands—have resettled in Connecticut, Rhode Island, Maine, New Hampshire, and Vermont.[17] Currently in Massachusetts, refugees are guaranteed cash and medical assistance for eight months. Medical assistance consists of basic state health insurance; cash assistance comes in the amount of $428/month for a "case" of one, with an additional $105 for each additional family member.

What is not guaranteed is a place to live after the first month. In theory, when a refugee arrives in New England, a safe and appropriately priced apartment (usually with a sponsor) will have been selected for them by their volag, which pays the refugee's rent for the first month. After that point, cash assistance is expected to cover the refugee's portion of the rent, leaving adequate money left over for utilities and other necessities. Still, given the cost of rent and utilities in New England, housing costs often far exceed the

16. Some of the most successful resettlement zones in the United States have been midsized US cities like Minneapolis and St. Louis, as well as some larger cities with relatively low unemployment and cost of living, such as Phoenix and Atlanta.

17. According to the Massachusetts Office of Refugees and Immigrants statistics at mass.gov/ori. Asma Khalid estimates that one in four refugees resettled to Massachusetts in recent years have been Iraqi. See "Iraqi Refugees Find a Complicated New Home in Mass," WBUR, April 9, 2013.

cost assistance allotted. As a result, refugees find themselves in dangerous and substandard housing or in apartments far too expensive for their budgets. Some discretionary funds exist to fill this gap or to cover utilities on a short-term basis, but they are not assured. During that first month, refugees undertake a flurry of paperwork: applications for rent and utility assistance; registration for a social security number in order to receive SNAP benefits (food stamps); and enrollment in school and job training classes. The support of caseworkers is indispensable in helping refugees apply for eligible supplemental benefits, releasing discretionary funds where available, and—most importantly—assisting them in finding work.

The caseworker is theoretically a refugee's go-to for nearly everything in their first months in the United States. Many caseworkers told me that their "number-one" task was to instill in refugees the importance of work, to help them develop the skills they need to become employable, and to find them jobs. One Iraqi caseworker I met, named Omar, underscored the importance of teaching refugees about the necessity of work in a "culturally appropriate way." Omar told me that an American caseworker had "scared a group of Iraqis to death" by telling them that they had to work— even if it meant "scrubbing toilets." Omar said that he had to intervene and explained to the group that he would help them find an appropriate job to get work experience, which is important to "move up." He also promised that there were government programs to help along the way. "No one is going to be stuck scrubbing toilets for the rest of their life," he told them. The need to balance these countervailing forces of neoliberal economic demands and "cultural appropriateness" led many volags to hire Iraqis to serve as caseworkers for other Iraqis. Usually, Iraqi caseworkers are refugees themselves—and in that case they are frequently former interpreters, as Terps are seen to have the unique professional and language abilities to do the job.

If no caseworker positions were available, refugee agencies would often help former Terps find work as interpreters for medical, legal, or other translating firms. One refugee agency that I encountered had formed its own for-profit translating business within the nonprofit organization, in which it employed recently resettled refugees among others. Professional interpreters from the Iraq War were prized translators in this and other translating businesses, serving the growing Iraqi refugee population. Husham, a former interpreter with the Marines, began working for the refugee agency-affiliated translation business when he could not find other work. At earlier points in our interviews, he had told me that working as an interpreter was a low point in his life, which he had hoped to devote to music and the arts. Once beginning work with the refugee agency's translation company, he quipped that he had gotten it all wrong. Working as a Terp was the best decision of his life: it set him on a path to become an interpreter for the nonprofit resettlement agency's for-profit business. It turns out that he had met his future Iraqi girlfriend while serving as her interpreter at the local hospital.

Most of the young people who worked as interpreters in the diaspora were men, and all but one of the Iraqi caseworkers I met was male. This disparity appeared to be a function of the volag's perceptions of "cultural appropriateness." The view that men were more appropriate authority figures than women was widespread among the refugee agency employees I met in New England, although not always explicitly articulated. I discussed this dynamic one summer afternoon with a woman who operated an independent Muslim refugee assistance group (in the back storeroom of a Middle Eastern restaurant in Boston). She informed me that refugee agencies tended to refer only Iraqi women to her group for the English as a second language (ESL) classes she offered or to visit her halal food pantry, although both were also open to men, explaining, "I guess they think brothers don't listen to women in power." When I asked her if there was any truth to that claim, she said with a sigh, "The issue is that the refugee agencies do not understand why or how to deal with it." She told me that such gender dynamics were not a matter of culture or religion but of history: women had a "big role" in Arab culture, but individual men might not have "personal experience" with women in power. That, she believed, could change—as it had in the past and was changing now.[18]

---

18. She cited the example of the Arab Spring, in which many women were participating, to oust male dictators. In her view, women had a greater public role in the Middle East prior to the era of (often US-backed) dictatorships.

Such a historical perspective on gender dynamics is generally lost in the refugee resettlement process in favor of reductive cultural explanations. As a result, Iraqi men became brokers of state benefits as caseworkers for the Iraqi diaspora. In a climate of waning resources, their role became a crucial and politicized one in the diaspora. The relationship between caseworker and refugee lent itself to feelings of paternalism and favoritism. Many refugees suspected caseworkers of giving differential treatment to clients and doling out resources only to their friends.

In order to avoid the possibly undesirable outcomes of being randomly assigned to a city and accompanying refugee agency, many members of the refugee network avoid the second round of roulette altogether. Instead, they avail themselves of the option to request a sponsor in the United States. A sponsor may be a relative, friend, or acquaintance. Much of the time, in fact, refugees only know their sponsors distantly—sometimes they have never met. Often sponsors were themselves resettled refugees—sometimes from the 1990s Iraqi refugee migration and sometimes from the 2003 war.

The responsibility of the sponsor is to house, feed, and assist the refugees—in other words, to be a quasi-refugee agency themselves. This strategy saves the state and refugee agency money, helps the sponsor financially with contributions to her rent, and enables the refugee to resettle in a chosen destination with a chosen point of contact. Because of these factors, sponsorship is a favored option by many volags, applicants, and sponsors alike. It is so preferable that sometimes volags connect sponsors and refugees who do not know each other. This is especially true for single women who immigrate alone.

Yet, the sponsor-refugee relationship is extremely challenging. Feelings of dependency and exploitation run in both directions of the relationship. Given the close quarters of urban apartment units, rooming with distant acquaintances or near strangers proves untenable for many, like Hiba and Frank. Rarely do these sponsorship-roommate relationships last longer than a few months. Sometimes newly arrived refugees have the chance to serve as a sponsor for someone else arriving from Iraq, presenting the opportunity to move into a preferable apartment of their choice, which they could then sublet. Other times, the sensitivity of the arrangements leads one of the two individuals to move out abruptly. Most interpreters were on their own within two months. Iraqi men and women continued to move frequently from one living situation to another, depending on circumstances and income, across the Boston area.

Apart from finding immediate work to pay the bills, finding affordable housing is the most urgent challenge that Iraqi refugees face. More broadly, they encounter the structural challenge of acquiring credentials, education, and job training in order to pursue careers with an opportunity of upward mobility. Many Iraqi refugees—and former interpreters in particular—possess higher degrees, and some had professional lives as doctors or engineers in Iraq. Neither their educational degrees nor professional credentials were readily transferable to the United States. While a select few have held out for a job in their field—acquiring college transcripts, getting them certified by international companies, and applying for graduate school in their field—the majority leave their earlier educational and professional lives behind and start again, usually at a much lower pay grade. For example, one former interpreter living in Providence with a bachelor's degree in English and aspirations for academia began volunteering at a local hospital in order to find work as a medical assistant and, eventually, as a cast technician. The hospital would ultimately pay for him to acquire a medical assistance degree. He was among a small group of steadily employed Iraqi refugees. More often, Iraqi refugees work part-time in service-sector work, without benefits or opportunities for future training. It is this job insecurity that led many former interpreters to join the military or to work in refugee resettlement for paragovernmental agencies—sometimes with misgivings.

Iraqi refugees receive legal permanent residency (their "green card") after one year in the United States. After receiving green cards, interpreters can apply for citizenship after four years. By 2012, the first round of interpreters was beginning to receive American citizenship. By that time, some others had already moved back to Iraq. Indeed a significant portion of the Iraqi network has returned home, sometimes visiting the United States just enough to maintain green cards and at other times not at all. Most interpreters, like Tamara, live distinctly transnational lives—their families, their pasts, their futures, and their identities span multiple continents. And even with citizenship, Iraqi youth face the structural and social threats of "de-Americanization."

Tamara: A "Liberation War" Refugee Rebuffs Salvation

Tamara, who arrived in Boston several months before Meena, served as Meena's sponsor and roommate. Like Meena, Tamara does not frequently see other Iraqis. A former Terp for several army units involved in training the Iraqi army at Camp Victory, she applied for refugee status in the United States with two goals: to find an engineering job and to eventually petition for her mother and siblings to join her in the United States. Tamara is from a large middle-class family in Baghdad, and her mother and younger siblings had decided to stay in the family home in Iraq for the short term unless the security situation worsened. More importantly, Tamara's mom wanted to limit the impact of the move on Tamara's brother, who had a severe developmental disability. The family decided it made sense for Tamara to go ahead of them, settle down in the United States, and try to find a job.

Tamara, twenty-eight years old, with a surprising life history full of grit and loss, found that her most personal experiences mattered little in the refugee resettlement process. The immigration process demanded that she perform a certain kind of "persecution story." The day-to-day details about her sacrifices with US Forces mattered not at all. Her own biography, views, or experiences were not vital, and her dreams for the future were of no concern at all. It was, as she said, all about "the story."

Tamara had heard about the P2 refugee program for US allies while working at Camp Victory, and she applied from Baghdad. She decided to apply because of the deteriorating security situation: she had not been directly threatened because of her work with US Forces but said she could not predict if she would be in the future. Indeed, it was because she could not predict the future that she wanted to apply for refugee resettlement. In her refugee interview, she learned that this was not sufficient for refugee status. To be considered a refugee, she had to articulate a specific type of narrative, in which dominant US categorizations of the conflict mattered more than her nuanced experiences.

Tamara and I frequently took long walks around the city. On one, she recounted her refugee interview to me in detail. "The officer's name was Mr. Smith," she told me. When Mr. Smith asked if she had been a target of any violence in particular, she said no. His eyes remained downcast, focused on his notes. Any threats? No. "Is it safe to stay in Iraq?" he asked in a routine voice. She reminded him of the dangers interpreters faced in Iraq. She said it was her mom who was most fearful that something might happen. He asked why she remained in Baghdad if it were potentially dangerous. She responded curtly that she was one of the only people in her family earning an income—and it was home. It is a big decision to leave one's home. Mr. Smith probed further: "Tell me more about the danger you might be in? Who would want to target you? Can you name any terrorist organizations in particular?" And it went on like that. Tamara found herself reducing her life experiences to what she described as "headlines." She acquiesced to his line of questioning: over the course of the interview, she became a "pro-American" single woman in danger from anti-American terrorists.

When the refugee officer asked about her family's political affiliations, Tamara again spoke telegraphically. "My family has a history of supporting America," she recalls telling the officer. She explained that her uncle was imprisoned, tortured, and executed by Saddam's government due to his membership in the Dawa Party and his participation in the Shi'i intifada in 1991. Her family hoped for American intervention in support of the uprising, and when it did not come, they lived in fear. "If you're my relative, they will believe that you and I think alike. They will hold you responsible for something that I did," she explained to the officer. So, she went on, the family's loyalties remained questionable and the subject of ongoing investigations. She was hopeful when the US-led invasion took place in 2003. She did not mention to her interviewer that her dad had died of kidney failure right before the 2003 invasion, and that this was what she most clearly remembered about 2003. She did not say that, after his death, she deferred her dreams of attending graduate school to earn money for her family. Instead, she noted that her mom referred to the US-led war as a "liberation war." She elaborated: "I grew up watching TV against America. I began listening to radio—BBC—that connected me to outside. After my uncle died, I felt trapped in Iraq. I was dreaming of leaving." When the officer asked about any family member's possible connections to militia groups, she said her family believed in the democratic process, not violence. Tamara became a double victim in the course of her interview: her family was persecuted under Saddam Hussein—awaiting "liberation"—and they were also now targets in the new Iraq. She told me that the officer began stamping her paperwork in front of her.

When Tamara arrived in the Boston area, her caseworker, a young Iraqi man, placed her with an Iraqi couple as her sponsors. A few years older than she, the couple had two children. She described the caseworker and the couple as very "protective" of her. She had not spoken to anyone about her work in Iraq, but figured they knew: single women alone were assumed to have worked with US Forces. Her caseworker told her that it was important that she live with a good family, because life in America was difficult alone. As it turned out, one of her greatest difficulties in the United States was the family she lived with—and the caseworker himself. Her sponsors did not approve of her going out of the house alone and, when the couple went out, they often asked Tamara to babysit. After working outside of the house for years in Iraq, being limited to four walls felt punishing. She tried to explain to her sponsors that, while she appreciated being taken in as part of their family, she needed to go out and get a job to earn money for *her* family back in Iraq. Her sponsors acceded to her request to go out and look for work. When she did, they strongly encouraged her to wear a headscarf, which she typically did not except to pray, so that neither American men nor other Iraqis would get the "wrong idea." When she met with her caseworker about finding a job, he informally suggested that she might have more success in the interview if she took off the headscarf. She was incredulous: "This is crazy! Which way is it? Who do they want me to be?"

Tamara did not want to work at the temp agency where her caseworker placed many other Iraqis. With the amount of money she could make there, Tamara would have to stay in her sponsor's apartment forever. So, she decided to look for work on her own. Time and again she hit the same wall looking for a job: she had no "work experience" in the United States. She found it deeply unfair. She reflected: "Coming to the US has always been good and bad. It got to a point where I felt like I didn't have any more good options in Iraq. I spent all my time with the military—all my time—I didn't even see my family. But here that does not count as 'work experience.' I knew coming to the US would be hard but I thought it would create some chances for my family. Now, I can't find anything for me here." Part of what struck Tamara as unfair was the fact that the intense pressures she felt in the United States—especially from her caseworker—had seemed directly at odds. On the one hand, she was expected to become an economically independent and productive member of society. In other words, she needed a job. But, on the other hand, she was expected to live with a "good" Iraqi family and be a "good" Iraqi girl who helped out at home. How could she be both? The incident around her wearing—or not wearing—a headscarf was particularly upsetting to her. She believed it was her decision, not her sponsors' or her caseworker's, and yet it had become the test of both her acceptability in the diaspora and her employability in the United States.

Eventually, Tamara took a bolder approach. She began approaching places of business and asking to speak to the manager. She would explain that she was a refugee from Iraq, that she had to leave her home and her family, and that she was trying to restart her life in the United States. Finally, she got a job reshelving clothes at a department store. She was not guaranteed more than twenty hours a week, however, which meant that she could not yet move out of her sponsors' home. She was stuck at home with a family that was not hers. She began to speak increasingly satirically on our walks about the "liberation war." She might be stuck in an apartment, Tamara quipped, but at least she was in a "free country."

She discovered that she had to do everything for herself, adding dryly that this was "the American way." Tamara found her Iraqi caseworker overbearing and unhelpful: he gave advice rather than assistance. "Really, I don't know how he got that job," she commented. Against his advice, once she saved enough money, she finally moved out of her sponsors' home into an apartment with another young woman whom she met at the refugee agency (an Eritrean woman). Though they came from different national, ethnic, and class backgrounds, she found her new roommate far more accepting of who she was. Now across town from her former sponsors in the suburb of Chelsea, she insulated herself from the pressures and gossip of the Iraqi diaspora.

She slowly got more hours at work but also began dreaming more and more about a career in her field: engineering. Realizing that a graduate degree in the United States was her only option if she wanted a career in engineering, Tamara began studying feverishly for the GRE and would take the test four times before getting a score with which she was satisfied. She then began the years-long process of getting her college transcript certified and applying for graduate school in engineering. Graduate school became the guiding dream and central focus of Tamara's life in the United States. When we spoke about graduate school, she would furtively remind me not to tell anyone else (i.e., other Iraqis) about her plans: they were *her* plans.

Meena's arrival made Tamara feel a bit more at home in Boston. For one thing, "I started speaking Arabic again," Tamara said. The two had met each other through their work as Terps in Iraq, but never directly worked together. Meena moved into Tamara's two-room apartment, sharing her bedroom. She told me, "I feel like Meena is my sister because she was here with me step by step. But at the same time I try to keep my distance. . . . It's hard to say why; it's everything. I feel a lot of pressure around other Iraqis. Sometimes I just want to get away from the pressure." Meena stayed with Tamara for four months before finding another multiroom apartment of her own. The two women remained friends but saw less of each other after Meena moved out. Tamara never identified precisely what kind of pressure she felt from Meena. She clarified that it was nothing Meena said or did: Meena was her sister. The pressure came just from being around other Iraqis in the United States: "It is unspoken, you just feel like people are watching you. I never feel totally comfortable."

Though Tamara avoided Iraqis in Boston, she, like Meena, traveled back to Iraq once a year to see her family. She brought medicines and electronics that they requested. She also took GRE test-prep books with her on the journey, she told me, and studied on the bus ride from Amman to Baghdad. She says, "I'm not really here and I'm not really there. I'm really a refugee." Many others in her very situation—former interpreters who applied for refugee resettlement via the P2 program from Baghdad—would not identify as a "refugee." For Hussein, whom we will meet shortly, a refugee is someone who has to "flee their homes," which neither he nor Tamara did. In his mind, they simply took advantage of an immigration benefit. Yet, Tamara identifies with the image of the refugee, betwixt and between, making her way through the world under challenging circumstances and more or less alone.

Tamara is uncomfortable asking for help, though she often asks for "information" and, sometimes, a fair "chance." Rather than asking other Iraqis or her caseworker for "help," Tamara opted to make her own way, negotiating with bosses and authority figures independently to get what she needs. She explained to me how she had lobbied her landlord to allow her to sublet her apartment when she returned to Iraq to visit her family and asked him not to report she had gone to the refugee agency, so that she could continue to receive cash assistance. (Though modest, this cash assistance helped.) He agreed. She described the process of writing her graduate application, in which she identified herself as a refugee looking for an opportunity to change her life—and to give her family a chance. After reading the application myself, it struck me that Tamara's personal statement about her journey as a refugee closely mirrored the "persecution story" that she had performed for the refugee officer. She was admitted to a master's program in engineering.

From the beginning of the resettlement process, Tamara has strategically positioned herself within variations of a "persecution story." Far from a passive victim, Tamara navigates the challenges of immigration and resettlement assertively. Feeling acute pressure from other Iraqis, Tamara navigates US society on her own. Rather than asking other Iraqis for help, she negotiates power structures in the United States—employment, housing, education—by herself, asking for a "break" from a landlord or from a graduate admissions office when she needs it—not only to better herself but to give her family a "chance." Tamara identifies as a refugee both instrumentally and affectively. Her identification as a single refugee emerges as an assertion of her duty to family, a reminder of individual strength and, in an important sense, a rebuke of her Iraqi sponsors' and caseworker's "protection." While she adopts the subject-position of a refugee in her travels through US power structures, she is clear that the US government has neither "saved" nor "liberated" her. What she has been able to achieve, she achieved by her own efforts—not from the help of the US state or her refugee agency, specifically. (Indeed she is critical of the state's lack of support for refugees and chides her caseworker's incompetence.) She says, "I can only depend on myself. And my family is depending on me." Tamara makes claims of cultural belonging not as a passive victim in need of the state's salvation but as a resourceful refugee making her way, despite and not because of the state's help, and all for the sake of family.

Though avowedly motivated by her family, Tamara responds to pressures of American individualism and neoliberal capitalist demands. Mirroring Ong's observations of Cambodian refugees, Tamara's identification as a refugee indicates her assumption of a subject-position as an individuated subject, a worker, and to some degree an aspirant toward the "American Dream." A hopeful observer might interpret her to be on the brink of fulfilling her American Dream—starting fresh in the United States, going back to school, and beginning a new life. Yet, her American dreaming—and the cultural currency it garners—comes with deep criticism of the United States. She critiques the lack of systematic support for refugees and the unfairness of the American economy more broadly. Further, she describes the conditions in the diaspora in which she must seek out work, crystallized for her in the debate between her sponsor and caseworker about *her* body, as "crazy." That she was expected to be both a good Iraqi girl and an independent, employed woman—and that pursuing one made the other impossible—infuriated Tamara.

Hussein: Rebuilding Iraq as a Refugee Caseworker

In contrast, young men like Hussein may make claims of belonging in the United States by assuming roles of authority within the US state apparatus. Apart from joining the military, a common avenue for employment in state (or parastate) agencies is as a refugee caseworker. Like interpreters-turned-soldiers in the US military, interpreters-turned-caseworkers occupy a position as both Iraqi and American. They assume a role of authority as decisive gatekeepers of financial assistance within US resettlement structures, but they also are gatekeepers of the Iraqi diaspora in an important sense. They are empowered to "look after" Iraqis—precisely in the sense that Tamara did not want to be looked after.

I met Hussein, a charismatic thirty-two-year old caseworker, at the refugee resettlement agency where he works in Worcester, Massachusetts. Hussein came to the United States in 2005 as a Fulbright scholar to study English literature in Missouri. Once he returned to Iraq, he began working as a high-level interpreter for a US Army command in Baghdad before working briefly as an interpreter for the newly reconstituted Iraqi Ministry of Public Works. After being threatened by al Qaeda in 2008, Hussein applied for refugee resettlement from Baghdad, where he lived in the Dora neighborhood with his parents. However, as a young professional who had lived in the United States before, he considered himself an immigrant rather than a refugee.

Soon after his arrival in Worcester in 2009, Hussein began volunteering as an interpreter for the refugee agency. Within a couple of months, as Iraqi refugee arrivals picked up, he was hired full-time as a caseworker. Both of his parents have joined him in Worcester, though he remains unmarried and expects that he will until his job slows down. He told me that his new job feels like the other side of the mission of "reconstruction" in which he participated in Iraq: with so many Iraqis in the United States, he believes it critical to build a strong Iraqi community here. Just as 1990s-era US-based exiles became the new leaders of Iraq, many Iraqis here could be the country's future hope. Yet the prospect of that community-building project remained far off; Hussein explains that in the immediate term Iraqi refugees are a "difficult population to deal with." He empathizes deeply with what his Iraqi clients have gone through, and he understands that their difficult pasts contribute to their challenges in acclimating to the United States. He was fortunate to have survived Iraq's wars with his family, property and life "intact," and this was not the case for many Iraqis. On my first visit to the refugee agency, Hussein told me: "Health care providers here ask me why Iraqis suffer so much from PTSD. I say, take it from the beginning. From 1980 we were at war. For eight years with Iran. About two years of rest and then Kuwait. Then the embargo. Finally in 2003, the invasion. No rest, no clearly seen future, no stability."

Hussein explains his job to be one of easing Iraqis' transition to their new life in the United States. He understands that the transition is not only a matter of adjusting to a new city, dealing with trauma and economic hardship, or missing family and friends. It is also a matter of acculturation. He sees his work as that of a "cultural adviser" for Iraqis, much like he had been a cultural adviser to Americans in Iraq. This position of authority does not always come easily.

> I am wearing two hats all of the time. I am an Iraqi and I should be accepted by the community here. But at the same time, I am their caseworker. I need to tell them things they don't want to hear. They must find a job; I cannot support them forever. They must not make issues with each other over small things, a bad word or a bad look. I cannot be there to solve every problem. I try to explain that we have to leave some things in Iraq: here we cannot interfere in other people's lives; we can't take matters into our own hands. We must respect everyone's rights. That means adjusting some of our traditions, especially for women. You know Iraq is a very patriarchal society. America is a free country. They have accused me of many things, of being a traitor. I tell them, this is all for your own good. I need you to succeed.

Hussein says that his Iraqi clients are suspicious of him at first but over time they begin to listen to his words. His authority—and the suspicion that surrounds it—stems both from his Iraqiness and his proximity to the US state. His role in the diaspora has become that of an advocate for Iraqis, an enforcer of American rules, a mediator of Iraqi problems, and an adviser on life in America. While Hussein speaks about the need to leave "some things in Iraq," such as certain patriarchal values, he also emerges as a sort of patriarchal figure himself, reconfiguring how that authority is reckoned and applied. He recounted animatedly: "People tell me, 'You are one of us, why are you doing this?' I was asking one Iraqi guy about his rent. He could not pay. When I talked to him he said, 'You should be siding with me. I have no money. You are my only hope.' I said, 'I am also your caseworker and I want you to learn to make it in America on your own.' America is a very, very hard life, but people must try." Rather than dispersing favors, Hussein wants to teach Iraqis to "make it" on their own. Both financially and socially, Hussein appears to want Iraqis to think about themselves as individuals rather than "blocs." Hussein evokes a sort of American individualism, based, in his estimation, on equality but also on individual initiative. Only with a respect for the individual, Hussein tells me, can Iraqis rebuild a strong community in the United States.

Hussein's ultimate goal as a caseworker is just that: to build an Iraqi community that features the best parts of Iraqi culture—arts and creativity, hospitality and generosity—but under a common "rule of law" and with respect for everyone's dignity. He sees this as an especially challenging goal because, as he says:

> The problem is we are used to close-knit community based on a tribal mentality. Since the 1990s we have begun to think in terms of tribal blocs, religious blocs, ethnic blocs. So they interfere with each other's affairs all the time. Even if families don't know each other, they interfere in each other's lives. It is one thing if your families go way back in Baghdad; it is another thing if you are interfering and gossiping with strangers. There is no trust. For example, we have three families living in the same building. One family was having a BBQ in the backyard with a few cans of beer. Another Iraqi went over to him and said, "You are turning this house into a bar and I will not allow it." The man was insulted. They could have talked it out if they knew each other, but they didn't and he was insulted. It escalated. The police were called. I was called. I receive calls like that in the middle of the night a lot.

Hussein believes that rebuilding Iraqi society in the United States is all the more crucial because of the ongoing challenges in Iraq. The reconstruction of Iraq, while difficult, may be more successful in the United States than in Iraq itself. He says: "Iraq is sinking. Once you play on the strings of sectarian and ethnic difference, it will be dark for years. Here we have a chance to begin again with the genuine Iraq. We are all protected by the same law."

Hussein sees that the Iraqi diaspora is an especially tricky place for women. He views the treatment of women as an important index of Iraqi society and culture throughout recent history. He recounts how women in Iraqi society had greater respect and power before the resurgence of "tribal thinking" in the 1990s. He says, "The Iraq we left is a very patriarchal society, they come to America and the transition is very sharp. They need to start a new notion about family here. For example, a husband called me recently about his wife. They just arrived not long ago. He told me, 'My wife all of a sudden has a lot to say about our relationship. She says she's going to call you. If she does, you know what you have to tell her.' I said simply: 'Brother, she is equal in every way here. Period.' He was very, very mad at me. He called me a 'pimp' of the Americans." Hussein is particularly concerned about single young women and hoped to prevent gossip and conflict in the diaspora by placing them within Iraqi families. For Tamara, among other women, it was just the kind of protection from which she tried to insulate herself. Having recently accompanied Tamara on her frustrating journey with her caseworker and sponsor, I was startled to hear Hussein talk openly about the cases of several Iraqi women who have "taken off the veil . . . even older women!" He was encouraged by this fact because he felt it was an indication that women had greater choice over their lives and control over their bodies. From Hussein's experience, it was the protective atmosphere of a supportive family that would enable a young woman to feel comfortable to do this within the wider diaspora: because a single woman alone may feel she had no choice but to veil in an effort to ward off any range of suspicions.

Hussein evokes a form of liberal feminism, which, coming from his positionality as an employee of a US parastate organization, appears as a sort of Western democratic doctrine. For him, "women's rights" appear as an index of acculturation to the United States—and not only of Iraqi societal shifts. As an Iraqi leader in the United States, Hussein appears to be rebuffing "Iraqi patriarchy" in favor of a liberal state-based patriarchy, in which authority figures like himself look after the "rights" and well-being of women. His goal to protect Iraqi women may be exactly the sort of project that young women reject. To hear him tell it, Hussein's earnest intention for women is far from keeping them trapped at home, despite the fact that this might be the felt effect. Yet, he remains a protective, patriarchal figure in his vision of the Iraqi diaspora, and it is his real patron–client relationship in the diaspora that lends him the platform to voice it.

Hussein's view of rights, triangulated through US liberalism and based on his idealized vision of the individual, represents his mode of claim-making and asserting belonging in the United States—as well as a technology of governing other people's views. The male caseworker is not the sole author of cultural scripts of claim-making for Iraqi refugees, but he is an important conduit of technologies of government—"policies, programs, codes, and practices . . . that attempt to instill in citizen-subjects particular values (self-reliance, freedom, individualism, calculation, or flexibility)" (Ong 2003, 6). As a broker of the state, his strategies of claim-making are also strategies of governance by which other citizen-subjects are formed.

Gendered Citizenship

Gendered dynamics of claim-making in the US resettlement process respond to orientalist biases in the US immigration system that empower men to be the spokespeople during the immigration process as well as diasporic leaders in the United States as a function of "culture" as well as histories of shifting gender ideals in Iraq. The encounter between male caseworkers and female refugees is particularly illuminating. Iraqi women like Tamara described feeling conflicting pressures: both to get a job as an independent working woman and to be a good Iraqi girl. Tamara identifies strongly as a refugee, sacrificing a great deal to start over in the United States. By contrast, male subjects like Hussein identify as Iraqi Americans, rebuilding Iraq in the United States as soldiers and caseworkers, among other state positions. Hussein becomes a spokesperson for women's rights, advocating greater "equality" among men and women. Yet, in such efforts for women's rights, Iraqi men remain the protectors of women's bodies. Much like in Iraq during its back-to-back wars and under occupation, women's bodies are the site of governance by patriarchal figures in the diaspora—but here taking the form of self-described "feminist" caseworkers. Despite the suspicion that he described feeling from his clients,

Hussein has sparked a positive buzz among many Iraqis I have met. His dream of opening an Iraqi cultural center has gained traction and may soon come to fruition.

Just as Hussein has laid down roots in the United States, assuming an authority position within the US resettlement infrastructure and becoming a leader of Iraqis in Worcester, he has also been targeted with racial and ethnic discrimination and profiling. Because of his "complexion" and his "name," Hussein tells me, he has received several slurs and was once detained by the police for hours after a simple traffic violation. He recounted:

> One day last fall, I was driving through "Sadr City" [the Main South neighborhood of Worcester][19] and I accidentally went through a yellow light. A police officer was nearby and he pulled me over. He said I was speeding too, but I don't believe we were. I was with another Iraqi guy, my client, and we were headed back to the office. I guess we looked suspicious to him—you know, dark guys, dark hair, sunglasses. But, they put us in the back of the car and kept us there for two hours. And then they called backup. Backup! In the end, they didn't even give us a ticket. Really, it doesn't bother me. I explained that we were on the way to the agency, where I worked. I called him "Sir" and "Mr. Officer" and told him, "Hey brother, I am very sorry about that." I understand it is their job. But my friend was really upset. And really I understand that too. It's not fair. But, you have to know how to deal with it. He doesn't have the same experience with those sort of people that I have from working in the US military.

Hussein speculates that he and his client looked suspicious because "you know, dark guys, dark hair, sunglasses." He adds that he dealt with the officers—by apologizing and addressing them as "Sir" and "Mr. Officer." Hussein tells me that it was not "fair" that he was pulled over and detained, but that he knew how to deal with the situation.

---

19. Here Hussein is referring to the Main South neighborhood of Worcester, which he dubs "Sadr City" because of Main South's crowded low-income housing.

Hussein's experience is part of a broader trend in the post-9/11 United States that targets Arabs and Muslims with special attention—and targets Arab and Muslim men and women differently. As Cainkar observes: "Gendered ideas were evident in the ways in which the American government . . . focused its policies on men. . . . American government agencies conducted widely publicized mass arrests and deported thousands of noncitizen Arab and Muslim men, who were referred to by the government as 'terrorists,' although they had been cleared of terrorist associations. . . . Only two females, both sixteen-year-old girls, were detained or incarcerated on suspicion of being terrorists, and women were wholly excused from the government's special registration program. Arrest, interrogation, incarceration, special registration, and removal were almost wholly implemented on male subjects" (2009, 231–32). This gender-inflected racial profiling exemplifies a reductive and orientalist view of Arab, Muslim, Middle Eastern—often homogenized as a monolithic threat. If Iraqi interpreters enacted a form of "military orientalism" in Iraq, they are encountering legal orientalism in the United States. Further, the scrutiny that Hussein and Tamara alike face in the United States was exacerbated by the media, which reinforced images of violent Arab men and alternately sexualized or victimized Iraqi women.[20] Thus, in addition to the orientalist underpinnings in the resettlement process itself, orientalist biases in law and media also aggravated state-based surveillance and mutual suspicion among refugees in the diaspora.

Hussein would later tell me that his job of "cultural advising" works in both directions in the United States: he helps Iraqis adjust to life in the United States, but he also helps Americans adjust to Iraqis in their cities. Over time, he hopes that seeing Iraqis on the streets will be "a normal thing" for people in Worcester. Much like he had as a Terp in Iraq, he sets out to humanize Iraqis for Americans—perhaps talking back to

20. Iraqi American Celia Shallal has observed: "Diaspora politics get me down. . . . So-called progressive American publications foster more damage; they often regurgitate Orientalist frameworks . . . images of charred bodies, men holding guns, and oversexualized identities thrust upon men and women are ubiquitous" (Al-Ali and Al-Najjar 2013, 144).

the culturally essentializing tendencies in American public discourse. Yet, it was similar tendencies within the refugee resettlement process that granted young men like him such authority, and it was emergent patriarchal regimes that enabled him to wield it. If and when he resists American discursive structures that essentialize Iraqis or Iraqi discursive structures that naturalize patriarchal control, it would be as if he enacted those structures to some degree.

Hussein asserts cultural belonging in the United States in and through his assumption of authority as an Iraqi American in the US refugee resettlement infrastructure, taking an assimilationist approach. In this capacity, he claims cultural belonging in part as a gatekeeper of state benefits and broker of Iraqis' acculturation. In response to the pressure Iraqi American caseworkers exert, certain other Iraqis in the United States, such as Tamara, make claims of cultural belonging as refugees, who survive despite and not because of state help and who insulate themselves from both the US state and the Iraqi diaspora.

Iraqis' experience of cultural citizenship in the United States is mediated by US constructions of Iraqi culture and by the translation (or invention) of Iraqi cultural dynamics in the United States, against the backdrop of neoliberal economic imperatives and foreign wars fought in the name of "freedom." As Talal Asad (2003) and Elizabeth Povinelli (2002) show, the seemingly paradoxical forces of liberal individuation and cultural difference fit hand-in-glove within prevailing late-liberal "multicultural" frameworks of citizenship. Under the vision of multiculturalism, subjects learn to be "different" within liberal structures of commonality, wherein the state administers and governs the boundaries of "difference."

In *Buddha Is Hiding*, Aihwa Ong observes a "clash" between Cambodian cultures and cosmologies and market individualism. She concludes that "Khmer-Buddhist ethos seemed to have become irrelevant; for the young especially, Buddha appeared to be hiding" (2003, 281). By contrast, in the case of Iraqi refugees immigrating to the United States after the "culture turn" in the war on terror, culture is not "hiding" but is acutely present in the resettlement process. Iraqi culture, in this sense, is a product of Iraqi interpreters' translation and American officials' orientalist orientations. Iraqis' cultural citizenship in the United States is now somewhat beholden to American constructs of Iraqi culture. Within that cultural construct, Iraqi men have been empowered to speak for the Iraqi people and the US state in a way that women have not, granting them a privileged position for laying claim to cultural citizenship. In parastate positions, men like Hussein govern other Iraqis' claims of belonging in and through making their own claims of cultural citizenship. In response, women devise strategies of their own, sometimes rebuking Iraqi protection or US government "help."

6

Inside the Refugee Network and across Borders

When I dropped Abbas at South Station in Boston to board the bus to JFK Airport, he told me, "Don't worry, I'll be back." He was headed to Baghdad to spend a month with his family. The joke among our group of friends was that Abbas was going to Iraq to marry his secret girlfriend. Husham— for whom Abbas served as a sponsor—said laughingly to Abbas at dinner the night before, "Have a nice life, buddy." He later told me he was only half-kidding: the easiest thing in the world was to lose touch with people in the refugee network. Abbas insisted with a smirk that he was going to see his mother and that he would return to Boston as planned. Husham turned to me and said, "Okay, well then, I promise you he's coming back with a big carry-on."

A month later, Abbas called me from JFK asking me to pick him up at South Station in a few hours. As I stopped the car at the curb outside the station, he tapped a gold wedding ring on the passenger window, grinning. I exclaimed, "Husham was right!" He told me excitedly that his wife's name was Noor. She was an old friend of the family and had just graduated from university; he would move back to join her in Baghdad in a few months' time. Several months later, on the eve of Abbas's return to Baghdad to begin a new life with his wife, our group of friends again gathered for dinner. Like many going-away parties I attended, this one was filled with more uncertainty than finality. Abbas told us again, "Don't worry, I'll be back." He planned on returning to the United States for several months each year to maintain his green card and earn money doing temporary work. Husham again said, "Have a nice life!" I could not guess which way Abbas would go. I had heard the equivalent of "Don't worry, I'll be back" from many members of the refugee network whom I would never see again. But I had also said goodbye to friends who told me they would stay in Baghdad forever (and others who were moving permanently to another state), who would later call me from the bus station in Boston out of the blue, asking for a ride.

The network of former interpreters in Boston was defined by this itinerancy, impermanence, and uncertainty. Because former interpreters generally immigrate alone and due to the complex relationships among them, this pocket of the Iraq War diaspora is less of an established community than a shifting network. With their migration back to Iraq or to other regions in the United States, the network appeared at times more like a revolving door. At the same time that these young men and women maintain relationships and commitments in Iraq and elsewhere, they also develop attachments in New England. Jobs, neighborhoods, friends, and partners tie them to Boston and its environs. What distinguishes this refugee network was that these connections could be made and left in the blink of an eye.

As an assemblage of individuals apart from their families, the network of former interpreters is distinct from much of the wider Middle Eastern diaspora in the United States as well as from other resettled refugee communities. While the wider Middle Eastern diaspora and other resettled refugee communities are equally defined by transnational commitments and identities, a novel form of transnational citizenship emerges out of former Iraqi interpreters' itinerancy. Especially against the backdrop of an occupation in which interpreters directly participated, what it meant to be an individual abroad had a very different meaning—and differed for men and women. With a greater precedent for men migrating independently, young men's itinerancy was more easily understood in terms of economic migration than young women's in the Iraqi diaspora. Historical precedent shapes young men's practice of transnational citizenship as a practice of temporary work abroad. Single young women's practice of transnational citizenship, on the other hand, reflects a more permanent resettlement in the United States and revolves around the maintenance of transnational family ties and obligations from afar.

Though they might appear at odds, the strategies of cultural citizenship that interpreters developed vis-à-vis the US state—as Iraqi Americans and as refugees—and the transnational citizenship practices they put to use vis-à-vis Iraq and the Iraqi diaspora are interrelated. While young men more widely identify as binational, potentially returning to Iraq, women identify as US-based Iraqi refugees. Even as these interpreters pursue assimilationist strategies in the United States, young men imagine futures in Iraq more readily than do Iraqi women. While they endeavor to insulate themselves from Iraqi authorities in the US state and the diaspora more broadly, young women in this network generally view their presence in the US-based Iraqi diaspora to be permanent. Simply put, many Iraqi women do not feel they have a long-term future in Iraq to which they might return. The prospect of returning to Iraq to marry is "impossible," as Meena had told me. "You don't recover from working for US Forces and living in the US if you are a woman," she said. Meena's connection with Iraq took the form of temporary visits, financial support, and long-distance caretaking for family members there.

Meena moved to Texas to "start over again" around the same time that Abbas moved back to Baghdad to enjoy his new family. I grew to communicate less and less frequently with her, aside from occasional messages from Texas and care packages of Middle Eastern sweets I would receive with the address of a Baghdad shop on the wrapper (presumably from her last visit home). Tamara would stay in Boston. She was buried in her graduate studies, however, and I rarely saw her. Mohammed or "Mo" would also move back to Iraq, and would marry shortly thereafter. Hussein remains in the United States but speaks seriously about returning to Iraq—and even about returning to work in the Ministry of Public Works (but, he says, perhaps as a minister rather than an interpreter). Hiba and Tariq remain in the United States, although Tariq has taken a job as an intelligence analyst on a military base in another state and Hiba stays in the suburbs of Boston, aside from occasional trips to Baghdad. Tariq has divorced his second, secret wife, and Hiba gave birth to twins. Despite her terrible experience as a sponsor to Frank, she agreed to be the sponsor to two other recently arrived Iraqis, one former colleague of Tariq's at Titan, a young woman, and her distant cousin, a young man, who also worked as an interpreter.

In this chapter, I juxtapose these unique lived experiences of transnationalism to the wider Middle Eastern diaspora, on the one hand, and to other resettled refugee communities on the other. I pick up with Hiba, examining her experiences of the Iraqi sponsorship network, her evolving connection with Iraq, and the diverging itineraries of the three refugees for whom she served as a sponsor. Finally, I return to Abbas's case, as he straddles Boston and Baghdad—before discussing more broadly how these individuals' transnational practices disrupt contemporary theorizations of transnationalism.

Middle Eastern Diaspora or Refugee Enclave?

That this refugee network is characterized by its youthfulness is not out of keeping with wider Arab and Muslim immigrant populations in the United States. Moustafa Bayoumi observes of first-generation Arab and Muslim immigrant communities: "Arab and Muslim Americans are younger than the general population. Twenty-one percent of the American public is between eighteen and thirty years of age, but 30 percent of American Muslims are. The median age of Arab Americans is twenty-one, compared to thirty-five for the whole of the United States" (2008 7). What distinguishes this refugee network from other Arab and Muslim immigrant communities is that while the network is part of a wider wave of refugees, its members are single young men and women who have immigrated alone and are usually strangers to one another. The Middle Eastern diaspora in New England contains large numbers of refugees (from Palestine, Lebanon, and elsewhere) as well as single young adults (students and professionals), but rarely are those single young adults refugees, nor are those refugees single individuals who have immigrated alone. In this sense, Iraqi former interpreters represent a unique position in the Middle East diaspora in Boston, and in the Northeastern United States more generally.

Former interpreters in the Boston area interact with the wider Middle Eastern diaspora on a limited basis and with fellow Iraqis even less. Most commonly, the young men and women I encountered in this refugee network report interacting with non-Iraqi twenty- and thirty-somethings who are in Boston working or attending university. Given the precedent of singles' migration for professional or educational purposes in the Boston-based diaspora, network members sometimes identify themselves as students or professionals. Whether or not they were attending classes or on a professional path, this was an aspirational identity with which Iraqis in the refugee network identified. Still, the experiences of these young Iraqis is considerably different from other single young adults in the area because of the conditions under which they left Iraq and the uncertainty of their future trajectories.

This refugee network's experience in Boston was also distinct from other refugee populations from Asia, Africa, and Latin America that settled in the region. While not without their own internal fractures and hierarchies, several refugee populations in New England have formed enclaves in cities and towns with strong community organizations and public profiles. Iraqi refugees have not as yet formed any comparable regional enclaves or communities. Further, because most young Iraqis do not meet the usual profile of a refugee—in their class and educational backgrounds, among other things—Iraqi interpreters have not followed the course of most refugee populations in the United States. We see this most dramatically in their unfolding plans to return to Iraq. As with most members of refugee groups, Iraqi interpreters live distinctly transnational lives. Unlike many other refugee populations, however, Iraqi refugees' strategies of transnational citizenship consist of frequent trips home and, for some, future plans of returning to Iraq.

Diasporas of Empire

Early Arab immigrants from Lebanon and Syria[1] were perceived as a "model minority" in their entrepreneurial initiative and assimilation into

---

1. Immigration from the Middle East to the United States has been a longstanding phenomenon, dating back to the late nineteenth and early twentieth centuries. A history

middle-class white America (Jamal and Naber 2008; Naber 2012).[2] These US-based Arab populations were part of a global diaspora that grew over the twentieth century, forming a transnational circuit. Levant Arab populations grew to be defined by their mobility and globality. By the twentieth century, for example, there were more Lebanese outside Lebanon than inside the country. The diaspora emerged as a way of life in many Middle Eastern communities.[3] For some life outside the Middle East was viewed as permanent, and for others it was a temporary arrangement, but with home and family spanning multiple continents, transnationalism became a normative mode of being.

As scholars like James Clifford have shown in his seminal contributions to scholarship on diaspora, diasporic identity changes as historical conditions shift.[4] With decolonization, postcolonial contests, and the formation of Israel, an increasing portion of Middle East migration was involuntary, and often resulted from wars in which the United States was directly or indirectly involved. Thus the profile of Middle Eastern diasporas in the United States changed into what Nadine Naber has called a "diaspora of empire." Palestinians, Iraqis, and Lebanese, among other populations, formed diasporic communities whose identities were tied to their embattled situations of exile, as Edward Said has powerfully captured in his 1979 essay "Reflections on Exile" (Said 2000).

Over the 1970s, 1980s, and 1990s, Arab Americans grew to be seen as a "problem minority" in the United States (Naber 2012, 36). Due to the political handling and media coverage of the Israeli-Palestinian conflict, the US-Arab oil crisis in the 1970s, and the rise of socialist Arab

---

of Arab migration to the United States can be found in Suleiman's *Arabs in America* (1999); for contemporary discussions of the Middle East diaspora see Shohat and Alsultany's *Between the Middle East and the Americas* (2013).

2. For more on race and class dynamics of early Arab and Middle Eastern immigrants, see Gualtieri (2001) and Jamal and Naber (2008).

3. Hourani's *The Lebanese and the World: A Century of Emigration* (1993) is a definitive text on Lebanese migration.

4. See James Clifford's "Diasporas" (1994). Also, an excellent summary of this literature is Braziel and Mannur's *Theorizing Diaspora* (2003).

governments (followed by Islamist governments), American perceptions of Arabs transformed radically in this time period. Many US-based Arabs found themselves in a country whose foreign policies toward their home countries struck them as deeply unjust. Some, especially young people and second-generation Arab Americans, felt torn between cultural pressures in the Arab diaspora (as well as political commitments in the Middle East) and life in the United States. After 9/11, the already scrutinized Arab communities of the United States found themselves under siege.[5] Membership in the diaspora of empire became more fraught than ever.

As a part of the larger diaspora of empire, the Iraqi diaspora has grown over past decades to contain nearly 150,000 people across the United States. Recent Iraq War refugees represent a new "layer" to the sizable Iraqi diaspora, to use Nadje Al-Ali's phrase (2013, xxxi). Iraqi Rashad Salim writes, "Since the mid-twentieth century Iraq has experienced successive waves of demographic dispersal, exile, and (forced) emigration," (2013, 237). The conditions under which each wave of forced migration occurred in Iraq have dynamically shaped how each diasporic "layer" constitutes itself in the diaspora of empire. For example, the relationship between earlier Gulf War refugees—including Shi'a refugees of the Ba'th's post-intifada retaliatory campaign, upper-middle-class or elite professionals, and creative intellectuals—and the new wave of refugees, with large numbers of US allies and a greater portion of middle-class Iraqis, is far from straightforward. Members of the refugee network describe feeling a sense of marginalization in the diaspora—even, if not especially, from earlier waves of Iraqi refugees. Just as important as their perceived political profile, the fact that members of the refugee network immigrated alone, rather than with whole family units, made the former interpreters feel suspect. Because they came apart from a family to ground and orient them in the diaspora, they did not fit the mold. Hussein observes that older, established Iraqi refugee communities want "little to do with" newly arriving Iraqi refugees.

5. See Cainkar's *Homeland Insecurity* (2009) and Haddad's *Not Quite American?* (2004).

As for their distinctive political profile in the diaspora, interpreter network members actually share the wider diaspora of empire's experiences of ambivalence about US government policy, despite their common fear of being perceived as apologists for US militarism. That this pocket of the diaspora is uniquely enmeshed in the US state, with many of its members continuing to work for the US state in some way, is evident—not least to the surrounding Iraqi refugee community. Network members' professional alliance with the US state and their perceived political views are the cause for their extreme caution vis-à-vis the larger Arab and Middle Eastern diasporas. For Max, the imagined indignation of other Arabs upon learning that he worked for US Forces kept him from even setting foot in an Arab café or market. My interlocutors took measures like Max's—sometimes more drastic—to conceal their work with US Forces and the conditions of their flight from Iraq. Nevertheless, the fact that Iraqi interpreters were part of a wave of Iraqi refugee migration was unmistakable in the view of the wider diaspora.

Said described contemporary situations of Palestinian displacement, and Middle Eastern displacements more broadly, as a "generalized condition of homelessness," leading to novel configurations of diasporic identity (1979, 18). James Ferguson and Akhil Gupta, among others, have broadened Said's analysis to theorize "deterritorialization" as a way of life for a wide array of translational actors. In their analysis, "identities are increasingly coming to be, if not wholly deterritorialized, at least differently territorialized. Refugees, migrants, displaced and stateless people—these are perhaps the first to live out these realities in their most complete form, but the problem is more general" (1992, 68). While enmeshed in larger questions of deterritorialization, the specificity of displacement experiences in the diaspora of empire must be underscored. In the post-9/11 era, the transnational ties that bind individuals in the diaspora to their home countries are highly policed. Further, those transnational ties come with complex personal "moral-political" negotiations. Much is written about the structural forces of empire—its military, economic, and political iterations—that have called diasporas into being. I agree with Aihwa Ong's observation, however, that what too often remains missing from discussions of diaspora are the intimate and personal disciplinary structures that govern diasporic subjects' lives and the moral-political dilemmas they face in every experience of those larger structural forces.[6] Young Iraqis' moral-political dilemmas of diaspora in the particular historical moment of "war on terror" America reveal themselves in turn as they navigate life in the Boston area, a region where other refugee communities have settled at different historical periods, facing distinct moral-political dilemmas.

Refugee Zones

New England has been a refugee resettlement zone for refugees of the Vietnam-era conflicts—especially Cambodian refugees—as well as other refugee populations since the resettlement program began in earnest in 1980. Due to the high cost of living in the Boston metropolitan area, refugees have begun resettling—both by choice and as a matter of policy—in mid-sized cities with more affordable housing options and greater employment opportunities in the region. One of the biggest and most reputable refugee agencies, the International Rescue Commission, closed its doors in Boston in 2009 because it felt it could no longer responsibly bring refugees to such an expensive city with dwindling resettlement funds. Today, dense refugee communities have sprung up in smaller cities and suburbs as a result of more strategic refugee resettlement and refugees' secondary migration to more affordable areas around the United States.[7]

Some of the refugee communities that have grown deep roots in the region over the past decades include Cambodians, Somalis, and Liberians. Despite US resettlement policies that have sought to settle refugees

6. Ong writes that "missing from these accounts [of diaspora] are discussions of how the disciplining structures—of family, community, work, travel, and nation—condition, shape, divert, and transform such subjects and their practices and produce . . . moral-political dilemmas" (1999, 14).

7. For more on resettlement strategies and outcomes in US urban areas, see Singer and Wilson's 2006 report for the Brookings Institution: "From 'There' to 'Here': Refugee Resettlement in Metropolitan America."

broadly across the United States to avoid "unassimilated" pockets, many refugee communities have grown into established "enclaves." For example, Cambodians in Lowell, Massachusetts, making up over 10 percent of the city's population, represent the largest concentration of Cambodian refugees in the United States.[8] This population has formed mutual assistance organizations and community organizations in several Lowell neighborhoods, becoming a powerful presence in the city. Similarly, thousands of Somali refugees have landed in Lewiston, Maine, and large numbers of Liberian refugees in Providence, Rhode Island, forming dense communities. Though not without internal generational, gender, and class fissures, these populations have developed robust communities with equally strong ties to the region.

Though still a recent population in New England, Iraqi refugees already display patterns of resettlement that differ considerably from other refugee populations in New England in several important respects. The experience of Iraqi interpreters is especially unique. First, due to the lack of cohesion and the solitary migration of many Iraqi refugees, no such enclaves as seen in Lowell or Lewiston have emerged among Iraqis. Further, because of a common language and cultural background with other Arab communities, some Iraqis have begun participating in other Middle Eastern communities rather than forging relationships with fellow Iraqis, particularly given the ongoing conflict in Iraq and climate of suspicion in many corners of the diaspora.

Second, Iraqi refugees have educational and class backgrounds distinct from most refugee populations with which resettlement agencies work, raising new challenges in the resettlement process. While many South Asian and African refugees have received job training to assume jobs in the industrial or service sectors, many Iraqis seek work in a specific professional field (though often unsuccessfully). As a result, Iraqi refugees often follow individualized tracks and move around looking for work or educational opportunities rather than settling in dense enclave

8. Background on Cambodian refugees in Eastern Massachusetts can be found in Smith-Hefiner's *Khmer-American* (1999).

communities. Third, unlike most other refugees, many Iraqis return to Iraq quite frequently, and some wish to move back to Iraq one day.

Highly individualized and itinerant lives distinguish Iraqi interpreters from many other refugee communities in New England. Members of the refugee network practice a form of transnationalism that stands apart from other refugee communities in their frequently binational lives and futures. Sunaina Maira has argued that transnational identities are not equally available to all immigrant communities in the United States: certain communities' assertions of transnational identities, especially global Muslim identifications, are perceived as a danger in the current political climate (2009). Etienne Balibar has similarly explored how transnational configurations are both a product of globalization and at times perceived threats to prevailing global hegemonies (2009).[9] In response, Iraqi interpreters have developed strategies of transnational citizenship—that is, claims of belonging to multiple, intersecting, or competing national bodies—that are situated and gendered, as we will explore further in the cases of Hiba and Abbas.

Hiba: From "Single Woman" to Perennial Sponsor

As a sponsor to three different Iraqi interpreters, Hiba grew rather accustomed to taking perfect strangers into her home. Several months before I first met her, Hiba had hosted her first refugee: a good friend of her husband named Frank. As discussed in chapter 4, Frank had worked as an interpreter with Tariq in Iraq; Tariq had asked Hiba to do him this favor. Hiba agreed to let Frank live in the couple's second bedroom "like a brother" while Tariq was on deployment. They would tell anyone who asked that Frank was Hiba's cousin. Everyone agreed that this situation, while unconventional, could be advantageous in that Hiba would no longer be viewed by the refugee network as a "single woman"—she now had

9. Etienne's *We the People of Europe?* (2009) is among the best theorization of transnational citizenship. Critical summaries of transnational citizenship scholarship can be found in Portes, Guarnizo, and Landolt (1999) and Castells and Davidson (2000).

family, if fictive family.[10] After several weeks, Frank got his own apartment in the same quadraplex building, and shortly after that Frank's parents joined him in the United States from Iraq. Hiba heard from a woman at the refugee agency that Frank had been speaking badly of her to other Iraqis and then, one day, Frank's mother confronted her in front of the apartment building. Hiba recalls: "One day I was getting out of my car and she [Frank's mother] started talking under her breath. I was respectful. I said: 'Is everything all right?' Then she called me . . . ugly words. The worst thing is that they never explained themselves. They just began to hate me."

It seemed to Hiba that Frank's mother began to resent her for the very thing that she had expressed great appreciation for earlier: that Hiba had taken in her son while she was still in Iraq. Hiba notes, "That is really not a usual thing in our culture, to take in a stranger—I did not know his family. But we are in a different country. He is my husband's friend. What was I supposed to do?" Perhaps, Hiba pondered, they believed that she had not acted like a "good" Iraqi girl in doing this. Maybe, she speculated, some rumors had started about Frank staying with Hiba, and the family felt they needed to protect their reputation by ruining hers. The tension grew unbearable and she decided to visit her family in Basrah. She stayed in Iraq for many months, and several days after she returned to her Boston apartment, she found a letter in her mailbox telling her that she had been evicted.

Frank's family had bought the entire apartment building. He allowed all of the other tenants to remain in their apartments except for Hiba: "He evicted me in the middle of winter, without my husband to help me move. I called the police, but they couldn't help me. I just didn't understand it, I helped him like a brother." Due to this experience, Hiba struggles with the limits of felt loyalty and perceived transgression. She grapples with her decision to open her home to Frank as an act of national loyalty ("We are all Iraqis") and as an act of cultural betrayal ("This is really not a usual thing in our culture, to take in a stranger—I don't know his family").

10. Though married, Hiba was widely viewed as "alone" (*wahdaha*) because her husband lived overseas and she had no other family nearby.

Over tea, I sat down with Frank and his mother. They knew that I was Hiba's friend, and while we would not discuss their falling-out explicitly, it was clearly on everyone's mind. Frank told me that he had begun to doubt the judgment of men who joined the US Army—especially those who left their wives alone: "09 Limas [linguists] in the Army aren't really soldiers. Okay, they have a rank, but they don't get any of the power that real army men have. They can't give orders. They don't get benefits. They are just temporary tools, like dogs. Even dogs have ranks in the military. The bomb sniffers. They have ranks, sergeant or staff sergeant. Did you know that?" Frank continued by asking rhetorically why anyone would leave his wife alone to take such a job. It is not right, he asserted vehemently, for women to live apart from their husbands, especially in a "foreign place" like America. Calling linguists "temporary tools, like dogs" conveys clear contempt directed at Tariq, and decrying single women in the diaspora plainly identifies Hiba's living alone as "wrong." Frank's mother, who was busy—almost frenetic—serving food, refilling tea, wiping down the kitchen counter—paused and interjected in Arabic: "Iraqi culture is beautiful. But people forget." Frank would later return to Iraq as a CAT 2 interpreter in the US Embassy in Baghdad—one of the best-paid civilian interpreting jobs available. After Hiba moved out, she never saw Frank or his family again.

Hiba found a small apartment in another suburb, Revere. Far from anyone she knew, she painted, furnished, and landscaped the apartment with the intention of staying for a while. When Tariq returned from his deployment and revealed the news of his second wife, Hiba bought a one-way plane ticket to Iraq, where she stayed for several months. We talked over Skype frequently while she was away. She was torn about her next move. On the one hand, she felt that she could not stay in Iraq. As she put it, "Life is not easy as a divorced woman." Further, she knew that after moving away to the United States as a married woman and then returning single, she would be "questionable." She felt suffocated by the idea of living in a neighborhood where everyone knew everything about her. But, on the other hand, she could not fully imagine what her life would be like in the United States. She could go back to school for a graduate degree, or find a good job; but these things would not come easily.

Eventually, she decided to return to the United States—come what may. After her decision, Tariq made one of his own: he divorced his second wife and opted to settle down in Revere for good. The couple took what they called a "honeymoon" to Montreal and decided to try and start again. Hiba became pregnant with twins. Tariq bought a minivan with vanity license plates that had both Iraqi and American flags on it. Then, Tariq moved away again, to work as an intelligence analyst at a military base in Arizona. Hiba was alone once more, and this time she was pregnant.

When Hiba was seven months pregnant, she hosted another refugee. Ahmed was her distant cousin and, at twenty-five years old, seemed more like a teenager to Hiba. He rarely came out of his bedroom, except to eat food that Hiba cooked. She trusted that he would not spoil her name as Frank had, but she also was not entirely happy with the situation. When she went into labor a month early with her husband away, Ahmed drove her to the hospital. He did not stay for the delivery. Hiba texted me right before going into an emergency C-section in the middle of the night: "Pray for me. I'm alone here." When I reached the hospital early in the morning, the twin baby girls were in the intensive care unit. She told me that she had not pictured her birth to be like this: without her mother or sisters. I sympathized and asked her if she wished she had stayed in Iraq. She said, "No, Madeline. I couldn't have stayed in Iraq. This is my life now." I took her words "This is my life now" to refer to a living situation in which she wavered between being alone and sponsoring strangers in her home, now with two babies. As the babies grew stronger over the following days, Tariq (still in Arizona) asked me over the phone to brainstorm names that "sounded" both Arab and American.

Ahmed returned to Iraq within six months of arriving in the United States. But one day, months later, he called Hiba from the bus station in Boston out of the blue saying he was back. He would stay only a few months and would leave again—this time, he said, to get married. Hiba did not believe he would return to the United States again. "It is different for men. He can move to a new area in Baghdad and start again. If I did that, people would ask: Where is your family?" Hiba asserts a double standard for women and men in starting over. While she feels she would be "questionable" in her hometown, and people would ask "Where is your family?" in another town, Ahmed can more easily start again in Iraq.

Most recently, Hiba has served as a sponsor for a young woman who worked as an interpreter for the Transition Team unit in which Tariq was formerly a soldier. Anwar was bubbly and cheerful; she helped with Hiba's daughters and was a real friend to Hiba. But there was also something mysterious about her. Hiba told me that she exercised obsessively at the gym. When Hiba asked her why she was so concerned about fitness—thinking that perhaps she had a boyfriend she had not told Hiba about—Anwar told her that she was preparing to enlist in the US Air Force. Hiba told me: "And people say I am crazy!"

Hiba did not disapprove of Anwar's decision exactly, but she also admitted that she could not fully understand it. She acknowledged that Anwar, like all Iraqi women, confronted an impossible challenge in trying to uphold the ideal of the "good Iraqi girl" in the United States. But it seemed like Anwar was rejecting the gendered ideal altogether. As we spoke more about it, Hiba reflected that, just as she felt that her only option was to start life over again in the United States, maybe Anwar was doing the same thing in her own way.

Anwar asked for my help arranging a meeting with a recruitment officer. At the meeting, the young recruitment officer told her she would have to pass the ASVAB within the next six months, as she was approaching twenty-seven—the age limit for enlistment. On the way home from the meeting, Anwar asked to stop at a bookstore. She bought an ASVAB study guide. She thanked me profusely and asked me not to mention a thing about our meeting to anyone except Hiba. After I dropped her off, I would never see her again. Several days later, Hiba told me, Anwar took a bus to New York and moved in with a friend who lived there. Hiba too lost touch with Anwar. Neither of us knows if she successfully enlisted.

Even after being evicted by onetime friends, living for years without any family nearby, and giving birth all alone, Hiba feels that living in the United States is her only option. After living in the United States and as a wife to a US soldier, she felt it would be impossible to start over in Iraq. She and Anwar—in very different ways—both had to begin again in the

United States. This was not, however, the case for young men like Ahmed, whom Hiba believed could move to a new area in Iraq and start a new life. Hiba now says she is grateful for all of the adversity: she is stronger than she ever knew she could be. She also has had a renewal of faith, saying, "Being all alone can make you feel very close to God." She misses her family—especially around holidays—but she has begun volunteering at an Islamic school, where she hopes to send her daughters one day. When I asked her if there were other Iraqis there, she said with a faint smile, "I hope not." Even if there are, she tells me, she is less afraid of what people could say about her: she has already been called the worst things possible. She added, "Actually, I'd like to work with the Iraqi girls"—to play some part in raising them to be strong women just like her own daughters. She has recently begun wearing a headscarf—not to appease anyone or "make a statement," she tells me, but because it makes her feel connected to both her faith and her cultural heritage. In contrast to Tamara, who experienced a "de-hijabing" of sorts by her male caseworker amid her efforts to balance imperatives of work and pressures to be a "good Iraqi girl," Hiba has made the choice to wear the hijab as she navigates feelings of diasporic detachment and cultural and religious attachments. She tells me she had been cursed by a young man at the grocery, and has noticed people she has known for some time treating her differently. She does not give much concern to these incidents, saying, "I am not American and I never will be American. But I have my life here. I am okay with that."

Hiba continues to visit Iraq periodically; her parents have also visited her in Massachusetts for several months.[11] She wants her daughters to speak and read Arabic fluently and to learn to cook Iraqi food. One day as she cooed her daughters to sleep, she joked about sending them to Iraq for their teenage years. When I asked if there was any grain of truth in the joke, she said, "No, no, not really. I just know how hard it is to be an Iraqi girl here." But, she elaborated, she knew that conflicting cultural pressures

---

11. Her father needed eye surgery, and Hiba insisted he come to the United States for it.

and possible gossip was somewhat unavoidable in the Iraqi diaspora. She could not shield her daughters from it; all she could do was raise them to be strong.

While Iraq remains a central part of her life, Hiba continues to keep some distance from other Iraqis. Her strategy for coping with the challenges she faces in the diaspora is to assert her own strength and raise strong daughters. When her children are a little older, Hiba hopes to begin working full-time at the Islamic school to be a role model for young Muslim girls in the United States. Hiba identifies as an Iraqi refugee—never quite American. Yet, she is more firmly rooted in the United States than many young men in the refugee network. Unlike for many of these young men, who plan their future lives around a return to Iraq, Hiba's practice of transnational citizenship paradoxically only roots her more and more in Boston. Her visits home only remind her of the challenges she would face if she moved home. Her cultural investments in both work and family in Boston solidify her attachment to the United States, while she keeps the US-based Iraqi community at a distance.

Abbas: Husband and "New Man"

Abbas and Husham—on-again-off-again friends—lived in a large five-bedroom apartment with a revolving door of other roommates. Abbas and Husham themselves took turns moving out—usually because of frustrations with the other. I first met Abbas at a Ramadan dinner during one of the periods in which he had technically "moved out," out of protest, though he came to the apartment for dinner. After that dinner, when he had played the *Sexy Female Interpreters!* YouTube video for me, he moved back into the apartment within a couple of days. The apartment was in a large, undermaintained complex with an absentee landlord. According to Abbas, all of the apartments were rented out to immigrants or refugees, who, in his view, could not "complain" about the disrepair of the building.

At various times, Abbas and Husham had Syrian, Iranian, Guatemalan, Salvadoran, and Nigerian male roommates. At different points, Husham and Abbas also were joined by Iraqi roommates. Husham had "vouched" for one of the Iraqis, and Abbas for the other. Both arrangements ended badly. In one, the new roommate refused to pay rent, did not clean up after himself, and used other people's food and property. Abbas and Husham called the landlord and then the police in hopes of evicting him, but they could not help. Finally, they arranged a deal for the roommate to move into another Iraqi man's apartment for lesser rent, strongly encouraging him to take it. On the second occasion, Abbas reported that the problems revolved around their Iraqi roommate's "lifestyle" (by which he meant dating and drinking). When the roommate refused to leave, they moved his belongings onto the sidewalk.

Abbas admits that neither of these issues alone warranted such dramatic actions. But when living in close quarters with other refugees of the Iraq War, issues around money and "lifestyle" take on a new valence. They become laden with significance surrounding Iraqiness and Americanness. In the one case, Abbas felt that the slovenly roommate had not accepted an "American way of life" and refused to realize that he had a responsibility to take care of himself. In the other case, by contrast, Abbas seemed to believe that his "wild" roommate had lost his Iraqi sense of respect and respectability.

Difficulties with roommates were the source of Abbas and Husham's most serious conflicts. But the friends also had internal conflicts of their own. Husham was dating an Iraqi woman of whom Abbas did not approve. Husham felt that Abbas did not share vital information on potential job opportunities from which he could benefit. And, most troublingly, the two men had profoundly diverging political views—especially relating to Iraq's new government. Abbas accepted Prime Minister Nouri Al Maliki's government; Husham deeply opposed it. Every time that Husham went to the bathroom, he would say, "I am going to the Maliki." This enraged Abbas. After every fight, the two would make up. Once when both vented to me so furiously on the phone, I thought their relationship's resiliency had found its limit. But within weeks of every confrontation, they decided to become roommates again. Even if they were not the closest of confidants, they could rely on each other more than anyone else in the Iraqi diaspora.

Over the years that I knew them, the two began to drift apart—a slow but more permanent distance than brought about by their previous bouts. Abbas began talking about going back to Iraq. Husham, reading between the lines, anticipated that Abbas was contemplating getting married and moving back for good. According to Abbas, Husham began to recount every single car bomb or kidnapping transpiring in Iraq in front of Abbas. Abbas was incensed by his insensitivity. He said, "My whole family is still there—so is yours," interpreting Husham's behavior as a way of coping with the guilt he felt for not returning to Iraq himself.

Abbas began speaking about returning to Iraq for a visit a full year before he purchased a plane ticket. He had been promoted at one of his jobs and had settled into a work schedule that allowed him to finally save money. He had saved enough in fact to send his mother on *hajj* (pilgrimage to Mecca). He did not want to risk leaving his job—and he was just beginning to make real friends in the United States. At a cookout with colleagues from his hospital job, which I joined, he regaled the crowd with stories about his time with the US military, much as he had the first time I met him over our Ramadan dinner. He told me that he finally felt at home in the United States, just as he began to make plans to visit Iraq.

Then tragedy in his apartment complex deeply impacted Abbas and accelerated his plans to travel home. One of his roommates, Luis, who was an undocumented worker from Guatemala in his forties, had died of a heart attack in their shared apartment. Luis had been alone in his bedroom and was not discovered until Abbas found him many hours—maybe a day—after he was thought to have died. Abbas would tell me that Luis, much like Abbas and Husham, was in the United States earning for his family, or "soldiering," as Luis had called it. Sorting through Luis's personal effects to find his family's contact information, he found a few thousand dollars in cash and an ID that listed "Marco" as Luis's real name. Abbas began to wonder if Luis ever knew his real name was not in fact "Abbas." This was the pseudonym he developed working for US Forces that he kept for his protection while living in the United States.

For weeks Abbas had nightmares about dying in the United States and his family never finding out. He expressed doubts that Luis had been in the United States to help his family at all; posthumously he began to consider Luis a selfish man who left his family alone in Guatemala, speculating that he spent most of his earnings on alcohol, gambling, and women. But then again, Abbas asked me one day, "How am I different?" For four years, he had been earning money with the intention of sending enough money to his family in Iraq to build a new house; in reality he found he was earning just enough to eke out a living in Boston and send a few hundred dollars home now and then. He told me he was beginning to have deep regrets about leaving his family to come to the United States at all. Much like men's military soldiering on the warfront in Iraq—or his fellow interpreters who leave family to fulfill a broader sense of filial duty—Abbas's economic "soldiering" in the United States meant that, in order to help his family, he actually had to leave his family. And now Abbas questioned how much "help" he could provide from afar: "Helping my family by leaving my family? It doesn't make sense."

A few weeks after Luis's death, Abbas had an upsetting dispute with his landlord, who insisted that Abbas and his other remaining roommate cover Luis's rent while they looked for a roommate to replace Luis. He was shocked: "A man has died, I told him, and all you care about is money?" He called the police. The police did not listen to him, concluding simply that they could not help him because the lease was "under the table." Abbas had wanted to say to the police: "You want to see under the table? Shady business? Look at the American war in Iraq."

As it happened, in this period he began having nightmares about the war in Iraq again, vivid and bloody nightmares of a sort he had not had in years. He told me about his visions of contracted laborers from Sri Lanka, Peru, and Uganda working for Halliburton and KBR—many of whom he imagined were undocumented—dying in Iraq. One vision was so powerful that he began to believe it was real: the image of undocumented workers being thrown into the old, manmade lakes Saddam Hussein kept for fishing, where their bodies would slowly decompose, eaten by the fish. Abbas's experience of "peacetime" America—where landlords shake him down for his dead roommate's rent and police wash their hands of the situation—made him see the Iraq War in a new way. He had long opposed the way that the United States handled the war, but he had still personally invested some hope in rebuilding Iraq. After several years of living in the United States, earning just enough from his multiple jobs to live, and upon seeing another man die of economic "soldiering" in the United States, Abbas started to feel that "America is only about money."

Abbas began to fundamentally doubt the strategy that he, and so many other interpreters, had lived by for years as an interpreter and now as an immigrant in the United States: to support one's family by living apart from family. Abruptly he decided to return for a visit to see the "situation" in Baghdad. While away, Abbas married Noor and made plans to move back home for good after saving a bit more money, filing his taxes, and collecting his things in Boston. He would miss his American friends and some aspects of his American life, but it was time to go home. He wanted to be near family and to start a family of his own. He wanted to return to the familiar sights and sounds of Baghdad. Abbas hoped to find work teaching English in Baghdad, and to return to Boston for a few months a year to work temporarily and maintain his green card.

As planned, eight months after moving back to Baghdad to begin his life with Noor, Abbas returned to Boston. He would stay for two months in Boston and work for the company for which he once worked full-time. He moved back into his old bedroom in the apartment he once shared with Husham and others. From the first week of Abbas's return, it was evident to both Husham and Abbas that any foundation of friendship that they once had was lost. Both men called me with complaints and concerns about the other. Husham told me of Abbas: "He's kind of made it clear that if you go back to Iraq then you're a good person, and if you don't, then you are an American, not Iraqi anymore. That's what he hates to death lately. He thinks we all should go back and marry Iraqi women like he did. Okay, if he thinks that, if he doesn't like America anymore, why is he here in Boston? Red flag!" Husham represents Abbas's view as one in which Iraqi men should go back to Iraq if they are "good people" and real Iraqis. Further, he articulates a suspicion that Abbas does not "like" America, saying dramatically, "Red flag!" When I asked what he meant by "red flag," Husham said: "I just don't like people who don't appreciate this country. I want to move home too, and someday I will, but I am here now. And this country has done a lot for me." Abbas, for his part, felt that Husham had "lost himself" since he last saw him, saying, "It doesn't even feel like I'm talking to an Iraqi anymore." Both men imagine futures in Iraq, but continue to have lives that tie them to Boston. But both also express suspicions about how the other navigates this binational life: Abbas views

Husham as too American, and Husham views Abbas as something like anti-American.

Though navigating the binational life has become another arena for suspicion, what is clear is that Abbas and Husham, unlike Hiba, Meena, or Tamara, could vividly picture permanent futures in Iraq—just as both (despite Husham's allegations about Abbas) had deep commitments to the United States. Abbas strategically identifies as both Iraqi and American, but in his confrontation with Husham, he faces a danger of identifying as "too American or too Iraqi." Husham and other men similarly face this dilemma. Their strategic self-definition as Iraqi Americans represents an attempt to identify as "both/and" rather than "either/or," a situated rejection of the binary thinking of "us" and "them" that has intensified with the war on terror.

Abbas's binational life has not only involved tumultuous visits to the United States, it has also brought about significant challenges for his new family in Baghdad. Abbas found that he and his new wife had divergent expectations of their life together: Noor had hoped to work in a lab at the university from which she had just graduated, but Abbas had hoped she would stay at home. She told him that it was unfair of him to expect her to stay at home if he was spending months each year in the United States. The couple divorced. He wrote telling me that he might return to Boston again sooner than expected; he missed everybody, he told me, and "even Husham," he joked.

Then, in his next message a month later, Abbas informed me that he and Noor had settled their differences and were going to remarry. This time they would have a big wedding, not a simple ceremony as they had before. He had still not been able to find work as an English teacher, but remained hopeful. When I asked him if he felt safe living in his old family home as violence escalated once again in Iraq, he said that he had "no problems at all." He joked that the United States had given him so many grey hairs that he looked like a "new man." With a new wife and plans to build a small house of their own, he appears to feel like a new man too.

Abbas's future is uncertain. Though his path has not been without roadblocks, it is evident that Abbas is able to start again in Iraq, reinventing himself as a "new man" in a way that many women in the Iraqi diaspora felt they could not. Abbas has developed strategies of transnational citizenship by which he maintains work opportunities in the United States and a family life in Iraq, laying the groundwork for a continued binational future. Hiba, by contrast, sees no permanent future in Iraq, but remains tied to the place because of her family there. Her strategy of transnational citizenship revolves around her commitments to her family in Iraq and, perhaps even more profoundly, her conveyance of Iraqi cultural heritage to her daughters.

This divergence in transnational strategies and capabilities for "new starts" reflects the gendered politics of identity and belonging in the refugee network of former interpreters. Both young men and young women confront suspicion and pressures from all sides; so too do they find themselves in processes of subjectivation in which they are to be individuated economic agents and disciplined cultural beings. Similarly, both young men and women exert agency and strategy in their navigation of these complex terrains. Yet, the available strategies and structures of agency vary for men and women in the Iraq War diaspora. An examination of Iraqi refugees' transnational lives shows that these strategies and structures contain a differential horizon of choices n—what Sarah Mahler and Patricia Pessar have called "gendered agency" (2001, 442). This differential is strikingly apparent in comparing the cases of Hiba and Abbas.

Young men can more readily start again, in part because in both the diaspora and the new Iraq young men's solitary migration is legible as economically motivated and temporary—more so than young women's. The circumstances that would lead to a young woman migrating independently are widely perceived to be more severe. What is more, young women confront an expectation—aggravated by refugee agencies—to be family-bound in a way that young men do not. Women apart from family in the United States are often placed with families through the sponsorship process. In theory this is to ease young people's entrance into the United States, but in practice this has meant that many women feel stifled by outsized cultural pressures that are exacerbated by resettlement practice. Further, if, as Hiba says, a woman returning to her family's community in

Iraq would be questionable, a woman who would start over in Iraq apart from her family would be even more suspect.

Gender Politics and Proscriptions

While Abbas can claim transnational citizenship that spans two continents and enables him to envision a future on either, Hiba's strategies of transnational citizenship revolve around her continued identification as an Iraqi in the United States. Though unique, this phenomenon speaks to larger patterns of gender in the current era of neoliberal globalization. It has been widely observed that experiences of migration are gendered. Male and female migrants—laborers, professionals, or refugees—have distinctly different family expectations and experiences of integration coming with their migration.[12] A variety of research has shown that men more commonly than women follow "social networks" to their destination and retain those networks while abroad, while women are found to be more tied to family relationships.[13] Patricia Pessar has argued that research "has eschewed female migrants owing to the widely shared assumption that women (and children) migrate to accompany or to reunite with their breadwinner migrant husbands" (2005, 2). Thus, if practices of transnationalism are gendered, then studies of transnationalism are too. According to Ong, "Women, who are half of humanity, are frequently absent in studies of transnationalism . . . [feminist scholarship] is seldom considered in the masculinist study of globalization" (1999, 11–12).

In the wake of the feminization of global labor markets, only recently have researchers shown interest in examining the lifeways of single female migrants. Yet, intellectual biases persist that imagine women as being a priori family-bound subjects. Research on Filipina domestic laborers, for

---

12. A great deal of literature on Filipino migrant workers has focused on such gender dynamics, for example. For a discussion of divergent gender expectations of strategies among transnational Filipino families, see Parreñes (2005); compare Tacoli (1999).

13. See Curran and Rivero-Fuentes's "Engendering Migrant Networks" (2003) and Hagen's "Social Networks, Gender, and Immigrant Incorporation" (1998).

example, has widely confirmed the view that single female migrants work principally to send money home under conditions in which nonfamilial "social networks" are either difficult to maintain or not prioritized. Many researchers have come to the conclusion that men tend to be more visible, empowered, and represented during processes of migration, and women more tied to home and family in the current configuration of neoliberal globalization, even despite the increased demand for female labor. As a result, many women's experiences and plans in global diasporas are observed to be more "provisional" and men's more permanent (Barber 2000).

Similar to some of these research findings, Iraqi women have not been as visible or represented as men in the diaspora (this is best exemplified by men rather than women becoming caseworkers). Women have also prioritized family commitments over other transnational "social networks." But, counter to such findings, so have Iraqi men. Further, quite unlike many of the case studies represented in this research, it is Iraqi women rather than Iraqi men who appear most firmly settled in the United States, and it is men who are more "provisional" in their diasporic plans—precisely because men wield a more empowered position and can choose to return to Iraq. Due to the inability to imagine futures in Iraq, many Iraqi refugee women are building new lives in the United States—though not often with the fellowship of other Iraqis. Men, by contrast, appear more likely to continue binational lives. In this way, a "provisional" condition contains its own privileges, just as permanency can reflect a reduced horizon of choices.

Configurations of "gendered agency" within this refugee network are such in the Iraqi diaspora that young men are able to identify as binational, while women—as Iraqis based in the United States—identify as betwixt and between both US and Iraqi identifications. Hiba cannot imagine a future in Iraq, but neither will she ever be an American. She says, "I am not American and I never will be American. But I have my life here. I am okay with that." Abbas, on the other hand, is able to begin again as a new man, though not without challenges of his own. Present gender configurations in the diaspora (aggravated by resettlement processes), which prescribe women to be attached to a sponsor family and empower men as professionals, make it such that single men are interpretable as economic migrants and single women as failed or potentially dangerous familial beings. In reality, both men and women assert that they have migrated to help their families in the immediate or distant futures. Further, both men and women appear to prioritize their family over other social networks— indeed both men and women hold themselves at a distance from others in the refugee network.

These case studies thus disrupt the normative view of prevailing research agendas that expect a priori for women's behavior to be more tied to "home," fulfilling restrictive gender prescriptions as cultural necessities. Overdetermined expectations can and do reproduce male-dominant biases in the resettlement process itself. The feedback loop that emerges at the nexus of scholarly or popular "expertise" and military and governmental policy and practice, most powerfully exemplified by the Human Terrain System, can reduce cultural complexities to caricatures. To base Iraqi resettlement policies upon such caricatures—about who is best fit to work as caseworkers (men) and who is best fit to live with an Iraqi family (single women)—can and does aggregate gender politics in the diaspora. In reality, practices of transnationalism and experiences in the diaspora are "are *situated* cultural practices" (Ong 1999, 17; emphasis added). Only in view of the situatedness of Iraqi men's and women's experiences within this refugee network—as single young Iraqis with war-torn pasts (replete with wartime gender proscriptions), deep historical ties to the US state and (its gendered war on terror), and persisting ties to refugee resettlement infrastructures (and its gendered practices)—do the network's complex diasporic gender politics come into view.

Conclusion

Two years after I left my work in the US Refugee Admissions Program, as my fieldwork in Boston was winding down, I received an alarming phone call. I had been subpoenaed to testify on a matter relating to an Iraqi refugee alleged to have participated in terrorist activity.[1] A refugee whose case I approved was a suspect in the case. The lead FBI agent sent me the young man's "A-file" (alien file), containing my adjudication, for me to review on the plane ride to the grand jury. When I arrived at the FBI office, I sat for an informal briefing session before the grand jury met. It became clear that the agent either did not have sufficient evidence to convict the individual, or he was not able to share that evidence with me. In either case, his intention was to pursue deportation rather than press criminal charges, and his hope was to invalidate my adjudication from years ago (outlining how the individual met the qualifications of a refugee) in order to withdraw his Legal Permanent Residence. Pursuing possible "terrorists" through immigration rather than criminal channels has become a trademark of the PATRIOT Act era; noncitizens' immigration status has

---

1. Since Iraqi refugee resettlement began, two Iraqis had been convicted of past terrorist activity in Iraq and sentenced to long prison sentences. The case I had been called to testify about was entirely unrelated to these cases. Apart from these two cases, the FBI has been found to be involved in multiple "sting" operations, which create false terrorist organizations and attempt to solicit supporters (among other operations) in Arab American communities. According to many legal scholars, this practice is ineffective in actually preventing terrorism and in some cases constitutes entrapment. See Sahar Aziz's "Caught in a Preventative Dragnet: Selective Counter-Terrorism in a Post 9/11 America" (2011); and "Policing Terrorists in the Community" (2013).

grown to be a crucible of addressing possible threat. Keenly aware of this as we sat in our briefing, and of the view that the man should be given a trial if evidence indicated wrongdoing, I declined to testify in the way the agent plainly wanted me to: I stood by my refugee adjudication. The agent sent me on the next plane home without ever going to the grand jury. As far as I know nothing ever came of the case.

Refugee resettlement in the PATRIOT Act era made for a schizophrenic and mutually suspicious relationship between Iraqis and the US state. Resettlement in this historical moment meant that one was both supported by and under the constant surveillance of the government. The so-called war on terror was the mantle that brought Iraqi interpreters to work for US Forces and made each member of the refugee network a possible suspect. Suspicion registered differently for men and women, presenting imperatives for men to identity themselves as nonthreatening protectors and for women to identify as victimized objects of protection within the US military, immigration channels, and resettlement structures. Simultaneously they face suspicion within the Iraqi diaspora, rooted in their past work for US Forces. In response, they devise strategies by which they perform and police filial duty across the refugee network, invoking models of male protection and female victimization akin to those they performed in encounters with the US state. With complex histories predating US occupation, the performance of such polyvalent models vis-à-vis both the state and diaspora have potentially subversive outcomes.

When network members perform models of the good Iraqi girl, for example, they also subvert these figurations and can deploy them in resistance to the projects out of which they emerge. As she identifies as a faithful daughter and "good girl," Meena strategically pushes to the limit that figure's coherence and regulatory power. She finally accepts the label as a "bad girl" if, as she forcefully asserts, she has earned that title by fulfilling her filial duties. She powerfully subverts the binarized good-versus-bad regime for women. Mohammed identifies as the brother to American soldiers in order to speak back to American power in Iraq. Further, as he reflects on the paradox that his role as patriarchal protector took him away from his own natal family, he arrives at the view that "a man's power, he receives only by tradition. I can't do anything a woman can't do for herself." He subverts constructs of masculinity that pin manhood to patriarchal protection and pin femininity to women's victimized status—figurations that run through both Iraqi wartime "traditions" and US imperial feminist "traditions." At the meeting point of disparate Iraqi cultural histories and US structures of power, performances of filial duty are active sites of signification and resignification.

The process of subject formation that unfolds at that meeting point—at the point of encounter between US structures of power and renderings of Iraqi "culture"—is what I have termed subject formation in translation. Iraqi interpreters are both subjects and agents of that encounter. As conduits of US power and translators for Iraqi culture, interpreters' subjective experiences of identity and belonging along the global route they forge, from US bases to Boston apartments, are uniquely borne out of their translation of American war on terror configurations of power and discursive formulations of Iraqi culture. As they speak, interpreters are forcefully translated; they also actively translate themselves. Interpreters' subjectivation represents the conditions for their strategic action. Interpreters' strategic identification with such polyvalent models of male protectors and female victims has formed the foundation of network members' assertions of cultural citizenship vis-à-vis the United States and transnational citizenship vis-à-vis the global Iraqi diaspora, but with sometimes surprising results.

Former US allies in Boston continue to hold profoundly complicated relationships with Iraq, especially with the rise of Da'ish (the so-called Islamic State) and the return of thousands of US troops to Iraq. Abbas tells me if he had not married Noor, he may have joined a Shi'i militia to counter Da'ish's campaign across Iraq. After a stretch of unemployment following his deployment in Arizona, Tariq has been rehired as a linguist in the US Army "because of Da'ish" and is stationed in Saudi Arabia. He has persuaded his cousin Ahmed, for whom Hiba was once a sponsor, to also join the Army to "fight for Iraq . . . again." In another unexpected turn, Tamara found that the only engineering job she could secure was at one of the largest US weapons contractors (Raytheon), supplying many of the weapons systems to Iraq, after she completed her master's program.

Iraqi refugees around the world represent an important global circuit. By UN estimates, nearly 10 percent of the total Iraqi population fled the country since 2003. Former US allies wield an especially fraught position within this global circuit. Reflecting on the tenth anniversary of the US invasion, "Riverbend"—the author of the famed blog "Baghdad Burning," now published in hard copy in the United States—wrote about what Iraqis had "learned" from the occupation. She writes: "We're learning that the biggest fans of the occupation (you know who you are, you traitors) eventually leave abroad. And where do they go? The USA most likely. . . . If I were an American, I'd be outraged. After spending so much money and so many lives, I'd expect the minor Chalabis and Malikis and Hashimis of Iraq to, well, stay in Iraq. Invest in their country. I'd stand in the passport control and ask them, 'Weren't you happy when we invaded your country? Weren't you happy we liberated you? Go back. Go back to the country you're so happy with because now, you're free!' . . . We're learning that the masks are off. No one is ashamed of the hypocrisy anymore." Riverbend labels the allies and advocates of the occupying forces "traitors" and considers the fact that the "minor Chalabis, Malikis, and Hashimis" have left Iraq as another form of betrayal. As it turns out, the position of US allies in the United States—as refugee caseworkers and members of the armed services—has proven as embattled as their initial work with US Forces. Those embattled positions may again bring former interpreters like Tariq and Ahmed back to Iraq to, in their words, "fight for Iraq."

The US-allied Iraqis also occupy a unique role in the post-9/11 United States, shedding light on the current conditions of legal and cultural citizenship in the United States. Iraqi interpreters have given much of themselves and their young adulthood to work for US Forces in Iraq. In the United States, they have struggled to make a living—leading many to once again pursue employment with the US state. They are subject to economic imperatives that make their continued alliance with the US state a necessary and even desirable step in order to "make it" in the United States. Even as they position themselves within the structures of US government, some like Hussein continue to face profiling; others like Hiba encounter slurs in the grocery store; and many "know [they are] not American," as Hiba put it. Iraqi refugees confront deep, longstanding racial and economic exclusions in the United States. Some are more able to cope with these inequalities than others. While men can more readily identify as hyphenated Americans, my research shows that young Iraqi women continue to feel isolated from cultural belonging in the United States. Further, men more than women have access to leadership positions within realms of the US state.

This reality reflects prevailing biases in immigration and resettlement structures that empower men to lead and speak for Iraqi women and children. Iraqi men are assumed and authorized in immigration proceedings to be the principal voice, and Iraqi men are similarly empowered to be refugee caseworkers for other Iraqis in the United States. Stemming from reductive views of Iraqi "culture," these practices translate fluid and historically situated gender arrangements into restrictive gender roles. To some degree, access to cultural citizenship in America has become beholden to American orientalist views of Iraqi culture, which systematically empower men. Both Iraqi men and women have faced prejudice and bigotry. The US-based Iraqis deal with these realities in a number of ways. Some, like Hussein, put the military manners he acquired in Iraq to use by addressing the officer who pulled him over as "sir," hoping to eventually educate Americans about Iraqis. Others, like Hiba, resign themselves to the reality that she will never be of this place. These responses, too, speak to a profound divergence in experiences of belonging and citizenship in the United States.

In an era of blind drone strikes, talk of the "clash of civilizations," and reduced civil rights for foreign-born Americans, how might we reimagine citizenship and civility in the United States? At a moment of militarism and persisting gender injustice in the United States, how might the stories and voices of Iraqis in America build an agenda for feminism and against militarism? Finally, in the wake of dictatorship, war, occupation, displacement, and continuing suspicion, how might the network of US-based Iraqis begin to build socialities of conviviality and community? These are open questions. I can begin to partially answer them with reflections on what some Iraqis in the diaspora are already doing to work for just American policy and convivial Iraqi communities.

Some Iraqis that I have met are speaking out against US militarism. Mikhaeil, Hiba's sponsor, for example, has participated in antiwar and antidrone protests in the Boston area. Though he identifies as having a "covenant" with America, Mikhaeil is outspoken in opposition to certain US foreign policies. He has given talks at several universities—including my own. Just after one of the biggest and most publicized antidrone rallies in Boston in April 2013, there followed the "Boston Marathon bombings" at the Boston Marathon. Mikhaeil—a Christian from the Middle East, not a Muslim from Chechnya—found himself in the uncomfortable position of answering questions about "extremist Islam." He attempted to both condemn the violence while also reminding audiences and friends of his larger message about global politics and US foreign policy. The challenge of changing the conversation from essentializing debates about Islam and totalizing discourse about foreign "others" to concrete discussions about US policy has been a steep one for Mikhaeil, but one that is as important as ever.

Other Iraqis in the Boston area have taken action by speaking directly to power. Just before John Kerry was confirmed as secretary of state, several Iraqi women, including Tamara, asked for a meeting with Senator Kerry's office to discuss the lack of educational and professional opportunities for former allies now in the United States. The group had drafted a compelling letter to the senator that enabled them to get on the office's schedule. In the meeting with Kerry's senior staff people, which I was able to join, the Iraqi women took turns telling their stories. They then outlined their proposals for better job training, recertification, and scholarships for Iraqi allies in the United States. The staff was encouraging, and the women left feeling heard. Though the project was shelved after Kerry left Massachusetts, the women have continued their work. For now, they have created an information sharing network for leads on jobs or education. After Tamara's success getting into graduate school (and her surprising job placement afterwards), she became a leader in this process. Along the way, she also developed some camaraderie with a few other Iraqis.

The best efforts at building communities have been those like Tamara's that connect diverse Iraqis in the diaspora over larger shared everyday needs and experiences. Similar small-scale, community-building work is underway in areas across New England from Portland, Maine, to Chelsea, Massachusetts. In the Boston suburb of Chelsea, Iraqi women have come together in a small-scale Muslim community center in the back of a Middle Eastern restaurant to celebrate Ramadan *iftars* and to take ESL classes—on one occasion inviting local news media to share their stories. In Maine, several Iraqi men have come together to start up a local business: an Iraqi bakery and café. The bakery has become a community center of sorts. In Lowell, several Iraqis have partnered with a local peace organization to develop strategies for older refugees to attend community college classes. Along the way, they have also started an Iraqi-American Cultural Center using donated space in a local office building.

The common thread among these examples is that they were not manufactured resettlement attempts to understand Iraqi "culture," but were initiatives developed by varied Iraqis. Certain immigration and resettlement policies that attempt to be culturally sensitive have regrettably played a role in reproducing gender inequalities in the diaspora. Rather than perpetuating reductive notion of gender that miss the mark of "cultural understanding," immigration and resettlement policies might strive to create similar opportunities for men and women alike. Such an effort might begin with the rethinking of strategies that empower Iraqi men as caseworkers and placing Iraqi women to live with families; they can continue with more robust support in the way of housing, job placement, and education, so that all refugees—men and women—could have the chance to realize the futures that they envision. These futures are imaginable beyond current policies that place single Iraqi women in a sponsor's custodial care and that make employment in the military or other state institutions one of the only viable professional options for single Iraqi men.

Iraqis in the United States are in the midst of carving out their futures. As many return to Iraq, some have remained in New England developing very small-scale communities. The future of Iraqi allies in the United States, as well as in the new Iraq, remains to be seen. What is clear is that their stories—revealing much about the occupation of Iraq, the war on terror of which it was a part, and the broader conditions of legal and cultural citizenship in the United States—are not stories that can be reduced to victims and villains; good and bad girls; protectors, traitors, or terrorists. The agency, strategy, and subjectivity of US-allied Iraqis, which I have attempted to share in these pages, cannot be boiled down to a metanarrative. These young men and women are as complex as the historical moment that they find themselves in, as multifaceted as the diverse currents of discourse they straddle, and as powerful as the unique processes of subjectivation they occupy as former US allies in Iraq, and now Iraqi refugees in the United States.

Glossary

Works Cited

Index

Glossary

'abāya—robe worn by women
al 'anf atāfi—sectarian violence
al-bin tala ala-umha—a girl takes after her mother
al-hamdulillah—thank God
al suqut—the toppling
awlad al-madaris—children of schools
barra—outside
bint Iraqiya—an Iraqi girl/daughter
'eb/'ar—shame
eurif—custom
hijab—headscarf
iftar—feast
ikhwani—my brothers
intifada—uprising
irhaab—terrorism
keffiyeh—a scarf
majmu'a—group
shabab—youth
sharaf—honor
sumud—steadfastness
tahrir—liberation
tajrubat al-harb—the war experience
taqshiish—a punning game
tawiil—tall (m.)
thabita—officer
yejib—to mask

Works Cited

Abrams, Lynn. 2010. *Oral History Theory*. New York: Routledge.

Abu-Lughod, Lila. 1986. *Veiled Sentiments: Honor and Poetry in a Bedouin Society*. Berkeley: University of California Press.

———. 1998. *Remaking Women: Feminism and Modernity in the Middle East*. Princeton: Princeton University Press.

———. 2002. "Do Muslim Women Really Need Saving: Anthropology Reflections on Cultural Relativism and Its Others." *American Anthropologist* 104, no. 3: 783–90.

Ahmed, Leila. 1992. *Women and Gender in Islam: Historical Roots of a Modern Debate*. New Haven: Yale University Press.

Al-Ali, Nadje. 2007. *Iraqi Women: Untold Stories from 1948 to the Present*. New York: Zed Books.

Al-Ali, Nadje, and Deborah Al-Najjar, ed. 2013. *We Are Iraqis: Aesthetics and Politics in a Time of War*. Syracuse: Syracuse University Press.

Al-Ali, Nadje, and Nicola Pratt. 2009. *What Kind of Liberation?: Women and the Occupation of Iraq*. Berkeley: University of California Press.

Al-Jabbār, Fāliḥ, and Hosham Dawod. 2003. *Tribes and Power: Nationalism and Ethnicity in the Middle East*. London: Saqi Books.

Al-Jawaheri, Yasmin Husein. 2008. *Women in Iraq: The Gender Impact of International Sanctions*. Boulder: Lynne Rienner.

Al-Khayyat, Sana. 1990. *Honour and Shame: Women in Modern Iraq*. London: Saqi Books.

Althusser, Louis. 1970. "Ideology and Ideological State Apparatus (Notes towards an Investigation)." In *Cultural Theory: An Anthology*, ed. Imre Szeman and Timothy Kaposy. Malden, MA: Wiley-Blackwell.

Appadurai, Arjun. 1990. "Disjuncture and Difference in the Global Cultural Economy." *Public Culture* 2: 1–24.

Asad, Talal. 1986. "The Concept of Cultural Translation in British Social Anthropology." In *Writing Culture: The Poetics and Politics of Ethnography*, ed. James Clifford and George Marcus. Berkeley: University of California Press.

———. 1995. "A Comment on Translation, Critique and Subversion." In *Between Languages and Cultures: Translation and Cross-Cultural Texts*, ed. Anuradha Dingwaney and Carol Maier. Pittsburgh: University of Pittsburgh Press.

———. 2003. *Formations of the Secular: Christianity, Islam, Modernity.* Stanford: Stanford University Press.

———. 2004. "Where Are the Margins of the State?" In *Anthropology in the Margins of the State*, ed. Veena Das and Deborah Poole. Santa Fe: School of American Research Press.

———. 2007. *On Suicide Bombing.* New York: Columbia University Press.

Avant Deborah. 2006. "The Privatization of Security: Lessons from Iraq." *Orbis* 50, no. 2: 327–42.

Aziz, Sahar F. 2011. "Caught in a Preventive Dragnet: Selective Counterterrorism in a Post 9/11 America." *Gonzaga Law Review* 47: 429.

———. 2013. "Policing Terrorists in the Community." *Harvard National Security Journal* 5 (Fall): 147–224.

Balibar, Etienne. 1994. "Subjection and Subjectivation." In *Supposing the Subject*, ed. Joan Copjec. New York: Verso.

———. 2009. *We, the People of Europe?: Reflections on Transnational Citizenship.* Princeton: Princeton University Press.

Barakat, Halim. 1993. *The Arab World: Society, Culture, and State.* Berkeley: University of California Press.

Baram, Amatzia. 1991. *Culture, History and Ideology in the Formation of Ba'athist Iraq 1968–1989.* New York: St. Martin's Press.

———. 1997. "Neo-Tribalism in Iraq: Saddam Hussein's Tribal Policies 1991–96." *International Journal of Middle East Studies* 29, no. 1: 1–31.

Barber, Pauline Gardiner. 2000. "Agency in Philippine Women's Labour Migration and Provisional Diaspora." *Women's Studies International Forum* 23, no. 4: 399–411.

Bashkin, Orit. 2009. *The Other Iraq: Pluralism and Culture in Hashemite Iraq.* Stanford: Stanford University Press.

Batatu, Hanna. 2012. *The Old Social Classes and the Revolutionary Movements of Iraq.* London: Saqi Books.

Bayoumi, Moustafa. 2008. *How Does It Feel to Be a Problem?* New York: Penguin.

Bearman, Joshua. 2011. "Baghdad Country Club." *Atavist Magazine*, vol. 10 (December).

Benjamin, Walter. 1968. "The Task of the Translator." In *Illuminations: Essays and Reflections*, ed. Hannah Arendt. New York: Schocken.

———. 1986. "On Language as Such and On the Language of Man." In *Reflections: Essays, Aphorisms, Autobiographical Writings*. New York: Random House.

Bilal, Wafaa. 2013. "Invisible Mirror: Aggression and the Thumb Generation Response." In *We Are Iraqis: Aesthetics and Politics in a Time of War*, ed. Nadje Al-Ali and Deborah Al-Najjar. Syracuse: Syracuse University Press.

Braziel, Jana Evans, and Anita Mannur, eds. 2003. *Theorizing Diaspora: A Reader*. New York: Blackwell.

Brown, Keith. 2008. "'All They Understand Is Force': Debating Culture in Operation Iraqi Freedom." *American Anthropologist* 110, no. 4: 443–53.

———. 2009. "Evaluating US Democracy Promotion in the Balkans: Ironies, Inconsistencies, and Unexamined Influences." *Problems of Post-Communism* 56, no. 3: 3–15.

Brown, Keith, and Catherine Lutz. 2007. "Grunt Lit: Participant-Observation of Empire." *American Ethnologist* 34, no. 2: 322–28.

Brunner, Claudia. 2007. "Occidentalism Meets the Female Suicide Bomber: A Critical Reflection on Recent Terrorism Debates, A Review Essay." *Signs* 32, no. 4: 957–71.

Buck, Lori, Nicole Gallant, and Kim Richard Nossal. 1998. "Sanctions as a Gendered Instrument of Statecraft: The Case of Iraq." *Review of International Studies* 24, no. 1: 69–84.

Butler, Judith. 1990. *Gender Trouble: Feminism and the Subversion of Identity*. New York: Routledge.

———. 1993. *Bodies That Matter: On the Discursive Limits of Sex*. New York: Routledge.

Cainkar, Louise. 2009. *Homeland Insecurity: The Arab American and Muslim American Experience after 9/11*. New York: Russell Sage Foundation.

Campbell, Madeline. 2010. "Dissenting Participation: Unofficial Politics in the 2007 Saharawi General Congress." *Journal of North African Studies* 15, no. 4: 573–80.

Castles, Stephen, and Alastair Davidson, eds. 2000. *Citizenship and Migration: Globalization and the Politics of Belonging*. New York: Routledge.

Chandrasekaran, Rajiv. 2007a. *Imperial Life in the Emerald City: Inside Iraq's Green Zone*. New York: Vintage Books.

———. 2007b. "Democrats, Bremmer Spar over Iraq Spending." *Washington Post*, February 7.

Clifford, James. 1994. "Diasporas." *Cultural Anthropology* 9, no. 3: 302–38.

———. 1997. *Routes: Travel and Translation in the Late Twentieth Century*. Cambridge, MA: Harvard University Press.

Clifford, James, and George Marcus. 1986. *Writing Culture: The Poetics and Politics of Ethnography*. Berkeley: University of California Press.

Collins, Patricia Hill. 2000. "It's All in the Family: Intersections of Gender, Race, and Nation." *Hypatia* 13, no. 3: 62–82.

Coulter, Chris. 2009. *Bush Wives and Girl Soldiers: Women's Lives through War and Peace in Sierra Leone*. Ithaca: Cornell University Press.

Crapanzano, Vincent. 1997. "Translation: Truth or Metaphor." *RES: Anthropology and Aesthetics* 32: 45–51.

Curran, Sara R., and Estela Rivero-Fuentes. 2003. "Engendering Migrant Networks: The Case of Mexican Migration." *Demography* 40, no. 2: 289–307.

Davis, Eric. 2005. *Memories of State: Politics, History and Collective Identity in Modern Iraq*. Berkeley: University of California Press.

De Certeau, Michel. 1984. *The Practice of Everyday Life*. Berkeley: University of California Press.

Deleuze, Gilles, and Felix Guattari. 1987. *A Thousand Plateaus: Capitalism and Schizophrenia*. Minneapolis: University of Minnesota Press.

Derrida, Jacques. 1988. *The Ear of the Other: Otobiography, Transference, Translation*, ed. Christie McDonald. Lincoln: University of Nebraska Press.

Dodge, Toby. 2003. *Inventing Iraq: The Failure of Nation Building and a History Denied*. New York: Columbia University Press.

Eco, Umberto. 1992. *Interpretation and Over-Interpretation*. Cambridge: Cambridge University Press.

Efrati, Noga. 1999. "Productive or Reproductive? The Roles of Iraqi Women during the Iran-Iraq War." *Journal of Middle Eastern Studies* 35, no. 2: 27–45.

———. 2013. *Women in Iraq: Past Meets Present*. New York: Columbia University Press.

Eltahawy, Mona. 2008. *Female Suicide Bombers in Iraq*. Washington, DC: Center for International and Regional Studies Publications, Georgetown University.

Enloe, Cynthia. 2000. *Maneuvers: The International Politics of Militarizing Women's Lives*. Berkeley: University of California Press.

———. 2007. *Globalization and Militarism: Feminists Make the Link*. New York: Rowman & Littlefield.

Fairclough, Norman. 2001. *Language and Power*. 2nd ed. London: Longman.

———. 2003. *Analysing Discourse: Textual Analysis for Social Research*. New York: Routledge.

Fancher, Peggy, Kathryn K. Knudson, and Leora N. Rosen. 2003. "Cohesion and the Culture of Hypermasculinity in US Army Units." *Armed Forces & Society* 29, no. 3: 325–51.

Fanon, Frantz. 1967. *Black Skin, White Masks*. New York: Grove Press.

Farouk-Sluglett, Marion, and Peter Sluglett. 1983. "The Transformation of Land Tenure and Rural Social Structure in Central and Southern Iraq, 1870–1958." *Arab Studies Quarterly* 5: 139–54.

Ferguson, James, and Akhil Gupta. 1992. "Beyond 'Culture': Space, Identity, and the Politics of Difference." *Cultural Anthropology* 7, no. 1: 6–23.

Flores, William V. 2003. "New Citizens, New Rights: Undocumented Immigrants and Latino Cultural Citizenship." *Latin American Perspectives* 30, no. 2: 87–100.

Forte, Maximilian C. 2011. "The Human Terrain System and Anthropology: A Review of Ongoing Public Debates." *American Anthropologist* 113, no. 1: 149–53.

Foucault, Michel. 1991. *The Foucault Reader*. Ed. Paul Rabinow. New York: Penguin.

Frisch, Michael. 1990. *A Shared Authority: Essays on the Craft and Meaning of Oral and Public History*. New York: SUNY Press.

Fuchs, Cynthia, and Joe Lockard, eds. 2009. *Iraq War Cultures*. New York: Peter Lang.

Giordano, Cristiana. 2014. *Migrants in Translation: Caring and the Logics of Difference in Contemporary Italy*. Berkeley: University of California Press.

Goffman, Erving. 1959. "The Presentation of Self in Everyday Life." In *Contemporary Sociological Theory*, ed. Craig Calhoun. London: Macmillan.

Gonzalez, Roberto. 2008. "Human Terrain." *Anthropology Today* 24, no. 1: 21–26.

———. 2009. "Anthropologists or 'Technicians of Power'? Examining the Human Terrain System." *Practicing Anthropology* 31, no. 1: 34–37.

———. 2010. *Militarizing Culture: Essays on the Warfare State*. Walnut Creek, CA: Left Coast Press.

Gualtieri, Sarah. 2001. "'Becoming White': Race, Religion and the Foundations of Syrian/Lebanese Ethnicity in the United States." *Journal of American Ethnic History* 20, no. 4: 29–58.

Haddad, Yvonne Yazbeck. 2004. *Not Quite American?: The Shaping of Arab and Muslim Identity in the United States.* Waco, TX: Baylor University Press.

Hagan, Jacqueline Maria. 1998. "Social Networks, Gender, and Immigrant Incorporation: Resources and Constraints." *American Sociological Review* 63, no. 1: 55–67.

Haj, Samira. 1997. *The Making of Iraq 1900–1963: Capital, Power, and Ideology.* New York: SUNY Press.

Hall, Stuart. 2000 [1996]. "Who Needs Identity?" In *Identity: A Reader*, ed. Paul de Gay, Jessica Evans, and Peter Redman. London: Sage.

Hasso, Frances. 2005. "Discursive and Political Deployments by/of the 2002 Palestinian Women Suicide Bombers/Martyrs." *Feminist Review* 81: 23–51.

Herzfeld, Michael. "Honour and Shame: Problems in the Comparative Analysis of Moral Systems." *Man* 15, no. 2: 339–51.

Hinojosa, Ramon. 2010. "Doing Hegemony: Military, Men, and Constructing a Hegemonic Masculinity." *Journal of Men's Studies* 18, no. 2: 179–94.

Hiro, Dilip. 1991. *The Longest War: The Iran-Iraq Military Conflict.* New York: Routledge.

Hoffman, Daniel, and Stephen Lubkeman. 2005. "Warscapes." *Anthropological Quarterly* 78, no. 2: 315–27.

Holtzman, Jon. 1999. *Nuer Journeys, Nuer Lives: Sudanese Refugees in Minnesota.* Boston: Allyn & Bacon.

Hourani, Albert Habib. 1992. *The Lebanese in the World: A Century of Emigration.* New York: I. B. Tauris.

Inghilleri, Moira. 2010. "'You Don't Make War without Knowing Why': The Decision to Interpret in Iraq." *The Translator* 16, no. 2: 175–96.

Isenberg, David. 2008. *Shadow Force: Private Security Contractors in Iraq.* Westport, CT: Praeger Security International.

Ismael, Shereen. 2004. "Dismantling the Iraqi Social Fabric: From Dictatorship through Sanctions to Occupation." *Journal of Comparative Family Studies* 35, no. 2: 333–49.

Jaber, Faleh. 2000. "Shayhks and Ideologues: Detribalization and Retribalization in Iraq: 1968–1998." *Middle East Review* 30: 28–31, 48.

Jamal, Amaney, and Nadine Naber, eds. 2008. *Race and Arab Americans before and after 9/11: From Invisible Citizens to Visible Subjects.* Syracuse: Syracuse University Press.

Jarman, Robert L. 1992. *Iraq Administration Reports.* Vol. 4. Slough, UK: Archives Edition.

Jeganthanthan, Pradeep. 2004. "Checkpoint." In *Anthropology in the Margins of the State*, ed. Veena Das and Deborah Poole. Santa Fe: School of American Research Press.

Jiwani, Yasmin. 2011. "Trapped in the Carceral Net: Race, Gender, and the War on Terror." *Global Media Journal* 4.

Joseph, Suad. 1991. "Elite Strategies for State Building: Women, Family, Religion and the State in Iraq and Lebanon." In *Women, Islam and the State*, ed. Deniz Kandioyti. Philadelphia: Temple University Press, 176–200.

———. 2000. *Gender and Citizenship in the Middle East.* Syracuse: Syracuse University Press.

———. 2005. "The Kin Contract and Citizenship in the Middle East." In *Women and Citizenship*, ed. Marilyn Friedman. Oxford: Oxford University Press.

———. 2008. "Familism and Critical Arab Family Studies." In *Family Ties and Ideational Change in the Middle East*, ed. Kathryn Young and Hoda Rashad. New York: Routledge.

Joseph, Suad, ed. 1999. *Intimate Selving in Arab Families: Gender, Self, and Identity.* Syracuse: Syracuse University Press.

Jowkar, Fourouz. 1986. "Honor and Shame: A Feminist View from Within." *Feminist Issues* 6, no. 1: 45–63.

Kandiyoti, Deniz. 2007. "Political Fiction Meets Gender Myth: Post-Conflict Reconstruction, 'Democratization,' and Women's Rights." In *Feminisms in Development: Contradictions, Contestations and Challenges*, ed. Andrea Cornwall, Elizabeth Harrison, and Ann Whitehead. New York: Palgrave.

Khalid, Asma. 2013. "Iraqi Refugees Find a Complicated New Home in Mass." WBRU, April 9.

Khalid, Maryam. 2011. "Gender, Orientalism and Representations of the 'Other' in the War on Terror." *Global Change, Peace and Security* 23, no. 1: 15–29.

Khoury, Dina Rizk. 2013. *Iraq in Wartime: Soldiering, Martyrdom, and Remembrance.* Cambridge: Cambridge University Press.

King, Erika, and Robert Wells. 2009. *Framing the Iraq War Endgame: War's Denouement in an Age of Terror.* New York: Palgrave Macmillan.

Kirk, Michael. 2006. "The Lost Year in Iraq: Inside the Green Zone." *Frontline*, PBS, October 17.

Kuhn, Annette. 2007. "A Journey through Memory." In *Autobiography: Critical Concepts in Literary and Cultural Studies*, ed. T. L. Broughton. Vol. 3. London: Routledge.

Kwok, James. 2006. "Armed Entrepreneurs: Private Military Companies in Iraq." *Harvard International Review* 28, no. 1: 34–38.

Mahler, Sarah, and Patricia Pessar. 2001. "Gendered Geographies of Power: Analyzing Gender across Transnational Spaces." *Identities* 7, no. 4: 441–59.

Mahmood, Saba, and Charles Hirschkind. 2002. "Feminism, the Taliban, and the Politics of Counter-Insurgency." *Anthropological Quarterly* 75, no. 2: 339–54.

Maira, Sunaina. 2009. *Missing: Youth, Citizenship, and Empire after 9/11.* Durham: Duke University Press.

Makiya, Kanan [Samir al-Khalil]. 1989. *Republic of Fear: The Politics of Modern Iraq.* Berkeley: University of California Press.

Marr, Phebe. 2010. "One Iraq or Many: What Has Happened to Iraqi Identity?" In *Iraq between Occupations: Perspectives from 1920 to the Present,* ed. Amatzia Baram, Achim Rohde, and Ronen Zeidel. New York: Palgrave.

Massachusetts Office for Refugees and Immigrants. n.d. "Refugee Arrivals to Massachusetts by Country of Origin." http://www.mass.gov/eohhs/gov /departments/ori/

McClintock, Anne. 1993. "Family Feuds: Gender, Nationalism and the Family." *Feminist Review* 44 (Summer).

McClintock, Anne, Aamir Mufti, and Ella Shohat. 1997. *Dangerous Liaisons: Gender, Nation and Postcolonial Perspectives.* Minneapolis: University of Minnesota Press.

McNutt, Debra. 2007. "Privatizing Women: Military Prostitution and the Iraq Occupation." CounterPunch, http://www.counterpunch.org/.

McSpadden, Lucia Ann, and Helene Moussa. 1993. "I Have a Name: The Gender Dynamics in Asylum and in Resettlement of Ethiopian and Eritrean Refugees in North America." *Journal of Refugee Studies* 6, no. 3: 203–25.

Mendelson, Sarah E. 2005. *Barracks and Brothels: Peacekeepers and Human Trafficking in the Balkans.* Washington, DC: Center for Strategic and International Studies.

Mercer, Korbena. 1994. *Welcome to the Jungle: New Positions in Black Cultural Studies.* New York: Routledge.

Miller, Christian. 2009. "Foreign Interpreters Hurt in Battle Find US Insurance Benefits Wanting." *L.A. Times,* December 18.

Mitchell, Timothy. 2002. *Rule of Experts: Egypt, Techno-Politics, Modernity.* Berkeley: University of California Press.

Mosse, David, and David Lewis. 2006. *Development Brokers and Translators: The Ethnography of Aid and Agencies.* Bloomfield, CT: Kumarian Press.

Naaman, Dorit. 2007. "Brides of Palestine/Angels of Death: Media, Gender and Performance in the Case of Palestinian Female Suicide Bombers." *Signs* 32, no. 4: 933–55.

Naber, Nadine. 2006. "Arab American Femininities: Beyond Arab Virgin/American(ized) Whore." *Journal of Feminist Studies* 32, no. 1: 87–111.

———. 2012. *Arab America: Gender, Culture, and Activism*. New York: New York University Press.

Omar, Suha. 1994. "Women, Honor, Shame and Dictatorship." In *Iraq since the Gulf War: Prospects for Democracy*, ed. Fran Hazelton. New York: Zed Books.

Ong, Aihwa. 1999. *Flexible Citizenship: The Cultural Logics of Transnationality*. Durham: Duke University Press.

———. 2003. *Buddha Is Hiding: Refugees, Citizenship, and the New America*. Berkeley: University of California Press.

Owens, Patricia. 2010. "Torture, Sex and Military Orientalism." *Third World Quarterly* 31, no. 7: 1041–56.

Pandolfo, Stefania. 2006. "Bġīt Nġanni Hanaya" (Je Veux Chanter Ici) Voix et Témoignage en Marge d'une Rencontre Psychiatrique." *Arabica* 53, no. 2: 232–80.

Parreñas, Rhacel Salazar. 2005. *Children of Global Migration: Transnational Families and Gendered Woes*. Stanford: Stanford University Press.

Passerini, Luisa. 1998. "Work Ideology and Consensus under Italian Fascism." In *The Oral History Reader*, ed. Robert Perks and Alistair Thomson. New York: Routledge.

Passerini, Luisa, ed. 1992. *Memory and Totalitarianism*. New Brunswick: Transaction.

Perks, Robert, and Alistair Thomson, eds. 1998. *The Oral History Reader*. New York: Routledge.

Pessar, Patricia. 2005. "Women, Gender, and International Migration across and beyond the Americas: Inequalities and Limited Empowerment." UN Expert Group Meeting on International Migration and Development, November.

Porter, Patrick. 2009. *Military Orientalism*. New York: New York University Press.

Portes, Alejandro, Luis E. Guarnizo, and Patricia Landolt. 1999 "The Study of Transnationalism: Pitfalls and Promise of an Emergent Research Field." *Ethnic and Racial Studies* 22, no. 2: 217–37.

Post, Jerrold M., and Amatzia Baram. 2002. "Saddam Is Iraq: Iraq Is Saddam." Air Univ, Maxwell AFB AL.

Posusney, Marsha Prispstein. 1997. *Labor and the State in Egypt: Workers, Unions, and Economic Restructuring.* New York: Columbia University Press.

Povinelli, Elizabeth. 2002. *The Cunning of Recognition: Indigenous Alterities and the Making of Australian Multiculturalism.* Durham: Duke University Press.

Project on Government Oversight. 2004. "Federal Contracting and Iraqi Reconstruction." March 11.

Raghavan, Sudarsan. 2009. "An End to Baghdad's Dark Era." *Washington Post,* February 28.

Razack, Sherene. 2005. "Geopolitics, Culture Clash, and Gender after September 11." *Social Justice* 32, no. 4: 11–31.

Refugee Council USA. n.d. "Terrorism-Related Inadmissibility Grounds." www.rcusa.org

Rikoski, Jennifer, and Jonathan Finer. 2009. "Out of Iraq: The US Legal Regime Governing Iraqi Refugee Resettlement." *Rutgers Law Record* 34: 46.

Riverbend. 2005. *Baghdad Burning: Girl Blog from Iraq.* New York: The Feminist Press at CUNY.

———. 2013. "Ten Years on . . ." *Baghdad Burning,* www.riverbendblog.blogspot.com.

Robben, Antonius. 2009. "Anthropology and the Iraq War: An Uncomfortable Engagement." *Anthropology Today* 25, no. 1: 1–3.

Rohde, Achim. 2006. "Opportunities for Masculinity and Love: Cultural Production in Iraq during the 1980s." In *Islamic Masculinities,* ed. L. Ouzgane. London: Zed Books.

———. 2010. "Revisiting the Republic of Fear: Lessons for Research on Contemporary Iraq." In *Iraq between Occupations: Perspectives from 1920 to the Present,* ed. Amatzia Baram, Achim Rohde, and Ronen Zeidel. New York: Palgrave.

———. 2014. *State-Society Relations in Ba'thist Iraq: Facing Dictatorship.* New York: Routledge.

Romano, David, and Lucy Brown. 2006. "Women in Post-Saddam Iraq: One Step Forward, Two Steps Back?" *National Women's Studies Association Journal* 18, no. 3: 51–69.

Rumbaut, Rubén G. 2001. "Vietnamese, Laotian, and Cambodian Americans." *Interdisciplinary Perspectives on the New Immigration: The New Immigrant in American Society* 3: 308.

Saghieh, Hazem. 2000. "Saddam, Manhood and the Image." In *Imagined Masculinities: Identity and Culture in the Middle East.* London: Saqi.

———. 2007. "Vie et Mort de la Débaassification." *Revue du Monde Musulmans et de la Méditerranée.*

Said, Edward. 1979. *Orientalism.* New York: Vintage.

———. 2000. *The Edward Said Reader.* Ed. Moustafa Bayoumi and Andrew Rubin. New York: Vintage.

———. 2001. *Reflections on Exile: And Other Literary and Cultural Essays.* London: Granta Books.

Sassoon, Joseph. 2010. "Management of Iraqi's Economy Pre and Post the 2003 War: An Assessment." In *Iraq between Occupations: Perspectives from 1920 to the Present,* ed. Amatzia Baram, Achim Rohde, and Ronen Zeidel. New York: Palgrave.

———. 2011. *Saddam Hussein's Ba'th Party: Inside an Authoritarian Regime.* Cambridge: Cambridge University Press.

Shallal, Celia. 2013. "(Dis)connectioned." In *We Are Iraqis: Aesthetics and Politics in a Time of War,* ed. Nadje Al-Ali. Syracuse: Syracuse University Press.

Shohat, Ella Habiba, and Evelyn Azeeza Alsultany, eds. 2013. *Between the Middle East and the Americas: The Cultural Politics of Diaspora.* Ann Arbor: University of Michigan Press.

Simpson, John. 1992. "The Aftermath of the Gulf War." *Asian Affairs* 23, no. 2: 161–70.

Singer, Audrey, and Jill H. Wilson. 2006. *From "There" to "Here": Refugee Resettlement in Metropolitan America.* Washington, DC: Metropolitan Policy Program, Brookings Institution.

Siu, Lok. 2001. "Diasporic Cultural Citizenship: Chineseness and Belonging in Central America." *Social Text* 19, no. 4: 7–28.

Sjoberg, Laura. 2010. "Gendering the Empire's Soldiers: Gender Ideologies, the US Military and the 'War on Terror.'" In *Gender, War and Militarism,* ed. Laura Sjoberg and Sandra Via. Santa Barbara, CA: Greenwood Press.

Sjoberg, Laura, and Caron Gentry. 2008. "Reduced to Bad Sex: Narratives of Violent Women from the Bible to the War on Terror." *International Relations* 22, no. 1: 5–23.

Sjoberg, Laura, and Caron E. Gentry, eds. 2011. *Women, Gender, and Terrorism.* Athens: University of Georgia Press.

Sluglett, Peter. 2007. *Britain in Iraq: Contriving King and Country.* New York: Columbia University Press.

Smith-Hefner, Nancy. 1999. *Khmer American: Identity and Moral Education in a Diasporic Community.* Berkeley: University of California Press.

Spatz, M. 1991. "Lesser Crime: A Comparative Study of Legal Defenses for Men Who Kill Their Wives." *Columbia Journal of Law and Social Problems* 24, no. 4: 597–638.

Spivak, Gayatri. 1988. "Can the Subaltern Speak?" In *Marxism and the Interpretation of Culture*, ed. Cary Nelson and Lawrence Grossberg. Urbana: University of Illinois Press.

Stein, Jeff. 2011. "Iraqi Interpreters Seek Punishment for Contractor They Say Sexually Harassed Them." *Washington Post*, April 22.

Suleiman, Michael, ed. 1999. *Arabs in America: Building a New Future*. Philadelphia: Temple University Press.

Tacoli, Cecilia. 1999. "International Migration and the Restructuring of Gender Asymmetries: Continuity and Change among Filipino Labor Migrants in Rome." *International Migration Review* 33, no. 3: 658–82.

Takeda, Kayoko. 2009. "War and Interpreters." *Across Languages and Cultures* 10, no. 1: 49–62.

Thompson, Elizabeth. 2000. *Colonial Citizens: Republican Rights, Paternal Privilege and Gender in French Syria and Lebanon*. New York: Columbia University Press.

Thompson, Paul. 2000. *Voice of the Past: Oral History*. Oxford: Oxford University Press.

Tripp, Charles. 2007. *A History of Iraq*. 3rd ed. Cambridge: Cambridge University Press.

United Nations Office for the Coordination of Humanitarian Affairs. 2003. "Iraq Focus on Widows." IRINNEWS.org, July 16.

USCIS Iraqi Refugee Fact Sheet. 2012. www.USCIS.gov.

Victor, Barbara. 2003. *Army of Roses: Inside the World of Palestinian Women Suicide Bombers*. New York: St. Martin's Press.

Watson Institute for International Studies. *Cost of War Project*. Brown University.

Wedeen, Lisa. 1999. *Ambiguities of Domination: Politics, Rhetoric, and Symbols in Contemporary Syria*. Chicago: University of Chicago Press.

Weidman, Amanda. 2003. "Beyond Honor and Shame: Performing Gender in the Mediterranean." *Anthropological Quarterly* 76, no. 3: 519–30.

Whitworth, Sandra. 2004. *Men, Militarism, and UN Peacekeeping: A Gendered Analysis*. Boulder: Lynne Rienner.

Wikan, Unni. 1984. "Shame and Honor: A Contestable Pair." *Man* 19, no. 4: 635–52.

Yurchak, Alexi. 2006. *Everything Was Forever until It Was No More: The Last Soviet Generation*. Princeton: Princeton University Press.

Zubaida, Sami. 2002. "The Fragments Imagine the Nation: The Case of Iraq." *International Journal of Middle East Studies* 34, no. 2: 205–15.

Zucker, Norman L., and Naomi Flink Zucker. 1992. "From Immigration to Refugee Redefinition: A History of Refugee and Asylum Policy in the United States." *Journal of Policy History* 4, no. 1: 54–70.

Index

Italic page number denotes illustration.

Madeline Otis Campbell is an assistant professor of Urban Studies at Worcester State University, where she directs the Center for the Study of Human Rights and sits on the Women's Studies and Global Studies faculty. A cultural anthropologist, Campbell specializes in Middle East refugee migration in urban contexts.